Writers Workshop
of Horror 2

WRITERS
WORKSHOP OF HORROR 2

EDITED BY BRAM STOKER AWARD-WINNER
MICHAEL KNOST

Hydra Publications
1310 Meadowridge Trail
Goshen, KY 40026,

ISBN Number: 978-1-948374-52-1

Printed in the United States of America

First Edition

Cover Design © 2021 by Greg Chapman

Dedicated to F. Keith Davis

Introduction

Over a decade ago I recruited some of the finest authors and editors to help create an anthology of essays and interviews focusing on the craft of writing, each covering a specific element as it relates to horror and dark fiction. My goal was to produce a book I wish had existed when I started my own writing journey.

Writers Workshop of Horror was published by Woodland Press in 2009 and received the Bram Stoker Award for Superior Achievement in Non-Fiction, as well as the Black Quill Award. The book has been through dozens of reprints and is still a popular resource for up-and-comers.

I have always been amazed at the number of people reaching out to me via email, social media, or in person, telling me that after having read the book, and putting the things they learned into practice, they finally sold their first short story—or that they recently landed an agent or had just signed a novel contract.

I was pleased with how the anthology turned out, especially with how it offered differing voices and opinions—sometimes even conflicting differences—because, let's be honest, every writer has his or her own method(s) with the craft. And because of that, the book's strength was its myriad ideas from which the learning writer could consider and/or put to the test.

I honestly never thought about doing a second book, but a few years ago I found myself thinking about elements of the craft I wish I would have included in the first one. And so I began recruiting more top voices and opinions to help us continue the journey in improving our craft and telling those dark stories we love to fear.

In this one, you will not only find legendary authors, but also veteran writers who have entertained us for decades, as well as newer names who are just getting their careers started. All are professional and have wonderful experiences and knowledge to share. As always, take what you can use and store what you can't for another day.

I truly look forward to hearing from you and your personal success stories as to how *Writers Workshop of Horror 2* helped make a difference in your writing and career.

Michael Knost
michaelknost@me.com
March 2021

To the Next Generation!
Ramsey Campbell

Why do we write horror stories?

If you write in this field you're bound to be asked that question, and in any case it does no harm to know your reasons. It must be the question I've been asked most often in my career, and I've amassed quite a few answers. However, I don't think it's possible to answer the question until we have defined what we mean by "horror stories", and so here goes my neck on the block.

Horror fiction is the branch of literature most often concerned with going too far. It is the least escapist form of fantasy. It shows us sights we would ordinarily look away from or reminds us of insights we might prefer not to admit we have. It makes us intimate with people we would cross the street to avoid. It shows us the monstrous and perhaps reveals that we are looking in a mirror. It tells us we are right to be afraid, or that we aren't afraid enough. It also frequently embraces, or at least is conterminous with, the ghost story. It flourishes here and there in the fields of science fiction and crime fiction, and not infrequently it bobs up in the mainstream, whatever that is. Despite its name, it is often most concerned to produce awe and terror in its audience, but it is not unusual for a horror story to encompass a wider emotional range.

All these reasons (and maybe more that you can think of) justify one answer I give anyone who wants to know why I write what I write: that horror fiction seems to me to be an extremely broad field—quite broad enough to allow me to deal fully with any theme I want to deal with. Another answer, perhaps the one most likely to strike an echo in any aspiring writer, is that I want to pay back some of the pleasure that horror fiction has been giving me almost since I learned to read. (Indeed, my very first memory of anything I read is of being terrified by a story, presumably intended to be charming, in a British children's comic annual, where a Christmas tree dissatisfied with its lot uprooted itself from the tub and creaked back to the forest, scattering earth on the carpet as it went.) Even simpler, and as true, is the answer that I write horror fiction because I'm proud of my field. If you aren't proud of the field you write in, I can see no point in doing it at all.

Pride in a field involves knowing its history. I've no room here for a reading list, but let me recommend three fine fat anthologies as representative: *Great Tales of Terror and the Supernatural,* edited by Phyllis Wise and Herbert A. Fraser in the late forties and still triumphantly in print, David Hartwell's *The Dark Descent*, and Ann and Jeff VanderMeer's *The Weird.* One reason to become familiar with the traditions of your field is to discover what has already been done; another is to learn from the masters. The notion that you should learn only from your contemporaries, on the basis that if you look to earlier models then your work is likely to be unsaleably out of date, seems to me to be nonsense, and inimical to the vitality of any field. A field whose writers relate only to their own peers is in danger of disappearing up itself.

I've seen it claimed that Lovecraft and earlier masters are irrelevant to today's writers in the field, on the basis that if they were working today they would bring themselves unrecognisably up to date. In Lovecraft's case the claim is demonstrably rubbish, and I have my doubts about Machen and M. R. James, but that's not the point. The techniques these writers have been imitated, but they have never been bettered as far as I'm aware. If you want to learn the technique of the glancing phrase of terror, the image that goes by almost before you notice and shows enough to suggest far more (and it's worth knowing), study M. R. James. If you want to examine the model of the tale of supernatural terror, where carefully graduated hints and glimpses build to an awesome pitch, Lovecraft is where to look.

Lovecraft is a classic instance of the writer who constructs strengths out of his weaknesses. He had little interest in, or talent for, characterisation, and so he wrote stories in which the insignificance of humanity is the theme and the source of his power. No wonder that his novels were essentially extended short stories. Here I should admit that I first saw print by imitating Lovecraft slavishly. With the benefit of hindsight I feel there's nothing necessarily wrong in beginning by imitation, since if you have any originality of your own to be brought out you will soon become aware of the limits of your model. It seems to me that it can be useful to develop the rudiments of technique by imitation, in order to have gained some fluency before you begin to write more personally. The aim of any literary apprenticeship is to allow you to tell the stories only you can tell.

I hope that doesn't sound more daunting than it is. I'm simply asking you to be true to your own imagination and experience. By all means read voraciously, and don't limit yourself by confining your reading to your own field, but read as a means to finding your own voice. There's only one Stephen King, for instance, but there are far too many writers trying to sound like him. Show us what only you have seen, tell us your secret thoughts and wildest imaginings. Above all, be honest.

I believe that good fiction, and good criticism, show us what we hadn't seen before or what we had overlooked. Sometimes they make us look again at what we had taken for granted.

It seems to me that, despite all the claims I made on its behalf at the beginning of this piece, horror fiction too often takes for granted conventions which the field needs to examine in order to develop. Who better than the next generation, yourselves, to do so? Let me suggest a few for you to attack.

Take the theme of evil, as the horror story often does. Writing about evil is a moral act, and it won't do to recycle definitions of evil, to take them on trust. Horror fiction frequently uses the idea of evil in such a shorthand form as to be essentially meaningless: something vague out there that causes folk to commit terrible acts, something other than ourselves, nothing to do with us. That sounds to me more like an excuse than a definition, and I hope it's had its day. If we're going to write about evil then let's define it and how it relates to ourselves. In my view fiction should disturb, and especially disturb the reader's prejudices rather than seek to reassure by indulging and confirming them.

All good fiction consists of looking at things afresh, but some horror fiction seems to have an inbuilt tendency to do the opposite. Ten years or so ago many books had nothing more to say than "the devil made me do it"; now, thanks to the influence of films like *Friday the 13th,* it seems enough for some writers to say that a character is psychotic, no further explanation necessary. But it's the job of writers to imagine how it would feel to be all their characters, however painful that may sometimes be. Perhaps it's a lack of that compassion which has led some writers to create children who are evil simply because they're children, surely the most deplorable cliché of the field.

Some clichés are simply products of lazy writing. Tradition shouldn't be used as an excuse to repeat what earlier writers have done; if you feel the need to write about the stock figures of the horror story, that's all the more reason to imagine them anew. For instance, we might have believed there was nothing new to be written about vampirism until Karl Wagner wrote "Beyond Any Measure," whose stunningly original idea was always implicit in the vampire tradition and waiting for Karl to notice. Again, generations might have thought that the definitive haunted house tale had been written, but it hadn't been until Shirley Jackson wrote *The Haunting of Hill House* (a statement guaranteed to make some of you try to improve on that novel, perhaps). Put it another way: one reason some folk recoil from my own novel *The Face That Must Die* seems to be that it confronts you with how I imagine it might be like to be a psychotic killer, rather than keeping a Halloween face or ski mask between him and the audience, the better to turn him into a bogey-man we can dismiss as being nothing like ourselves. It's only fair to warn you that many readers and publishers would rather see imitations of whatever they liked last year than give new ideas a chance. But I've always tried to write what rings true to me, whether or not it makes the till ring. If you don't feel involved with what you're writing, it's unlikely that anyone else will.

There's another side to the field which is overdue for attack by a new generation: its reactionary quality. A horror writer I otherwise admire argued recently that "it has been a time-honoured tradition in literature and film that you have a weak or helpless heroine"—implying, I assume, that we should go on doing so. Well, tradition is a pretty poor excuse for perpetrating stereotypes (not that the author in question necessarily does); time-honoured it may be, but that doesn't make it honourable. In fact, these days so many horror stories (and, especially, films) gloat over the suffering of women that it seems clear the authors are getting their own back, consciously or not, on aspects of real life that they can't cope with. Of course that isn't new in horror fiction, nor is using horror fiction to define as evil or diabolical whatever threatens the writer or the writer's life-style, but at the very least one should be aware as soon as possible that this is what one is doing, so as to be able to move on. I have my suspicions too about the argument that horror fiction defines what is normal by showing us what isn't. I think it's time for more of the field to acknowledge that when we come face to face with the monsters, we may find ourselves looking not at a mask but at a mirror.

Now all this may sound as if it requires some discipline and dedication, and my experience is that it does. After all, the best way for a writer to compete is with oneself, to do better than one did last time. I'm not the first to say that the most important thing for a writer to do is to write, but I'll add that you should work on whatever you're writing every day until it's finished; to do otherwise is to court writer's block, every blank day adding to the hurdle that prevents you from getting back into the story and making the task seem more impossible. An example of this is my story "Litter", where six months elapsed between my first day's work and my return to the story, which I took up by writing the line "That's how he enters the story, or this is." I should have rewritten the story to improve its shape, of course. Now I rewrite more and more severely, and take great pleasure in cutting thousands of words out of first drafts; I think that's a pleasure worth learning as early as possible in one's career, not least because realising one can do it helps one relax into writing the first draft, where it's better to have too much material for later shaping than not enough. Learning to relax enough with the technique of writing novels comes easier to some than others; you may feel you need to plot a novel in advance (maybe all the way to breaking it down into chapter synopses) before you begin the first chapter, but it's worth trying to regard the synopsis merely as a safety net once you begin writing, trying to let the novel develop itself as it takes on more life. I did that first in *Incarnate,* and since then I've avoided plotting or constructing too far ahead, trying to know only as much as I need to know to start writing and head in the right direction. It can be fearsome to find yourself losing your way halfway through a novel, all by yourself in the unknown, but I find that the solutions are usually somewhere in what you've already written, and I can tell you that the bad days are worth the days when you feel the novel come to life.

I'm still stressing the arduousness, but let me see if I can pass on some tricks I've learned. We all have an optimum period of creativity each day, and it's worth beginning work then if you possibly can. Mine is from about six in the morning until noon or so. It's easy to get distracted away from your work, but music may help; my desk is between the speakers of the hi-fi on which I play compact discs (which last longer than records and keep me there longer) of all sorts of music from Monteverdi onwards. (Steve King uses rock, Peter Straub jazz.) Don't be too eager to feel you've exhausted your creative energy for the day, but if you sense you're close to doing so, then don't squeeze yourself dry: better to know what the next paragraph is going to be and start with that next time. Scribble down a rough version of it rather than risk forgetting it. Always have a rough idea of your first paragraph before you sit down to write, and then you won't be trapped into fearing the blank page. If you must take a day or more out from a story, break off before the end of a scene or a chapter, to give yourself some impetus when you return. Always carry a notebook (which of course your phone may be) for ideas, glimpses, overheard dialogue, details of what you're about to write, developments of work in progress. If an idea or something larger refuses to be developed, try altering the viewpoint or even the form: if it won't grow as a short story, it may be a poem. Sometimes two apparently unproductive ideas may be cross-fertilised to give you a story. Then again, you may not be ready technically or emotionally to deal with an idea, and it can improve with waiting.

What else can I tell you? Only to write. Surprise us, astonish us. Enjoy your work. Above all, don't despair. The frustration you will inevitably experience sometimes, the feeling that you don't know how to write, may be the birth pangs of something genuinely new. I know I still suffer that experience every time I write a story. Believe me, it's preferable to playing it safe with a formula. Good luck! I look forward to reading you!

Ramsey Campbell was born in Liverpool in 1946 and now lives in Wallasey. The *Oxford Companion to English Literature* describes him as "Britain's most respected living horror writer". He has received the Grand Master Award of the World Horror Convention, the Lifetime Achievement Award of the Horror Writers Association, the Living Legend Award of the International Horror Guild and the World Fantasy Lifetime Achievement Award. In 2015 he was made an Honorary Fellow of Liverpool John Moores University for outstanding services to literature. PS Publishing recently brought out *Phantasmagorical Stories*, a sixty-year retrospective of his short fiction. His latest novel is *Somebody's Voice* from Flame Tree Press, who are in the process of publishing his Brichester Mythos trilogy.

Reasons Why a Story Doesn't Grab Me

Ann VanderMeer

So, you want to write a horror story and you want to submit it for publication. Writing is a worthy endeavor and getting published is a truly wonderful feeling. You are probably asking yourself what are some of the things that make an editor reject stories when reading submissions, right? You're in luck! Here are some of my top irritations.

Nasty Little Characters and/or Stereotypical Characters

In other words, bad characterization. The reader wants someone to root for, or at the very least, someone interesting enough to continue reading. In my role as a short fiction editor, I've seen far too many stories that start with nasty people doing horrible things, There's nothing special in that. Even if you can think of the most creative ways to torture or kill another person, that doesn't make the characters interesting or the story worth reading. Use your creative imagination to bring some realism to your characters. Don't give me the stock players; i.e. the school jock who is a jerk, the cute but cold cheerleader, the loner serial killer, etc.

And it doesn't even have to be a person. One of my favorite haunted house stories is "Renovations" by Matthew Pridham. This story is told from the point of view of the house itself. The story begins when the house tells us how lonely they are without people there. It's truly one of the more compelling stories I've read. And the reader roots for the haunted house, as feelings of empathy for the loneliness move us strongly.

Violence and explosions are not the only way to create drama

Many times, I will see a story resort to gratuitous violence as a way to increase the drama. This is a shortcut, at the very least. There can be a lot of tension in a family holiday gathering (just watch one of the many movies that depict this), not to mention a conversation between two people. Ratchet up the drama in other ways besides going in for the jump scare. It will last longer and be more forceful, if the scenes are cut properly to enhance the tension.

Don't give me a shocking scene for no reason except to shock me. Same holds true for something gross. Whatever clever idea you come up with, make sure it is in service to the story and not just to shake your reader.

Don't follow trends

Don't write yet another XXX (fill in the blank) story just because it's popular right now. Write the story you want to write and worry about markets afterward. I can usually tell when a writer is forcing a story to match some perceived preference in the marketplace, editorship or publishing venue. It won't ring true for the editor or the reading audience if the story is forced to fit into a neat package.

Don't try to be the next Stephen King, Anne Rice or Clive Barker. Instead seek your own voice and be the next XXXX (fill in your own name here).

Too many characters and/or POVs

Ideally a short story should rest firmly in the point of view of one character. The reader needs to know whose story this is and a shift to different characters will result in reading whiplash. It's one thing to have a break in the story and introduce the thoughts of different characters, but in the end, you need to know who is telling the story (and by the way, they can't die at the end either, otherwise how are they telling the story? This mistake annoys me every time.) In addition, if your story has too many characters, it's difficult for the reader to keep track of everyone. Make sure to limit the number to what is necessary for the story.

A story doesn't start when a person wakes up!

Yes, I know that is when the day starts, but that's not when a story starts. You have to write an opening scene that engages the reader and compels them to turn the page. There's nothing exciting or compelling in the character's morning routine, unless their process of brewing the coffee is so fascinating that we can't turn away. I oftentimes will find myself lopping off several paragraphs at the beginning of a new writer's story and tell them "The story actually starts here."

And don't start the story inside someone's dream either. That makes me want to pull my hair out! When you begin this way, the reader is unsure of where they are, who they are with and what's going on. If you do need to have a dream sequence in your story, make sure that the reader is well grounded first. Then they are more likely to go follow you into a dream.

Nothing much happens and/or the ending just trails off

Two common problems here. A story that doesn't go anywhere and an ending that isn't an ending. No, you don't have to tie up every loose end to properly end a story. You just need to leave the reader with a sense of satisfaction. As a matter of fact, it's better to leave them wanting a bit more, but not if the reader is so consumed by unanswered questions that the story is not gratifying.

As for stories that don't go anywhere, think about movement. Where is the character going, what are they doing and what's happening around them?

Where are we?

The reader doesn't need long paragraphs of description of setting, but they still need to know where the story is taking place. Frequently, I see such generic descriptions that I have no idea what the character is seeing around them.

Keep in mind that the setting can also set the mood of your story. I've seen many successful stories where the town itself is somehow cursed, or ominous. The place where your story takes place can be almost as compelling as other characters.

Domestic revenge stories

I have certainly seen my fill of these. A timid, put-upon husband/wife/boyfriend/girlfriend with an overbearing husband/wife/boyfriend/girlfriend appear in the story and of course the character that has suffered the most gets some kind of revenge on their oppressor, either on purpose or by accident. This formula does not work for me.

A few other items I'd like to share; when an editor passes on a story that doesn't necessarily mean it's a bad story. There are many reasons. Perhaps they're overstocked, or the story doesn't quite fit their vision, or they've recently acquired a similar type of story. Try other markets and write more stories. Don't put all your publishing eggs into one story basket. The more stories you have out there in submission, the better your chances for publication. Keep the long game in mind. Writing is a profession that lasts a lifetime. Good luck and keep writing!

Ann VanderMeer is an award-winning editor & anthologist. She currently serves as an acquiring editor for Tor.com and Weird Fiction Review and is the Editor-in-Residence for Shared Worlds, a Science Fiction and Fantasy writing camp for high school students. Her latest anthologies include *The Time Traveler's Almanac, Sisters of the Revolution, The Big Book of Science Fiction, AVATARS, INC* (an online XPRIZE anthology), *The Big Book of Classic Fantasy* and *The Big Book of Modern Fantasy*.

Who Is that Walking Beside You? Haunted by the Horror Tradition

John Langan

Introduction: Overdetermined

In 2012, together with Brett Cox, Sarah Langan, and Paul Tremblay, I taught an online workshop on writing horror fiction. (We did it as a fundraiser for the Shirley Jackson Awards.) Each of us picked a different aspect of the subject to discuss and then ran the class for a week. We began with a written lecture, then gave an assignment related to our topic. It went reasonably well, and has continued to be offered—with a rotating slate of instructors—on a roughly annual basis to raise money for the awards.

I chose to address the horror tradition and the writer's relationship to it. Indeed, if memory serves, I called dibs on the topic from the start. Notions of tradition, canonicity, the classic(al), and the like have long fascinated me. I have a grade-school-era memory of reading and rereading Lin Carter's study, *Tolkien: A Look Behind the Lord of the Rings*, loving its attempt to identify the various literary sources on which Tolkien drew for his trilogy. Carter made a few interpretive mistakes, but they pale beside the sheer number of new texts he introduced me to.

During my teenage years, Stephen King's *Danse Macabre* provided a virtual syllabus for my reading in (his version of) the horror tradition. As an undergraduate English major with ambitions of writing fiction, I went around to several professors whose opinions I respected and asked them to give me lists of the books I should read if I wanted to be well-read. Later on, the literary critic with whose work I wrestled the longest in my graduate studies was the late Harold Bloom, who was deeply engaged with ideas of the canon and of what he called strong writers, which was to say, those central to the western literary tradition (as he saw it) and who therefore had to be reckoned with by any writer wishing to join its ranks. (I continue to have a love-hate relationship with Bloom, which I am sure he would find only appropriate.

To paraphrase Derrida on Sartre, I find myself asking, How could someone who was so wrong about so many things be so important to my critical consciousness?) When working on my still (and probably never) to be finished dissertation, I first wrote about a hundred and seventy pages meticulously examining the influence of Robert Browning's great poem, "Childe Roland to the Dark Tower Came," on a trio of H.P. Lovecraft's stories and then, when my committee rejected that project, another hundred or so pages on Lovecraft's influence on stories by Ramsey Campbell, Stephen King, and Thomas Ligotti. (Parts of this latter work went on to be published as separate articles.) Over my years of teaching college, I taught section after section of classes with titles like "Great Books: Western" and "Western Classics." More recently, I've been interested in Jonathan Lethem's essay, "The Ecstasy of Influence," which attempts to reframe influence as something a writer should welcome and embrace.

All of which is to say that I was, as Freud might have put it, overdetermined to tackle this subject. Both essay and assignment seemed to go over well enough, and I had ideas about returning to the piece and expanding it, developing some of its ideas. I didn't, although its subject continued to interest me. Then, this year, Michael Knost invited me to contribute to *Writers Workshop of Horror 2*, and suddenly it was time to return to my long-ago essay and see what I could do with it. Somewhat to my surprise, I found I still agreed with much of what I wrote for the class. Even so, there was a certain amount of it in need of fleshing out, especially regarding its approach to the notion of the (horror) tradition and, by implication, the classic.

I have the feeling this is not my last word on this subject; indeed, this may not be the last version of this essay. But I'm happy to have had the chance to think about its subject once again.

1. Three Pieces of Advice (and a Little Autobiography)

During my twenties, I went to hear (published) writers read their work whenever I had the chance. (Most of them under the auspices of the New York State Writers' Institute, one of the great ongoing successes of SUNY Albany.) After each writer was done, while I was having them sign their book for me, I'd ask variations on the same question: "What's your advice for a young writer?"

Probably the most brutally practical response came from T.C. Boyle, who advised me to marry a rich girl. The replies that stuck with me in a more profound sense, though, came from the somewhat unlikely trio of Terry Brooks, Barbara Kingsolver, and Nahid Rachlin. Brooks told me, "You have to write what you can write." Kingsolver said, "Write about what obsesses you," Rachlin, "Write about your passion." I think those three pieces of advice may in fact have been the same advice, but I find it useful to distinguish among them.

At the spot where your abilities meet your proclivities, where what you cannot escape coincides with what you don't want to escape, that's the heart of your strength as a writer.

Of course, you'll have found your way to this destination through your reading: perhaps a single work that strikes you like a thunderbolt, or perhaps a writer whose efforts resonate with you, or perhaps a group of writers who help you to see the possibilities of a genre—or, most likely, I think, a combination of all three. "If you wanna write it," Ursula Le Guin said, "you gotta read it," which I might parse, it's through reading a genre that you discover what kind of fit it makes for you, and also that you begin to learn how it does what it does.

An autobiographical illustration: if there's a single book that made me a writer of horror, it was Stephen King's *Christine*. I read it in paperback during the fall of 1983 (probably late October-into November, since the book would have had its paperback release in time for Halloween). It was not the first novel by King I'd read: this was *Cujo*, earlier that summer. *Cujo* hadn't made an impression on me. *Christine* transfixed me; it enveloped me. I found in it a world which contained the mundane and the fantastic, and King's portrayal of one was as hurling as his portrayal of the other.

By the time I was done with *Christine* (actually, it was probably long before I finished it), the course of my life had shifted and I knew this, writing fiction, writing horror fiction, was what I wanted to do. I sought out all of King's work I could find, either in paperback or through my local library. At the library, I came upon his nonfiction study, *Danse Macabre*, which sent me back to *Frankenstein*, *Dracula*, and *Strange Case of Dr. Jekyll and Mr. Hyde*, and then out to *The Haunting of Hill House*, *Ghost Story*, and *Shadowland*. These last two introduced me to Peter Straub, who became extremely important to me, to the extent he would exert as much influence on my writing as King.

2. Theoretics (I): Horror as a Genre (with Slightly More Autobiography)

In interviews over the last couple of decades, I've been asked variations on the same fundamental question, namely, What does the horror genre in particular have to offer a story? The shorter answer to the question is that the genre itself is the biggest strength horror provides a story's writer. I recognize, though, that while it pretends to be some kind of Zen profundity, my response treads the line between obfuscation and obnoxiousness, so a longer answer may be of more use:

There have been essays written claiming that horror is, in fact, not a genre, but an emotion (cf. Douglas Winter's famous "The Pathos of Genre"). This claim and variations on it continue to be bandied about (often by people I respect very much); in my view, however, it's wrong. Horror is, in fact, a genre, which is to say, a *kind* of fiction, a selection of stories and novels we can group together because of certain family resemblances.

Those similarities occur at all levels, from plot to setting to character to style to theme. What results is a sort of fuzzy set, at whose center we can place works on whose identity as horror the majority of us will agree: *Dracula*, say, and *The Haunting of Hill House*, and *The Shining,* and at whose margins we can locate those works over which people of good will may disagree: *Wuthering Heights*, say, and *1984*, and *The Collector*. The yield of this set is a list. Arranged chronologically, it's a history. Seen in relation to itself, it's a tradition with which the writer interacts. (I almost typed "with which the writer may interact," but there's nothing conditional about it: even if you're not [consciously] aware of it, when you enter into a genre, you've entered into a relation with its history. [Which is not a bad thing.])

In a sense, so straightforward a description simplifies what is a more complex process, as books hitherto un- or under-recognized are recovered and accorded their place in the tradition. Sometimes a book written decades ago may not achieve its full effect until a much later moment. In *Aspects of the Novel*, E.M. Forster suggests thinking of all the writers who have ever lived sitting in an enormous room, writing, which is not a bad image for the way the texts in a tradition exist in a kind of radical present, always ready to be ready, always ready to be read anew in relation to one another.

(For one idea of the parameters of this tradition, you could do worse than check out Stephen Jones and Kim Newman's *Horror: 100 Best Books*, which is a compilation of one hundred short essays written by one hundred writers on their favorite works of horror. Subsequently, Jones and Newman published *Horror: Another 100 Best Books*, which continues from the first book. As its title indicates, Lisa Kröeger and Melanie Anderson's *Monster She Wrote: The Women Who Pioneered Horror and Speculative Fiction* focuses on the women whose contributions to the foundation and formation of the genre have all too often been overlooked. You also might take a look at the first appendix to Stephen King's *Danse Macabre*, in which he recommends one hundred books published between 1950 and 1980 [the parameters of his focus in the book]. Brian Keene has written excellent appreciations of writers from William Hope Hodgson to Joe R. Lansdale, a number of them collected in *Trigger Warnings*. And of course, in the background is the granddaddy of all such surveys, H.P. Lovecraft's *Supernatural Horror in Literature*.)

It's the interaction with a history that I feel is the strength the horror genre—any genre, really—offers the writer. It brings them into contact with the efforts other writers have made with the stuff of the field, offering examples to be learned from, whether in imitation, rejection, or some balance of the two. It shows how other writers have met the challenges posed by the material of horror, the lengths to which they've stretched that material, the range of subjects they've found a place for in their work.

While it's my view that the horror genre is as capable of profundity of expression as any other kind of fiction, I also believe a horror story must always concern itself first and foremost with being a horror story. Before your vampire story can be a clever trope for the relationship of big business to the consumer, it must succeed in evoking our unease at the general manager whose skin always appears too white under the buzzing fluorescents, whose suit never fits him properly, who listens to his customers' complaints without once blinking his bloodshot eyes.

I'm aware I've been bandying about terms such as history and tradition rather uncritically, as if there's one received history and tradition for everyone. At this point in time, it would be naive and arrogant to insist on either. I've tried to work such an acknowledgment into my discussion through my use of the idea of the fuzzy set. However, at the center of the fuzzy set are texts to which the term classic is almost certainly to have been applied. (This is true for the books I mentioned above, *Dracula*, *The Haunting of Hill House*, and *The Shining*.) Unless we embrace Mark Twain's definition of the classic as a book everybody wants to have read but nobody wants to read, the term is likely to be no less fraught with interpretive peril.

Even as I acknowledge this potential trap, though, I want to access an escape hatch from it with the help of an essay by Italo Calvino, "Why Read the Classics?" Calvino begins his wonderfully lucid discussion by defining a classic as a book which has not finished saying what it has to say to us. He spends the rest of the essay expanding upon his opening statement. For my purpose here, the notion of the classic as a text in which a reader continues to find meaning (or with which a reader continues to generate meaning) will do. In the case of a writer, this includes a particular kind or maybe dimension of meaning, namely, that having to do with the construction of fiction. The classic in this regard is a text whose usefulness to writers is ongoing.

Another autobiographical example may be helpful. Some years ago, I had to teach a course in western literature post 1600. The focus of the class was supposed to be on non-English language writers, but an exception was made for Shakespeare and a couple of other poets. Since there was already a course devoted entirely to Shakespeare in the English department's offerings (not to mention, he was included in the English Literature I survey), I decided to omit him from my class in the interest of covering more non-English writers. But as the weeks progressed, I found that just about every writer who came after Shakespeare and was able to read him, either in English or translation, had been influenced by him. Reading Shakespeare had helped writers such as Goethe, Flaubert, and Dostoyevsky create their own works. Shakespeare was a great writer, I realized, because he had helped other writers achieve their greatness.

In his essay, "Tradition and the Individual Talent," T.S. Eliot answers the complaint that we know so much more than the writers who came before us first by agreeing with it and then by clarifying that they are what we know. A writer such as Shakespeare helps other writers make themselves possible. The same thing might be said of figures from Bram Stoker to Shirley Jackson to Stephen King. Their works are classics because they continue to speak to us and, in listening to them, we learn how to form our own sentences.

Speaking about genre in narrative, I tend to compare it to form in poetry, and there's enough usefulness in that comparison for me to mention it in closing. Just as the sonnet brings with it certain formal requirements and thematic traditions, so does the horror story, and the writer of either benefits from an awareness of them.

3. Theoretics (II): Narrative Gene-Splicing

In his essay, "Whom Do We Write For? or The Hypothetical Bookshelf," Italo Calvino (who seems to be more central to my thinking on this topic than I appreciated) answers the question posed by his title by declaring that we write for readers who are familiar with a number, even a great number, of other literary works. At the level at which we're working, no reader comes to a story or novel for the first time; in fact, I'd take the statement a bit further and say no reader comes to a horror story or novel for the first time. Even the reader who claims not to like the material of horror, not to read it, will have had some exposure to it, whether from encounters with Poe's stories in school or from exposure to those works situated nearer the margins of the fuzzy set to which I've been referring.

A novel, Calvino says, suggests a bookshelf on which it should be placed, a selection of other novels in whose tradition it positions itself. He goes on to say that, in his view, the most interesting novels are those which create the most unlikely bookshelves, which tuck themselves in between the oddest companions. It's a contention with which I agree, one I would argue is borne out by the career of a writer such as Ramsey Campbell. In his fiction, Campbell has continuously explored the ways in which a horror story might be written, to the extent that his work offers a catalogue of approaches to constructing a narrative in the genre. This catalogue arose from Campbell's ever-wider reading of the horror tradition, of both the writers whose work lies near its heart (i.e. Lovecraft and Leiber) and those whose work skirts its very distant edges (i.e. Greene and Nabokov).

Campbell has spoken of his admiration for this same aspect of Lovecraft's fiction, its ongoing investigation of the possibilities of the horror narrative, one rooted in Lovecraft's reading of Poe, Lord Dunsany, Arthur Machen, and Algernon Blackwood, to name a few. Jorge Luis Borges puts the matter another way in his essay, "Kafka and His Precursors," suggesting that every writer *creates* their predecessors. First, we recognize the presence of previous writers in what we are reading. Then, the more we consider the flow of that influence, we seem to perceive it running backward, so what has come after causes us to see what came before in a new way. We're back to E.M. Forster's image of all the writers who ever lived in the same room together, their works affecting one another in apparent defiance of time.

For this reason, I find myself especially interested in those stories or novels which limit themselves to reproducing the surface effects of a single writer, such as Lovecraft or M.R. James, as closely as they can. These kinds of efforts have their place as part of a writer's development, much as a garage band begins by playing covers of their favorite songs, but they strike me as a stage to be passed through, and not a final destination. To take Calvino's metaphor a little further, I'd argue our task as writers is to assemble our own bookshelves, to bring together those works that comprise our individual libraries.

(Note my emphasis on reproducing surface effects: what a writer such as the late Wilum Pugmire does in his use of Lovecraft's style and conceits is of another order altogether.)

4. Praxis: The Example of Ghost Story

I know: it's all fine and well for me to talk about literary gene-splicing in the abstract, but what about the specific? What does it look like when a writer puts this into practice, especially one working in the horror field? One answer is that it looks like most of the successful works of fiction you've encountered—which, I realize, isn't very much help. How about an example? Peter Straub's *Ghost Story* should do nicely, in part because he makes so much of his technique in the novel so obvious. At the macro level, he constructs a novel whose alternation between a small set of central characters and representatives of the community at large was strongly influenced by Stephen King's use of the same model in *Salem's Lot*.

The narrative threading throughout, about a company of men pursued by and pursuing a deadly, shape-shifting woman, is indebted to Arthur Machen's "The Great God

Pan." Within that overarching plot, Straub inserts a number of shorter—though related—stories, the longest of which is a fairly obvious rewriting of Henry James's *The Turn of the Screw*. He also employs motifs lifted from sources such as Walter de la Mare's "Out of the Deep." As the very title suggests, Straub makes engaging with the horror tradition a conspicuous part of his novel, such that you might say the novel itself is haunted by the very tradition it's exploring. And it's a stronger book for it.

When I undertook to write horror fiction seriously, at the end of my twenties, Straub's example was very much in the forefront of my mind; to this day, he remains a personal hero. I wasn't up, though, for the rigors of constructing a work like *Ghost Story*. Instead, I decided to focus on revisiting the archetypal monsters to see what I might do with each of them. I figured that the werewolf, the mummy, the evil magician came trailing enough baggage for me to rummage through it for inspiration, for something(s) to bounce my work off. The approach worked well enough for me to return it on numerous occasions; indeed, it's still one of the narrative tools I reach for most frequently.

5. An Assignment

All right: less chatter, more matter, as my friend Jack Haringa likes to say. Here's something for you to try. Select one of the following horror tropes and see what you can do with it in a scene of between seven hundred and fifty and fifteen hundred words. Think about the way in which the figure has been presented so far, its history. You may want to try to work in the center of the tradition, or you may want to approach the figure from a less-traveled direction. I'd recommend a scene in which the figure reveals itself/ is revealed to another character, but feel free to go in whatever direction most interests you. The scene should be complete, but the larger narrative it's part of may not be. Your choices are:

- ☠ The werewolf

- ☠ The vampire

- ☠ The witch/wizard

If you're up for more of a challenge, try this: select one of the following classic horror stories and write your own version of it (new setting, characters, possibly a different outcome) in no more than fifteen hundred words. Our knowledge of the original story should not be essential to the success of yours. Your choices are:

- ☠ Edgar Allen Poe "The Tell-Tale Heart"

- ☠ Shirley Jackson "The Lottery"

- ☠ H.P. Lovecraft "The Outsider"

(n.b. I've selected these stories because they're readily available online. If there's another you'd like to tackle, feel free.)

Finally, if you're feeling even more ambitious, frame either the scene or the re-telling from above with a variation on the club story. If you've read a lot of stories from the late nineteenth and early twentieth century, then you've probably run across the device of the group, usually of men, who, after dinner at their club, retire to the lounge for port, cigars, and a story or two. James uses it in *The Turn of the Screw*; Conrad employs varieties of it in several of his stories, most notably *Heart of Darkness*; Straub uses it in *Ghost Story* as part of the traditional materials he's engaging. What I'd like you to do is to present, in no more than five hundred words, a contemporary equivalent of those long-ago supper clubs, a location where a smallish group of people might meet and exchange stories. It might be an improvised affair—say, a group of guests sitting around a pool at a holiday barbecue—or it might be something slightly more formal—say, Thanksgiving dinner. Either way, it should lead into the scene or story that follows.

I'll also offer a coda. I realize everything I've discussed here may seem to be taking you in the direction of a great deal of self-consciousness about the relationship between your writing and a number of larger contexts and away from the emotion with which you seek to charge your story. It's been my experience that fostering such an awareness leads to an expanded sense of the possibilities available to you as a writer working within the horror genre, providing you with more characters, plots, and figures in which to invest the emotion.

Good luck, everyone, and good writing. I can't wait to read what you write.

John Langan is the author of two novels and four collections of stories. For his work, he has received the Bram Stoker and This Is Horror awards. He lives in New York's Mid-Hudson valley with his wife and younger son.

Interview with Bentley Little
Elizabeth Massie

Elizabeth Massie: *Hey, Bentley! Thanks for taking the time to answer some questions about you and your craft. I'm sure you know that I'm one of your longtime, biggest fans (though I have no urge to confine you in a cabin and chop off one of your feet if you don't write what I want you to write.) You craft stories and novels that have stayed with me long after I've read the last page, and have given me more than my share of genuine chills. I appreciate you taking the time to answer a few questions.*

A number of authors say they knew they wanted to be a writer from the days of their childhood. Is this true for you? If so, did you spend a lot of time either imagining stories, sharing stories, and even writing them down? If not, what jobs did you imagine yourself doing as an adult, and when did you decide to steer your ship in the literary direction?

Bentley Little: I've always written. In elementary school, I had two terrific and very progressive teachers—Miss Druiff and Miss Kasalek—in fourth and fifth grades. Both had tables in the backs of their rooms where students who finished their assignments early could write stories or draw pictures or make crafts. I usually finished my work quickly, and would go back there to write horror stories (often plagiarized from books I had recently read or movies I had seen). My friend Stephen Hillenburg would draw illustrations for those stories, and the two of us would stand in front of the class, me reading aloud and Stephen holding up his pictures. Stephen went on to create the cartoon *Spongebob Squarepants*.

I continued to write as a teenager, although I never showed anyone anything. I just shoved my stories in a box in the closet (although one time my mom found one of my discarded first-person stories in the trash and mistook it for a suicide note. My parents sat me down to have a Very Serious Talk, and, embarrassedly, I admitted to them that it was a story I had written).

I always wanted to be a writer—as an occupation not just as a hobby—but it wasn't until I was a freshman in college that I took a real step-in that direction. I'd been writing articles for newspapers since I was fifteen, but that involved telling other people's stories. I wanted to tell my own stories. As it happened, I saw an ad on TV for Harlequin romances. According to the commercial, the publisher released five titles a month. That meant they needed a lot of books. I figured I could easily write one, and with the arrogance of youth—I had never even read a romance novel—I sat down and wrote a story about a young woman moving to a small town and falling in love. It was embarrassingly bad. But I went to the library, got a copy of *Writer's Market*, and sent out my manuscript. Harlequin rejected it. Silhouette rejected it. Then I sent it to a publisher that printed books for adults with learning disabilities. They asked me to simplify it—no words over three syllables, no sentences over ten words—and I sat in the library between classes and rewrote the whole thing. The publisher showed it to clients—and promptly decided not to publish any more fiction. Romance was clearly not my forte. So, I decided to concentrate on writing what I liked, what I knew, and started submitting horror stories to various magazines. I've never looked back.

Massie: And your readers are so very glad you chose to focus on horror. Now, when you were just getting started, did you take creative writing classes of any sort? If not, how did you train yourself to write well?

Little: I did take creative writing classes in college, and was fortunate enough to have a professor—Keith Neilson—who was a horror fan. He was extremely helpful and encouraging. I don't know what would have happened if I'd ended up in the class of the other creative writing instructor, who hated horror.

Massie: I can't imagine taking creative writing from someone who detests a student's favorite genre. Glad you could give Keith Neilson a nod. Now here is something I know horror writers and readers will want to know. What scared you as a kid? And what scares you now?

Little: Everything in my youth directed me toward horror because everything I saw scared me—and I loved it. I enjoyed that feeling of being frightened. I remember being terrified by a children's picture book my parents read to me that had an illustration of a grinning moon, I recall being scared by the metronomic sound of the pendulum on a cuckoo clock my grandparents had given me. Dr. Seuss books stressed me out, things like Green Eggs and Ham or The Cat in the Hat, where this chaotic figure would come into people's lives and turn everything upside down. The first movie I ever saw in a theater, Mary Poppins, terrified me because an old bearded banker in a dark boardroom started laughing and began floating up toward the ceiling. His equally old sons later said, "He died laughing."

My mom used to watch the horror soap opera *Dark Shadows*, and I loved it, but it scared me so much that I had to watch it from outside the house, looking in through the screen door. So, fear, and the attraction to fear, has been with me from the beginning.

Haunted houses have always scared me the most. They still do. When I was growing up, there were very few supernatural books for children (hauntings always had a logical Scooby-Doo-ish explanation), but some of the haunted house books had scary parts. Two of my favorites were *Cobbler's Nob* and *The Happy Hollisters and the Haunted House*. I reread them many times. As an adult, my two favorite horror novels are *The Haunting of Hill House* and *The Shining*. Ghosts just seem scarier to me than monsters, and I don't care who you are or how old you might be: if you're alone in a big house at night, and the lights go out, and you hear unexplained noises from another room, you are going to be scared.

Massie: What a small world! I remember very well The Happy Hollisters and the Haunted House! *In fact, I give the Happy Hollister series credit for being a big inspiration to me, for lighting a fire that was already smoldering and spurring me on to make "being a writer" a reality. Speaking of writing successes, what was your first published work? Who was the publisher? Do you remember how it felt to see your name in print for the first time?*

Little: I suppose, technically, my first published work was a short story called "Ivy," which was about vines of ivy growing and killing people and eventually taking over the world. It appeared in a mimeographed newspaper at my junior high school.

But my first professional sale was the story "Pray 4 Baby," which appeared in the late great David Silva's seminal magazine *The Horror Show* in 1984. When I received my copy in the mail and saw my name in print, I thought I was on my way. I received a whole $8.75 for the story, but I felt as though I'd gotten a million-dollar advance. A real editor actually believed in my work! From then on, nothing was going to stop me.

Massie: The Horror Show *was fantastic, a ground-breaker back in "the day." I was lucky to have gotten my start there, as well. New and up-and-coming horror writers should seek out old copies of the magazine—there were plenty of kick-ass horror stories to be found within the pages. And a number of well-known horror writers of today got their start thanks to David Silva. So, your first pro sale was "Pray 4 Baby." And you plowed ahead and have produced an incredibly impressive body of work. Could you tell us who or what encouraged you during the early years of your writing career? Please expound on the Dean Koontz connection, if you want, or mention others if there are others.*

Little: For a long while, I was encouraged by rejection letters. Even editors who would not buy my work were generally complimentary, telling me that they might not like this particular story but to keep submitting because one day I'd come up with something that would get into their publication. And one day I did. Those kind rejection letters gave me a lot of confidence and inspired me to continue on.

I met Dean Koontz at a signing for his book *Twilight Eyes.* I'd graduated from college and had written my first novel, *The Revelation,* as my Master's project. But I had no idea how to find a publisher and was living with my parents, working temp jobs and sending out short stories to the same small press magazines that had been publishing me for the past few years. My mom saw in the newspaper that Dean Koontz was going to be signing at a local bookstore and suggested that I go. "Talk to him," she said. "Ask for advice."

There was no way I was going to do that, but I lied and told her I would. I couldn't afford the new hardcover novel he was promoting, so I gathered up some of my paperbacks and went to the signing. As it happened, we'd both had short stories in the same issue of *The Horror Show*, and when he asked who he should sign the books to, I told him, "Bentley." He recognized my name, we started talking, and he asked if I'd written anything longer. I told him I had a novel collecting dust, and he asked if I had an agent. I said I had no clue how to even get an agent. He offered to help, and wrote down my phone number. "I'll call you," he said.

Right, I thought.

But a week later, I was in the alley behind my parents' house, changing the oil on my car, and my mom came running out. "Dean Koontz is on the phone!" she said. I dashed into the house, grabbed some paper towels for my greasy hands, picked up the phone, and, sure enough, it was Dean Koontz. True to his word, he had found someone he thought might be a good agent for me: Dominick Abel, whom he had met on a convention panel. He not only gave me a name and address, but dictated the letter he thought I should send. I did exactly as he instructed . . . and Dominick has been my agent ever since.

Massie: *Not all writers are "full-timers." Many have day jobs and write in their spare time. This is a perfect situation for many who enjoy the variety that comes with two careers. Others hope to take the plunge and make writing their sole profession. Tell us a little about your experience becoming a full-time author.*

Little: It is because of Stephen King that I was able to make a living as a full-time writer. Like most mid-list authors, I had a day job for the first several years of my career. King had been kind enough to provide me with a blub for my novel *University*, and while I'm sure that helped sales, I still wasn't making enough to earn a decent living.

Then, one day, my aunt called me and said, "Stephen King was almost killed and he was reading your book!"

"What?" I said.

It turned out that she was in an airport and had picked up a copy of *USA Today*, which reported that Stephen King had been struck by a van while walking on a rural road. The article mentioned that, at the time, he had been carrying my novel, *The House*. After that one mention, my sales took off, and I was finally able to quit my day job. King subsequently mentioned my work in both his book *On Writing* and in an *Entertainment Weekly* column he had at the time. So not only am I a huge fan of his writing, but I owe him a massive debt for boosting my career.

Until several years ago, however, I had never met him. Then a friend scored some tickets to a Writer's Block event in downtown Los Angeles, where the *Los Angeles Times'* book reviewer was going to interview Stephen King on stage. Four of us went, and we all brought books to be signed. Unfortunately, it was announced at the beginning that there would be no signing afterward. After the formal interview, though, there was a Q & A session with the audience. My friends encouraged me to stand up, state my name, and ask something, but I felt too self-conscious to do that, so one of them raised her hand, planning to ask the embarrassing question, "What do you think of the horror writer Bentley Little?" Thankfully, she was not called on. The event ended and the crowd began filing out, but one of my friends stopped me.

"Stephen King's still here." He pointed to an exit to the side of the stage. The curtains covering the exit were blowing a little and, sure enough, we could see Stephen King standing right there.

"Go talk to him," my friends urged me. They pushed me in that direction, and I found myself walking up the aisle and through the curtains. I'm sure he thought I was some crazed stalker, but I quickly introduced myself and told him I just wanted to thank him for his support. Apparently, he'd been waiting for his ride, because immediately a door opened on the other end of the short passage, and a woman hurried in and said, "Let's go." I could see a limo in the alley outside.

"Nan," he said to the woman, "this is Bentley Little, a very talented writer."

"Hello," she said brusquely, then told him again, "Let's go."

And they were gone.

Massie: What a great connection! Thanks for sharing it. Too bad King didn't have some time to hang out following the interview; I know you two would have had a fascinating conversation, one during which a lot of horror fans and writers would have loved to have been flies on the wall.

Now to the issue of writing every day. Some writers advise newer writers to push through any real or perceived interference and write sometime every day, even if they don't feel like it. Do you agree with that? Why or why not?

Little: Writing every day is probably good advice, but equally important is to submit everything you write. If you're a great writer and no one sees your work, you're not going anywhere. If you're a terrible writer and you keep writing terrible stuff day after day, you're not going to get any better. Submitting your work will provide you with feedback. Editors, even editors who don't like your work, often give free—and very helpful—advice that you can incorporate into your writing. You will also learn that different editors have different tastes, and while one may not appreciate what you do, another might think it's terrific. So, write a lot and submit a lot. And don't give up if something gets rejected. Send it out again to someone else. If it's any good, it will eventually find a home.

Massie: *Do you have a regular writing routine? Care to share a brief look at the routine, if you do? If you don't, can you tell us how you tend to get into the writing flow?*

Little: I actually don't have a regular writing routine. I write when I can. To be honest, starting my career by working for a newspaper was probably the best training I could have had. As a reporter—even a teenage reporter working for free—I was exposed to a lot of people from different walks of life, and I learned a lot about the way people talk, which is very useful when writing dialogue. I was also forced to write under deadline pressure. Which is why I don't have to wait for inspiration to strike—I can write anything at any time. This skill is particularly important when you're first starting out and have no set writing time but have to write while juggling job, friends, family, and whatever else real life throws at you.

Massie: *Do you only write at home, or do you sometimes go elsewhere to pound out your tales of terror?*

Little: I only write at home. Writing to me is a private activity, and whenever I see people writing in a coffee shop or a park or a McDonald's, I always think they're phonies. When I was in college, I knew students who would talk about writing and think about writing. and plan to write—but never actually write anything. I had no respect for those poseurs. Other people I knew would write, but would always do so in public in order to make sure that other people knew they were writing. None of those wannabes ever went anywhere. My advice? If you're going to be a writer, take it seriously.

Massie: There have been articles, blogs, and even books written on the topic of writer's block, a term created in 1947 by psychoanalyst Edmund Bergler. Some claim writer's block is real while others say there is no such thing. What do you think?

Little: I don't know. I've never actually had writer's block, but every time I come up with something that I think is a good idea, I write it down and store it—just in case I get writer's block some day and can't come up with a story.

Massie: Speaking for myself (and, I know, for other writers as well), I have a few never-finished manuscripts, partial books that I started with a burst of energy but then, for one reason or other, the stories dwindled and died on the vine. I left them there and moved on to other books that I did get into totally and finished. Perhaps I'll go back to the orphans someday. Who knows? I'm wondering . . . do you have any abandoned partial books or short stories that just weren't working as you wanted them to and so you let them go and put your energies into another project? If so, do you still have them somewhere accessible, with the thought of perhaps going back to them someday?

Little: I have the first paragraph or fist pages of dozens of short stories I've started and not completed, and I'll probably get back to most of them eventually, but I don't really have any unfinished novels. Somewhere in my house or garage is the first horror novel I wrote (although it's more of a novella. I think it's about 120 pages). I have no idea where it is and don't care, because it will never see the light of day. It was terrible (and very derivative of John Maxim's novel *Platforms*, which greatly impressed me at the time.) But the truth is that I don't abandon novels once I start them. I have a bad habit of trying to write my way out of a problem, so rather than give up on something, I just plow forward. Which is probably why some of my books are better than others.

Massie: *For inspiration or just entertainment, do you ever visit haunted destinations or take part in ghost tours? Personally, I've always wanted to tour the Winchester Mystery House in San Jose, California, but have enjoyed others closer to home, such as the Trans-Allegheny Lunatic Asylum in Weston, West Virginia. If so, what have been some of your favorites?*

Little: Inspiration? No. Entertainment? Yes! I did go to the Winchester Mystery House when I was a kid, and it's as amazing as you would expect it to be. Our local museum has a "haunted walking tour" each fall, where a guide takes participants to places around town that are supposed to be haunted, and I take that tour every few years.

But my favorite place by far is the Whaley House in San Diego. It's the first (and possibly only) California historic site to have been officially recognized by the state as being haunted, and when I initially went there as a child, it closed at dusk. No one was allowed in at night. It's not a large building, but it is creepy. It was the home of a judge, and it's connected to his courtroom. It was also built over the site of a gallows. When I went there as a child, my cousin and I heard footsteps in a spot where many people have reported hearing footsteps, and after that we were afraid to go upstairs. As an adult, I returned with my wife. She was also afraid to go upstairs, but I dragged her with me. Weirdly, there was an old photograph on the wall that looked almost exactly like a woman we knew. I pointed it out to her—and she screamed. She then turned around, saw a mannequin wearing a historic black dress—and screamed. Embarrassed, we quickly went downstairs, past the other tourists who were wondering what all the racket was, and escaped through the back door. The place is spooky, and it usually shows up on Top Ten Haunted Houses in America lists.

Massie: When you write a novel, do you have a clear idea as to each character's personalities, likes, dislikes, strengths, weaknesses, backgrounds, etc. before you get started? Or do you have a more general idea and then the character comes into fuller being as you write (which would then mean going back and making tweaks to the earlier portions of the book?)

Little: I generally know the personality of the main character, and maybe that of his or her significant other. But the others evolve during the writing, sometimes for reasons that are necessary to the plot, sometimes because I have a vague feeling that a certain type of person is needed in the narrative at that point. Even the main character changes, however. Just as people in real life are affected by incidents in their lives, my characters change in response to the actions of the novel. Sometimes they don't actually change, but I discover deeper layers or new information about their pasts when they are confronted by events or interact with others. This affects the way I write about them going forward. It's very fluid, however, and nothing is ever set in stone.

Massie: Have any of your characters ever done anything in a story that caught you by surprise? If so, care to share one or two?

Little: Sometimes characters do surprise me. In *The Bank*, for instance, I gave a small town police chief a wife and two daughters so that he would have something normal to come home to after experiencing craziness on his job. But his wife . . . well, she decided to do things that the real estate agent spouse of a police chief wouldn't ordinarily do.

Massie: Do you write an entire first draft and then go back and edit? Or do you edit as you go along?

Little: I'm essentially a one-draft writer (another after effect of having worked as a reporter). When asked how often he rewrote his first drafts, Mickey Spillane supposedly said, "Rewrite 'em? Hell, I don't reread 'em." I'm not quite that bad, but I don't edit as I go. Generally speaking, I write until I've finished the story, then I go back and proofread it. At that point, I might clean up a few awkward sentences, or correct a spelling error here and there, but that's about it.

One time, however, as I was proofreading my novel *The Handyman*, I felt as though the story ended too abruptly. I tagged on an epilogue, but it didn't work, so I sent the manuscript to my publisher in its original form. After reading it, the editor, too, thought there needed to be more of a conclusion. By this time, I'd been away from the story long enough that I was able to come up with a decent epilogue that seemed to solve the problem. Unfortunately, the original version was sent to the printer, so the book as it exists today is the one both my editor and I thought seemed incomplete. Maybe if there's a paperback edition, they can add the epilogue.

Massie: Some writers believe that outlining kills the spontaneity of their writing. Others say laying down some "tracks" ahead of time can be helpful in giving themselves direction as they write. Do you use any sort of outlining?

Little: I do not outline. I just sit down and start writing, often with only a vague idea of where I'm headed. That said, if I suddenly come up with an idea that I think will work well later in the story, I'll write it down and then write toward it. That's the advantage of writing on a computer instead of on a manual typewriter (which is the way I started out). For the novel I'm working on now, I have probably 200 pages of straight consecutive story—and another five pages of random phrases that will be incorporated into the second half of the novel.

Massie: A number of creative people I know create in more than one way. An artist might also play a musical instrument. A writer might also enjoy cooking creatively or gardening. A musician might dabble in poetry. I realize that writing takes up a lot of your time as it is your career, but are there any side activities you do that draw on other creative aspects of yourself?

Little: I'm a voracious consumer of media. I read a lot of books, watch a lot of movies, listen to a lot of music, watch a lot of television. But as for a creative outlet: I'm a writer. Period. It is my one talent, and it fulfills all of my creative needs. I have neither the ability nor the desire to do anything else.

Massie: I'm not at all surprised that you read a lot, along with consuming movies, music, and television. I've read and heard some newer genre writers say they only read horror novels. What advice would you give to them?

Little: It's not really my place to critique a person's reading habits. Life's short, and I think people should read what they want to read. That said, I tend to read a wide variety of books.

To me, reading only one type of fiction is like eating the same meal day after day. Ice cream's great, but I don't want it for breakfast, lunch, and dinner. So, I don't limit my reading to horror fiction. Besides, there are a lot of great authors who write in other genres, and if I restricted my reading palate, I would miss out on them. Not to mention the fact that if I've spent all day working on a horror story, sometimes I want a break from the subject.

Massie: Thanks so much for taking time to talk with us and giving us some insights and advice. Keep on writing the good write and we will keep on reading!

Bentley Little is one of the most prolific and talented horror authors around. He's been entertaining horror fans with his story skills since the 1980s. His novels include, among many others, *The Revelation, The Mailman, University, The Store, The Town, The Ignored, The Association, The Academy, The Handyman*, and the newest release, *The Bank* (Cemetery Dance, 2020.) His works have been praised by Stephen King and in particular Dean Koontz, who was impressed enough by Little's writing abilities to help him learn some of the publishing ropes. Little has been called an "enigmatic" author (according to "Book Series in Order"), and that enigma "has allowed the mystery of his persona to grow." This seems, in part, because he doesn't take part in social media nor even have internet access.

Elizabeth Massie has been drawn to horror ever since her pre-school days when she read that Cinderella's stepsisters cut off toes and heels (respectively) to win the prince's hand in marriage. I mean, whoa. Those are some fascinating, creepy mindsets there. Inspired by fairytales as well as the original *Twilight Zone* and *Outer Limits*, Massie grew up (well, kinda) to become a Bram Stoker Award-winning and Scribe Award-winning author of novels, collections, short fiction, and more. Her works include *Sineater, Hell Gate, Desper Hollow, Madame Cruller's Couch and Other Dark and Bizarre Tales, Wire Mesh Mothers, Homeplace, Naked on the Edge, Afraid, It Watching, Dark Shadows: Dreams of the Dark* (co-authored with Mark Rainey), *Versailles, The Tudors: King Takes Queen, The Tudors: Thy Will Be Done,* and many others. She is also the creator of the *Ameri-Scares* series of spooky novels for middle grade readers which was optioned by Warner Horizon. Massie lives in the Shenandoah Valley of Virginia with her husband, illustrator Cortney Skinner. She loves geocaching and the beach and can't stand cheese and mean people.

What are You Afraid Of?

Lee Thomas

Creators are in a time of tremendous opportunity, but they are also in one of the most conservative phases of publishing. With publishers and editors in absolute terror of getting called out for insensitive representations, cultural appropriation, as well as straight-up prejudice, while simultaneously trying to address a socially aware audience that demands diversity, many folks in the book business are walking on eggshells.

Good. They need to get it right.

For so long, diversity was managed poorly or left out completely. Travel on back a couple of decades and see how many characterizations in speculative literature included People of Color (PoC) and those who sexually identify as not straight (LGBTQ+) you can find. Shout out those titles.

Let the crickets commence.

Suddenly, this dearth of diverse voices and experiences became a problem (it was finally noticed), but the reaction from certain sectors of the publishing industry was weak. For years, the argument had been, "There isn't an audience for those stories." They clung to that rationale. So, the audience had to let itself be known; it had to be heard. The mechanism they used to amplify their voices, social media, exploded, and it gave creators and readers the platform they needed.

Granted, certain areas of publishing were keeping up. Literary fiction tended to follow about a step behind social movements, and science fiction often speculated on "the other," creating vast opportunities for analogy. Further, niche publishers emerged, focusing their efforts on works of particular groups (PoC, LGBTQ+) that otherwise would not have found distribution. But alas, my best beloved genre, horror, was way behind the curve.

This chapter is going to offer a bit of context, a bit of history, and some advice for creating stories with LGBTQ+ content. It's important to acknowledge brilliant works have been and are being created with lesbian, bisexual, trans, queer, a-sexual, and other oriented characters, and these stories are contributing significantly to the literary canon and the advancement of the LGBTQ+ community. That noted, the primary examples here reference the gay male experience. However, I believe much of the content is transferrable.

If you're a member of the LGBTQ+ community, you know there are thousands of stories that need to be told, but you may wonder if there's an audience for the work. If you're not a member of the community, you might well wonder if you should (or even have the right to) write inclusive stories, particularly since the chance of getting called out is ever present. The answer to both is: Yes. Absolutely. One of the joys of writing is putting ourselves in other people's shoes, but, you want to put the work in. You want to do it right.

Over the years, questions and comments about my work have been posted that include such confounding phrases as—"The story would have been better without all the gay stuff;" "I couldn't relate to the gay parts;" and "Why don't you just write mainstream horror? You'd sell a lot more books."

This last comment (or some variation) has come from colleagues, publishing professionals, and readers. I find it the most confounding. What is the mainstream? Weren't Poppy Z. Brite, Clive Barker, and Peter Straub mainstream horror? Didn't they all write books featuring gay protagonists? (Yes, I understand that truly brilliant writers will receive a different response in the market than some of us shlubs, but still . . .) Even more importantly, why the hell wouldn't I write about those people and situations that were important to me? Aren't young writers always offered (somewhat iffy) advice like: "Write what you know?" and "Write the stories you want to read?"

In the late 80s and early 90s several exceptional works, featuring gay men and lesbians in the roles of protagonists, arrived to some fanfare, suggesting horror readers might be ready to embrace diverse characterizations. Among these groundbreaking authors were Clive Barker with the *Books of Blood* (1984), Peter Straub with *Koko* (1988) and *The Throat* (1993), and Poppy Z. Brite with *Lost Souls* (1992) and *Drawing Blood* (1993). As we moved into the new millennium, however, it seemed the momentum they had begun, had ground to a halt. LGBTQ+ representations in horror were few. So, not only could I write what I knew, but there was a whole lot of unexplored territory to write the kinds of stories I wanted to read. (There's still a ton of it, so get on that.) And as I began to get published, people started asking me why I wrote about that stuff.

Which brings me to the words of Toni Morrison, who said, "I never asked Tolstoy to write for me, a little colored girl in Lorain, Ohio. I never asked [James] Joyce not to mention Catholicism or the world of Dublin . . . It is that business of being universal, a word hopelessly stripped of meaning for me . . . If I tried to write a universal novel, it would be water. Behind this question is the suggestion that to write for black people is somehow to diminish the writing. From my perspective there are only black people. When I say 'people,' that's what I mean."

It's there in the phrases about universality and diminishment. The world doesn't need my take on heterosexual life. There's more than enough out there; it's been drenching our culture for centuries. If one of the purposes of fiction is to explore unknown settings, situations, conflicts, and characters, why should a story be of *less* value when it comes with perspectives external to the norm? Though the inclusion of LGBTQ+ content might have seen by others as diminishing the work, I understood this was what set my work apart, made it interesting. Made it valuable.

In recent years, I have been thrilled to see more and more authors, both LGBTQ+ and straight, creating other-oriented characters. I've also been disappointed to see how many deep-rooted cliches remain. So, let's look at a few of these.

As a young man, if I had based my perception of gays and lesbians exclusively on the actions and thoughts of homosexual characters in horror literature, I would have been left with the damaging impression that gays existed solely as lonely, embittered, suicidal, often deviant, individuals who resided in the shadowy fringes for good reason. Naturally, these characterizations were exploitative, playing to the overarching culture. So, rather than expressing traits inherent in homosexuals (whatever those might be), these works expounded on the worst traits formed and reinforced by a homophobic society. Of course, things have changed, but many of these cliches persist, and we even have some new ones.

The first few we'll look at briefly. These were once highly prevalent, but have since been addressed so many times, they don't appear nearly as often as they once did.

The effeminate male has long been the standard for gay representation, and it persists in varying forms. What's interesting about this cliché is that, in many ways, it's been reappropriated by the drag community and sent back out to the world, through popular media properties like Ru Paul's *Drag Race*, promoting the strength of the feminized man. We've also seen the chirpy, ever-supportive best friend character; the snobby, young (nearly always white) purveyors of clenched-jawed disapproval; and the victim.

The victim is a damaging cliché that lingers. Its origins are deeply rooted in our culture, and it manifests in a number of ways.

One of the most pervasive is the "Bury Your Gays" device. This approach to gay characterization was born of necessity in the 19th Century, since promoting "perversion" was discouraged, even outlawed, in both Victorian-Era Great Britain and the United States. These laws made it damaging for authors to write positive storylines for LGBTQ+ characters. If they tried, they could face jail, fines, and the complete destruction of their careers and personal lives. So, when a creator wanted to include gay characters, they had to do so by writing characters in misery: sad, corrupt, melancholic, depressed, and often suicidal, which gives the trope its name. Reaction to this predictable cliché has gotten so vehement that a writer can get called out online, rather loudly, for killing off a gay character.

Now, here's the thing, I write horror fiction. Considering the title of the book, I expect that you do as well. In horror, people die. Sometimes, a lot of people die. Sometimes they're gay. Intent and execution (the other kind of execution) are important here. If you've created a strong, fully realized LGBTQ+ character, and their death is part of the story, you've done your job. If you've sketched out a flimsy stereotype, included for the simple act of sacrifice, then you should expect to be excoriated for it. Truth is, if you do that with any kind of character you should be excoriated for it.

When not portrayed as melancholic, lovelorn, or on the brink of self-destruction, gay men were depicted as unwholesome and a moral threat. This is clear in the stereotype of the gay man as sexual predator, often enough suggesting a shallow life devoted to base pleasures or presenting the more damaging indictment that gay men were out to recruit their straight counterparts. By this social equation that connected LGBTQ+ behaviors to immorality, characters that exhibited overtly homosexual tendencies were often cast in the role of villain since homosexuality was presented as a marker signifying profound and consuming deviance above and beyond mere sexual orientation. From Chandler's characterization of the pornographer Geiger in *The Big Sleep* (1939) to the mutinous, ultimately cannibalistic Caulker's Mate, Cornelius Hickey, in Dan Simmons' *The Terror* (2007) homosexuality has often been conflated with debauched and grotesque acts, used as a reader's cue that the character is vile and dangerous.

This is a good point to ease away from the discussion of cliches and begin to look at how those cliches have persisted in horror fiction.

Historically, horrific stories—whether fairy tales, myths, or works of literature—have been, at their core, morality plays. Be good. Obey your parents. Forsake the demons of drink and fornication. Uphold the status quo and all will be well. If you follow temptation, retribution awaits. Contemporary horror fiction has clung tightly to this heritage. Time and again horror authors pit upstanding, wholesome, "normal" characters against persons, forces, or creatures intent on upsetting the status quo. As such, one sees that the puritanical palette from which horror is inked contains little in the way of gray space between the blacks and whites of good and evil.

While such tales are entertaining and can indeed serve as cautionary analogies, they can also perpetuate and promote suspicion toward groups perceived as "other." Xenophobia is defined by Merriam-Webster as "fear and hatred of strangers or foreigners or of anything that is strange or foreign." Through the 1970s and 1980s Homophobia was certainly present, and even far reaching, but in a broader sense, on a cultural level, people were dealing with a minority group that was for the most part a mystery, so the overarching term of Xenophobia seems more appropriate, as there can be little doubt that understanding of this group, when attempted at all, was minimal.

As such, it is no surprise that during the horror fiction boom of the 1970s and 1980s genre authors rarely included gay characters in their stories, and when they did incorporate them, the representations were flat and predictable. Often enough if a horror author decided to use a gay character in his or her work, they pulled a cardboard cutout from the closet and dropped it onto the page. For instance, in James Herbert's *The Fog* (1975), a teacher suspected of being homosexual is sodomized and mutilated by his all-male class, while a lonely and dejected lesbian contemplates suicide at the beach. Herbert's book was not alone. Konvitz's *The Sentinel*, King's *It*, and many other titles presented LGBTQ+ characters through cliché and judgement.

The trend of denigrating what few gay characters appeared in horror fiction continued through the 1980s as pulp writers churned out one horrific tale after another and found the need to populate their books with easily identifiable characters whose only roles were to serve as disposable victims or villains. Stereotyping made this an easy task. Horror authors didn't need complex characters to move their plots but were able to populate their works with such general "types" as the whore, the junkie, the black man, the Asian, and the gay. No further exploration of character was necessary, as readers were invited to bring their own understanding of these types—promoted and reinforced by popular culture—to the text.

As we moved into the new millennium, social acceptance advanced considerably, but LGBTQ+ representations in horror dwindled. Occasionally, a title would find an audience and make some waves, such as David Thomas Lord's *Bound in Blood* (2001), but for the most part, we'd been pushed back into the closet. This was not true elsewhere in the literary landscape. Representations in other categories were pushing forward, and they were changing dramatically. Gay stories were becoming about more than just being gay.

Author David Leavitt, in his 2005 essay, "Out of the Closet and Off the Shelf," for *The New York Times*, asserts:

More and more, gay fiction is giving way to post-gay fiction: novels and stories whose authors, rather than

51

making a character's homosexuality the fulcrum on which the plot turns, either take it for granted, look at it as part of something larger or ignore it altogether ... In most of these works being gay is not central; these are just people living their lives.

Post-gay characters have a different set of conflicts than their predecessors. AIDS is still a devastating force in the gay community, but pharmacological advances have transformed the discussion from one of certain death to one of health management. Social tolerance of gays by the straight community is not universal, but it has progressed significantly in the past thirty years, so that adults in the LGBT community have a different perspective of the world around them.

Both Clive Barker and Peter Straub presupposed the post-gay characterization long before Leavitt coined the phrase. During my first reading of Barker's *In the Hills, The Cities*, I had to reread a certain paragraph several times, because it seemed the two male characters had just had sex, but the idea of that content in a horror story was so alien to me, and Barker had never announced the homosexuality of his characters, I had to go back. In Peter Straub's *Koko* (1986), one of the protagonists, Tim Underhill, is tagged as gay early on. In a brilliant stroke, Straub sets up the character with the probability that Underhill is a villain (an expected role for a gay character), only to confound reader expectations later in the story.

What also set Underhill apart was his distance from gay conflicts. He was gay in a more incidental way. Straub has explained, "Really, I just liked the idea. A big, physical guy, totally masculine, a bit profane, a bit scary, very smart, really well-read, brave ... and guess what, gay."

Now, it's important to note that Underhill worked very well as an "incidental gay," simply because the character was so far removed from major issues that plagued other gay men during this time. He was not a political creature with the shadow of gay rights hanging over him, nor was he proximate to the effects of AIDS on the gay community. He simply wasn't a part of that world.

Even so, the idea of an "incidental gay," is tricky when writing contemporary fiction, for the same reason writing "incidentally Asian" or "incidentally African American" characters would be. Whether we like it or not, LGBTQ+ lives are political, because the culture has politicized us. Things have improved immensely in the past 50 years, but there are still total strangers in powerful positions at the state and federal levels, who believe they have the duty to strip away our rights. Churches preach against us, and discrimination is a matter for the courts to decide. Gay bashing still exists. As recently as 2018, the "LGBTQ+ panic" murder defense was successfully used to mitigate murder charges. So, attempting to create a character that is incidentally gay suggests a shallowness, or at the very least, a missed opportunity to create textures for a character.

This is not to say that stories or novels have to tackle LGBTQ+ issues. In fact, the conceit behind the Post Gay movement is that the issues aren't the focus of a story. That doesn't mean these issues don't exist and color our characters; it means the issue isn't at the core of the primary conflict. As an example, Paul Tremblay's *The Cabin at the End of the World* (2018) introduces a gay couple and their daughter, who endure a terrifying home invasion. The intruders have not targeted the characters because they are gay; the primary conflict has nothing to do with the protagonists' sexuality. Even so, one of the protagonists processes the event through his own experience with a brutal gay bashing.

Now that we have a brief history and a few ideas of what not to do under our belts, let's move forward.

Any good character is going to be fully realized, with a past, a vision for their future, and an emotional component, that can go from dead-inside to frantically sensitive. Though we have evolved past the "issue" novel, some awareness of the issues a character faces because of their race, religion, or sexual orientation can add depth and texture. In horror, we're dealing with psychological, emotional, and physical assault in a variety of forms. Think about the real-world threats to characters of diversity and imagine how they might equate or weigh the fictionalized abuses with those they face by simply existing in our society. By doing so, you're providing readers with points of empathy for the character, making any threat to that character all the more affecting. You're also grounding the story in what we understand to be the real world (if that's relevant to your tale).

If you're not a member of, or highly familiar with a particular group, then you should invest in research. If you were writing about a profession you didn't know, you'd hit the books or Google, so your microbiologist didn't sound like a cartoon character. The same effort should go into creating members of diverse groups. As previously noted, representations in media have advanced significantly, but watching a few television programs isn't the best way to get a handle on a minority group.

Several of my novels have been, in part, Historicals. When researching a particular era, I make the effort to immerse myself in the popular culture of the time. I read newspaper articles, listen to the music, read short stories and books, listen to radio programs. It's all available at the library or online. What I don't do is look for information in current popular culture that comments on that era, except for nonfiction pieces. I don't want to include information that has already been processed through another creator's mind. So, instead of watching *The Deuce* for details about 1970s New York City (though admittedly, the show does a fantastic job of recreating the time), read newspaper articles and watch movies that were created in that time. Listen to the music that was growing out of that period, and not just the hits. From this, you can gather small details that are specific to an era and not as obvious to readers.

This same process works when laying the groundwork for representations of diverse characters. Read works *by* LGBTQ+

writers, not just stories *about* them. Check out blogs and YouTube channels. Find out what is going on in that group and the art, entertainment, and issues, big and small, that are relevant and talked about. You'll find quite a few cultural touchstones beyond on just politics and sex.

And speaking of sex . . .

I'll only devote a few lines to the necessity of sex in a story. Your characters may have sex, they may not, but keep in mind sex is never *about* sex, at least not in fiction. It's about emotion, situation, and power. Sure, a scene can be added strictly for titillation, but that's missing an opportunity, since one scene can reveal much about your characters.

So, if you're a member of the LGBTQ+ community, tell your stories. An audience is waiting. We need to read them. If you're not a member of the community, you should explore any stories and characters you choose, even those including diverse lives and points of view. We want to read what you come up with.

For a very long time, LGBTQ+ readers never saw themselves in horror stories, at least they never saw anything to which they could aspire. Representation is important, and accurate representation is essential. The community is made up of heroes and villains and everything in between. When our stories are told and read and shared, understanding grows and the uncertainty (the fear) burns away. Of the hundreds of things your readers find threatening in your stories, the LGBTQ+ community should not be one of them.

Lee Thomas is the Bram Stoker Award- and two-time Lambda Literary Award-winning author of the books *Stained, The Dust of Wonderland, The German, Parish Damned, Like Light for Flies, Down on Your Knees*, and *Distortion* among others. His work has been translated into multiple languages and has been optioned for film. Lee lives in Austin, Texas with his husband, John.

Working from the Subconscious
Joe R. Lansdale

The most important thing I learned as a writer was to work from the subconscious. This sounds easy, and pretty much is once you are able to tap into it, but it takes practice. The subconscious is thought of as disorganized, and I suppose it can be, but I've found that since I don't plot my work, unless working in collaboration with others, where you kind of have to, that learning to rely on the subconscious is necessary, and though you may not be plotting in a conventional way, there's still plotting going on, but you are not as aware of it.

There's a lot of stuff there in the subconscious, and the disorganized materials have to be trained to line up, and this is a primary duty of the conscious mind, which for me works best after the subconscious has sorted things, and has in fact done a lot of secret plotting. The conscious mind scrapes off the edges, jettisons the useless, the materials that will not work in your story. Sometimes, however, the dream-like aspects of subconscious thinking, meaning the sort of thing where it all makes sense while dreaming, but not so much when awake, may have their purpose, may give your story a specific feel that can make a mundane scene seem more luminous.

Reading novels, stories, comics, non-fiction and viewing films and TV shows are fuel for the subconscious, as well as talking with others, if by phone, email, or in person. Before Covid, one of my joys was sitting and talking with people and hearing their stories. Having other interests besides writing and reading are important as well. For me it has been martial arts, even though I can't do much during Covid, as far as training my students, I have a martial artists mind, which I believe is about curiosity, free form, and learning what truly works for you through trial and error.

I have said before, to be the kind of writer you want to be, you have to write for you. Write like everyone you know is dead, so that you don't worry about what others think. It's about what you think. If you write for yourself, at least in my personal experience, you do better. Writing for yourself doesn't mean it's good, but with time you are more likely to arrive at the place you want to go, where the material is good.

I found that if I sat down to plot in a conventional manner, I would look at the ceiling, think about what was out in the yard, which books I wanted to read, and nothing developed other than boredom or some forced idea that was about as exciting as being forced to sit on and hatch a chicken egg. But, during the day, if I could learn to relax and think about anything but story, ideas would develop, and certainly at night a seed would be found. I don't immediately try and whip it into shape. I let it spill out, and after all these years my subconscious has learned to give me a story, and each day when I awake it has sorted it for me. I try to quit writing when I feel there are at least fumes in the tank, then start afresh the next day.

I try to write only about three hours a day. I stay fresh that way, and don't get so tuckered out that next day I do nothing. I set a reasonable number of pages. Three to five. I nearly always achieve that, or more. Sometimes a lot more. I let the idea flow, but I never let it turn into a vomit draft, which doesn't work for me at all, which explains the short work space daily. I polish as I go. I avoid multiple drafts, and when it's all done, I do a polish. I work better that way.

Do I ever violate this? Of course. I'm a grown man. I can make decisions. Have I ever been let down by my subconscious? From time to time, it will take a holiday and will fail to leave contact information. Still, there is enough residue in the house of my subconscious, I can, on my worst day, write a story. It may require more of my conscious mind than my subconscious during those periods, and I don't like it, but I can write a professional story. Sometimes the residue in my subconscious actually gives me a far better one than I expected.

That's the next trick. Showing up. I try to work five to seven days a week, and it takes something special to throw off that approach. Even on holidays, by working my short burst, in the morning, as soon as I wake up, I can be through for the day and any plans for the holidays are pretty much on course. Again, there are exceptions, but not many.

When I worked other jobs, I had to be sure and work either in the morning or afternoon or night. It might only be an hour in the morning, or an hour at lunch time, usually less, and primarily I read during that time or listened to people talk and tell stories, some of them wonderfully mundane. I enjoyed those too. Then at night I would work some more.

But now, after forty-seven years of writing, and now reaching forty years of full-time writing, I have been able to work my method successfully. I love writing. It can be hard sometimes, but mostly I find it fun. I think you should. It beats working in the aluminum chair factory and suits me right down to a tee.

I also bring a lot of my prewriting experience into my subconscious, let it bunch up until it wants out, and go for it. I borrow from my life, that of others, stories I've heard, etc., and then I make the rest of it up, or at best, my subconscious does. It seems far more clever than the conscious mind.

Wake up. Explode on paper with whatever comes to mind, and over time what comes to mind will make more sense. Sometimes just a line, or a deep memory or thought will blossom into a story idea. For me, nine times out of ten, after years of tapping into the subconscious, when I put my fingers on the keys, it's like a sensation of being electrified, and away I go.

Again, this is my method. It might work for you, or might even help you find a method that works for you. I will say this. This method has been good to me.

Joe R. Lansdale has written novels and stories in many genres, including western, horror, science fiction, mystery, and suspense. He has also written for comics as well as "Batman: The Animated Series." As of 2020, he has written 50 novels and published more than 30 short-story collections (maybe 40 by now!) along with many chapbooks and comic-book adaptations. His stories have won ten Bram Stoker Awards, a British Fantasy Award, an Edgar Award, a World Horror Convention Grand Master Award, a Sugarprize, a Grinzane Cavour Prize for Literature, a Spur Award, and a Raymond Chandler Lifetime Achievement Award. He has been inducted into The Texas Literary Hall of Fame, and several of his novels have been adapted to film.

Interview with Graham Masterton
JG Faherty

JG Faherty: *Over the years, you've earned a reputation as a writer who embraces many different genres, from horror to non-fiction. Do you feel this type of multi-faceted writing can help someone who's trying to build a career, or do you think a writer will develop their skills better by sticking to one genre in the beginning?*

Graham Masterton: With the benefit of hindsight, I think it's essential if you're thinking of becoming a full-time writer that you should stick to one genre . . . at least in the early days of your career. My first horror novel *The Manitou* was published around the same time as Stephen King's *Salem's Lot*, and sold more than half a million copies in its first six months. *The Manitou* was picked up by the late Bill Girdler and filmed with Tony Curtis playing the lead role. I went on then to write *The Djinn* and *The Revenge of the Manitou* and both sold tremendously well. But in those days, I had no concept of 'genre.' I had little understanding of building a 'fan base' and I didn't fully grasp that booksellers have so many thousands of books to deal with that they like to know which category to slot you into without actually having to read your book.

I wasn't bored with horror, but I wanted to expand my horizons and write about other topics that interested me. I was trained as a newspaper reporter and so I saw fascinating stories everywhere, not only personal and social but political. I wrote a romance novel, *Heartbreaker,* and then a huge historical saga, *Rich,* and then a disaster novel, *Plague,* and several political thrillers, *The Sweetman Curve, Ikon* and *Sacrifice.* All of these books sold well. My historical epics made the *New York Times* bestseller list. But I was neglecting my horror readers, and I lost the tremendous kind of momentum that Stephen King was building up.

Eventually, after three or four years, I returned to horror with a novel called *Tengu,* about Japanese demons taking revenge for Hiroshima. I have continued to write horror novels successfully ever since. But I have no doubt at all that I could have achieved much greater success if I had stuck to the genre consistently in those early days.

Faherty: *Switching genres the way you do, is it easy to move from one to the next, such as from horror to comedy, or do you have to really force yourself to work to keep things scary, or humorous, or whatever the book might be?*

Masterton: I have been writing novels since I was about eight years old. My first was inspired by my excitement at seeing the movie of Jules Verne's *Twenty Thousand Leagues Under the Sea*. I rushed home and wrote a novel in a school exercise book about a harpoonist called Hans Lee and how he fought a giant squid. I bound the book in cardboard, drew a picture for the cover and sold it to my friend for a penny. That was my first-ever royalty. I have been writing obsessively ever since, because I have so many fascinating ideas and the best way in which I can share them with other people is to write books and short stories about them.

I think basically that I am a born entertainer. If I had not become a novelist, I would probably have become a comedian, but I thank the muses that I didn't because being a comedian is very much harder and more stressful than writing novels. My great-grandfather was Polish and when he came to England from Warsaw, he became one of the most successful theatrical impresarios in London, managing Queen Victoria's favourite comedian Dan Leno. I have always enjoyed making people laugh, because I have always understood that laughter is one of our greatest defenses against fear and depression. So I find no difficulty in introducing humor into my horror or crime novels, because real people do often use jokes to deal with situations that worry or frighten them.

Here's some advice: I study the acts of top comedians to see how they handle their audiences—Jackie Mason for instance, or Don Rickles. Technically one of the best for timing and audience response was a British comedian called Max Miller. His timing was spot on, and he had a way of telling a suggestive joke without actually being explicit . . . he would lead the audience into thinking the ribald punchline without saying the words themselves and then accuse them of having filthy minds. You can use those stage techniques in your writing, encouraging your readers to think beyond the actual words that they see on the page. A typical example was a woman reader who complained to me about a scene in *Family Portrait* in which two little girls are beaten to death. She said it was too bloody and too explicit. I suggested that she go back and read it again. All I actually wrote was that the girls were killed like two seal cubs being clubbed in a cull. She had obviously seen a cull on television and visualized the blood and the cruelty for herself.

Faherty: *Many of your books require extensive research, such learning about Native American mythology for the Manitou series, or police procedure for the Katie Maguire* *books, or medical protocols for Plague. What's your process for research when it comes to a new book?*

Masterton: It used to mean regular visits to the local library, but of course these days we have the blessing of Google and other search engines on the internet, which saves a huge amount of time and effort. There are some details of course which you can't find online. For the Katie Maguire novels I talked to officers of An Garda Síochána (the Irish police) about their experiences and the Garda press office was always very helpful. What was most important for those novels, though, was actually living in Cork for five years and getting to know the community intimately. The only problem about that experience was that when I returned to live back in England, there was still some Corkinese stuck in my brain, both in terms of language and of logic, and I still can't stop myself from saying 'thanks a million' when I am being served in a shop or saying 'langered' when I mean 'drunk.'

For me, accurate research is absolutely vital, although I rarely share very much of it with my readers, as some writers are tempted to do, because that would be tedious and slow down the story. The more far-out the story, the more important it is to sound believable and have your characters and your setting rooted in reality. I have only once invented a town, and that was Granitehead in *The Pariah*, a thinly-disguised version of Marblehead, Massachusetts. Otherwise, I always set my books in real places. I am currently writing a horror novel based in Reseda, in California, and I have had some very useful help from the West Valley police department. It is probably my training as a newspaper reporter, but most of my novels are inspired by real events—my new horror novel *The Children God Forgot* was sparked by the massive fatbergs blocking London's sewers, hundreds of tons of solidified cooking fat and all the extraordinary debris that people flush down their toilets, including jewelry and live puppies.

I love writing historical novels, but the research is incredibly time-consuming. I recently published two crime thrillers set in the 1750s, set both in New England and London—*Scarlet Widow* and *The Coven*. For those novels I had to find detailed maps, as well as menus from restaurants of the time and newspaper reports. I had to research clothing and how it was worn. Did women wear knickers at the time? (No.)

Faherty: *I had a professor in college who always used to say, "Success is 1% inspiration and 99% perspiration." What's your take on what makes a good book—is it more the execution or the idea?*

Masterton: Your professor was simply repeating a cliché which bears no relation to the creation of a successful novel. Inspiration is everything. The plot has to be stunningly original, and hit readers completely from left-field. *The Manitou* was so successful because almost nobody had written a horror novel about Native American mythology before (with the exception of Algernon Blackwood's *Wendigo*). I fail to understand why people are still writing about vampires and werewolves and zombies when there are so many fantastic and terrifying demons and phantoms in world mythology. I have written only two vampire novels—*Descendant*, based on painstaking research into Romania's *strigoi* and not on tall men with fangs and black cloaks who bite fainting women on the neck—and *Manitou Blood*, in which vampires and Native American demons were combined.

Throughout the course of writing your story, you should constantly seek fresh inspiration to keep your readers surprised and shocked. You need to keep thinking throughout the writing process of new and entertaining ideas—bring in new characters that you hadn't thought of when you were starting out. They will change the course of the plot and make it more enjoyable for *you* as well as your readers.

Of course, writing is hard and tiring work—much harder and more tiring than non-writers ever imagine—and of course you can't sell a book until you've written it. But the inspiration is everything.

Faherty: What's your approach for writing a new novel? Once you have the idea, do you let it germinate slowly, or dive right in? Outline or just get started?

Masterton: It depends on whether I am writing a novel on commission or whether I am simply writing it because an idea has come to me. For instance, I wrote the first crime thriller about Detective Superintendent Katie Maguire because we had been living in Ireland for a while and I realized that I had never seen or heard of a crime novel set in Cork, which is a fascinating and highly idiosyncratic city, with its own accent which bears no resemblance to the smooth lilt you hear in Dublin and its own extraordinary slang—dowcha, boy! I also realized that there were very few female senior officers in the Garda (which was very Masonic and misogynistic) and that would make for some terrific character conflicts. I mixed those ingredients with some Irish mythology and then just sat down and let the story develop. When it came to the following ten novels in the series, all of them were commissioned by my publishers, so I would check with my friend Caroline Delaney at *The Irish Examiner* and see what scandalous stories were topping the news and construct a novel out of those.

My latest horror novel *The House of a Hundred Whispers* came from a request by my publishers for a haunted house story. I know that haunted house novels are very popular, but they are quite restrictive to write because they are mostly set in one location, and I do like multiple locations and multiple intertwining stories. However, I found an inspiring setting (Dartmoor, where *The Hound of the Baskervilles* was set) and a completely different breed of ghosts. Not ghosts at all, in fact, but something much more harrowing.

I wrote a page-and-a-half synopsis, which my publishers liked, and then just sat down and wrote it—but carried on researching local legends and local language all the time that I was writing it.

Ghost Virus, on the other hand, came from an idea, which occurred to me while I was visiting my author friend Dawn G Harris at the cancer charity shop which she used to manage. Donors bring in bags of clothes and some of those clothes used to belong to people who have passed away. It occurred to me that perhaps something of their spirit and something of their resentment at having died might have been absorbed into those clothes . . . with unnerving consequences for anybody who buys them and then wears them. I simply sat down and wrote about that spooky possibility, and as I wrote it new characters kept popping up and developing the story for me. I also researched what happens to clothes that can't be resold but are sent to Estonia as 'shoddy' to be ripped up and woven into new fabric. Most people don't realize how many 'new' clothes are made out of recycled fibers.

However, it is not worth rushing through a story. Sometimes it's worth taking a day or two off just to let the plot mulch for a while. You can often surprise yourself with what striking ideas you can come up with to enhance your book.

Faherty: *When you're writing, what kind of atmosphere or environment do you prefer? I know I like to write in silence, but some writers prefer music. Some like a bright office, some dark. Certain writers have to write at a specific time of day. Some prefer to write in public. What is your modus operandi?*

Masterton: I need absolute silence. I am creating a completely different world in my head and any outside noise is distracting.

I have a neighbor who has a vintage motorcycle and every now and then he takes it out and revs it up for about fifteen minutes. I have a large hammer and he is on my hit list. But for me, writing prose is like writing music. It is vital for me that readers should not be aware that they are reading, but are carried away into the world that I have imagined, believing while they are reading that it's real. If there is music in the background, Mozart's rhythm will interfere with mine, and the emotions expressed in his score will affect the emotions that I am trying to write about. William Burroughs and I spent hours discussing how to choose words and write sentences in such a way that we were rendered invisible—El Hombre Invisible, he called it. That is why we cut up language and put it back together in a different order—the novel we wrote together *Rules of Duel* is the result of some of that discussion. We never really intended it to be published, but it has been, and while much of it appears to be incomprehensible, most authors will understand how its structure works, and learn something from it. It is like looking at the inside of an automobile engine and seeing the pistons and the valves going up and down.

I don't care if my writing room is light or dark, but I do like a view out of the window. In Ireland I could see the River Lee below my writing room, with ships coming and going, and the green hills beyond. I have one mug of espresso in the morning—'horseshoe coffee' it was called by the engineers who built the transcontinental railroads in America, because they said that it was so strong that a horseshoe could float in it. Then I just get on with it until I reach a point in the story where I think it's time to stop and think about what's going to happen next.

Faherty: *One of your trademarks is the ability to build suspense. What are the key points to accomplishing that?*

Masterton: The real secret to building suspense is not to know yourself as an author what is going to happen next. I have just written a scene in my new novel in which my protagonists have to interview a key witness in a movie studio in LA. While they are there, they are tracked down by some baddies who have been told to silence them. They escape from one sound stage into another, and they burst right into the middle of the shooting of a spectacular horror movie. Before they entered that sound stage, I had absolutely no idea what they were going to find in there, but it turns into one of the most chaotic and dramatic scenes that I have written in a long time. As William Burroughs used to repeat: '*Be* there!'

Faherty: Tell me about your writing style. Do you try to put down a certain number of words per day? Do you work on more than one project at a time?

Masterton: I don't believe in word counts. I shake my head when I see writers saying 'I've reached my daily target of 3,000 words' or whatever. You're writing a novel, not shoveling manure. How much I write in a day depends on how the story is developing, and also of course on other factors like going for a haircut or meeting Dawn for lunch. One of the reasons I find it hard to read the novels of other writers is because I can almost always tell when they're slogging on for the sake of reaching a word target, or when they're following their synopsis without stopping to think if the development of their plot could be more amusing and less mechanical. I can also tell when a writer is growing impatient with their story, or tired, or even when they're hungry (I guessed that from a Len Deighton novel and when I asked him about it, it turned out to be true. He had hurried the ending of a chapter because he was starving!).

I don't usually work on more than one novel at a time, but while I am waiting for the contracts to be signed for a new commission, I have once or twice been tempted to start work on a new (uncommissioned) novel. That happened with *The Children God Forgot* and I had to park it halfway through to write *The House of a Hundred Whispers* before returning to finish it off later.

Faherty: What is your take on writer's block? Is it real? Do you ever have problems getting from the beginning to the end of a novel, or getting one off the ground to start with?

Masterton: I know that some authors do get stuck, but that has never happened to me. In fact, I used to think that Writers' Block was this big building in downtown San Francisco where dozens of writers sat staring glumly at blank sheets of paper. I was trained as a newspaper reporter and then became a magazine editor for ten years and when you're in those jobs you have to deliver the goods on time whether you feel like it or not. I have one unfinished novel, *If Pigs Could Sing,* which was going to be a humorous story about two brothers from Iowa who hit it big in the music business because they discover that the pigs on their uncle's farm can sing in harmony. My New York agent at the time, Richard Curtis, absolutely hated it, so I shelved it, but you can still read what there is of it in the Fiction section of my UK website www.grahammasterton. co.uk.

Faherty: Which of your own books are you most proud of, and why?

Masterton: Hard to say, because I like most of them and all for different reasons. Probably, though, *Trauma,* which is a shortish novel that was inspired by an article I read about a woman who had set herself up as a crime scene cleaner. After a murder, the police won't clean the brains off the walls for you—you have to pay for a private contractor, and that is what this woman did. I was originally going to write it under a female *nom-de-plume* but Pocket Books wanted it under my own name. It is written with great simplicity, very sparsely. I am proud of it because it appears to be a supernatural story but in reality, is just the story of a woman who is falling apart. The director Jonathan Mostow (*U-571*) optioned it for a movie and it got as far as a script but Universal diverted the finance to another project.

Faherty: *What books or writers have influenced you as a writer, and how?*

Masterton: When I was young, Jules Verne first of all and then Edgar Allan Poe. In my early teens I discovered Nelson Algren (*The Man with the Golden Arm*) and Herman Wouk (*The Caine Mutiny*). I loved their toughness and directness, and particularly in Wouk's case, his ability during the course of his story to turn the readers' sympathies completely upside-down. After that I discovered the Beat writers: Jack Kerouac, Allen Ginsberg, Lawrence Ferlinghetti, and Gregory Corso. And, of course William Burroughs. I was deeply impressed by their bravery and how outspoken they were, and especially by their use of language. I wrote a great deal of poetry in those days and I still do. Poetry is the best possible exercise for an author to try out varying rhythms and precise vocabulary and how to convey the maximum emotion with the minimum number of words. Short stories are the same: much harder to write successfully than novels.

Faherty: *You've mentioned in the past that you don't read much horror, because it's hard to write horror all day and* *then read it as well. Yet many writers and writing instructors tell beginning authors to read as much in the genre as you can. What's your take on that?*

Masterton: Bollocks. You need to talk to real people and have the courage to ask them how they think and feel and what their lives are like. How do you think I managed to write 29 bestselling sex instruction books? When I was editor of *Penthouse,* I talked to the girls who appeared in the magazine about every aspect of their love lives. How do you think I can write a series of crime novels about a woman like Katie Maguire? All of my life all of my closest friends have been women and I have never held back from asking them about their feelings and their relationships. What can you learn from reading some other horror author's books? Nothing. What you need is personal experience and an understanding of other people's lives. And of course, you need be to be literate—to hone your grammar and your spelling so that you don't have to rely on Grammarly or Word; and to have an extensive vocabulary. You expect the pilot who flies your plane to know how to lower the landing gear. You should be equally professional as a writer. And above all—be totally original.

Faherty: You've written in so many different genres, but you've said in the past that horror is your favorite. Why is that?

Masterton: I like writing horror because it has no boundaries. I enjoy plunging very ordinary people into weird and terrifying situations and see how they're going to react. It's what happens in real life. We're all jogging along quite nicely and then Covid-19 comes along and turns our lives into an inexplicable nightmare. So many thousands of people dying. The scale of such a sudden tragedy is beyond comprehension.

Faherty: What words of advice would you give to someone who's looking to improve their writing?

Masterton: If you can, find somebody to whom you can read your stories or your chapters out loud. You will be surprised how much that will help you to pick up awkward rhythms, repetitions and plot developments that could use clearer explanation. Above all, be yourself. Don't take any notice of other authors who say 'the road to hell is paved with adverbs' or some such twaddle. If you feel the need to use an adverb, use an adverb, as long as it isn't tautological or a Tom Swifty ('I really like you in that sweater,' he said, pointedly.) Even if you found out all manner of fascinating stuff when researching your novel, don't bore your reader with it. The reader wants a story, and if you manage to impart a few titbits of interesting knowledge while you're telling it, good for you, but the story comes first.

Faherty: Thank you so much! I always enjoy having the chance to interview you and catch up in general.

Masterton: I look forward to it, JG! Meanwhile, if you have the space for it, let me leave you with a poem I wrote only recently about the worlds that Dawn G. Harris and I create when we're writing either separately or together, which I think illustrates my point about the value of writing poetry for every author seeking to improve their style.

SECRET WORLDS

But while you carry out your daily chores
Shopping; or chatting; or chopping onions;
or scrolling on your phones

We two go travelling, in secret
To worlds that you may never know exist.

Ordinary, some of them, these worlds, and drab
With rundown terraced houses; and blistered plane trees
And wheelie bins lined up behind their walls.

Yet others where a cyan sea rolls in
On salt-white sands; and where the stars
Sparkle all night like shattered glass.
Where lilac blooms in darkness; and funerals are held
And grey cats stare from windowsills with yellow eyes.

When we arrive in those worlds, calm and sure
Like two professors walking into school
People still speak in shadow-language:
Lovingly sometimes, cooing like pigeons; sometimes
spraying spit with spite.
But meaningless. And they have seen themselves
Only as blurred reflections in a passing car, or a stagnant
pond.

When we arrive, we teach them sentences to speak,
Or when to hold their tongues.
We dress them, men and women, and we hold a mirror up
So they can clearly see their faces, faultless or grotesque,
And understand the world in which they live, this secret
world
With skies, and ragged clouds, and winds that you will never
feel

Unless, that is, we choose to write
and tell you what these worlds are like:
Their hills, their gloomy forests and their rippling fields
And introduce who lives there:

Warm-hearted, hostile, passionate or cold
Hopeful or grieving; or bewildered; or alone.

Otherwise, those worlds stay secret, in our minds
Until we widen our horizons and make other worlds
Further, stranger, but even more believable
And those worlds are forgotten, still unknown.

Multi-award-winning writer **Graham Masterton** is best known for his *Manitou* series, but that's just the tip of the iceberg for this incredibly prolific writer. He's had more than 100 novels published over the course of his career, and in addition, he's put out 5 short story collections, written several movie tie-ins, two humor books, and more than 60 short stories. His latest novels include *The Last Drop of Blood* (Katie Maguire Book 11), *The Children God Forgot*, and *The House of a Hundred Whispers*. You can follow him on Facebook (graham.masterton.3) and visit him at www.grahammasterton.co.uk.

A life-long resident of New York's haunted Hudson Valley, **JG Faherty** is the author of 7 novels, 10 novellas, and more than 75 short stories. He's been a finalist for both the Bram Stoker Award® (*The Cure, Ghosts of Coronado Bay*) and ITW Thriller Award (*The Burning Time*). His most recent novel is *Sins of the Father*, a Lovecraftian tale of love and revenge set in 1800s Innsmouth. He grew up enthralled with the horror movies and books of the 1950s, 60s, 70s, and 80s, which explains a lot. Follow him at www.twitter.com/jgfaherty, www.facebook.com/jgfaherty, and www.jgfaherty.com.

Am I Really a Horror Writer?

Michelle Renee Lane

In the introduction to *Writers Workshop of Horror* (2009), Michael Knost shares his personal experience as a novice writer and the fact that he didn't have a reliable community of writers to draw from as peers and mentors. His goal in putting together that collection of essays from some extremely talented writers, was to provide some of the lessons he wished he'd had while getting started, and to create a reference for writers—novices and experts—to gain some solid insight about the craft of writing. There is a surplus of books on how to write covering everything from genre to chosen format (novels, short stories, screenplays, blog posts, etcetera), to how to find a publisher, and how to deal with rejection. Many of these books are very informative and inspiring; however, no matter how good a how-to book might be, it is no substitute for belonging to a community of writers.

Writing is a solitary pursuit. Even if you are in a crowded place like a coffee shop, a library, or even a classroom, you still have to rely on your own ideas and pull from your experiences, what you've read, and your own imagination. Writing can be lonely. It forces you to sit down with yourself and face the contents of your own head. This isn't always an easy thing to do. Especially if you've dealt with trauma of any kind, or addiction, or even the constant undercurrent of systemic racism, sexism, classism and homophobia.

Speaking of systemic racism, sexism, classism and homophobia, each of these "isms" prevented many horror writers who were not white or male from finding a safe and supportive community within the genre in the past. I don't think this culture of exclusion was limited to the horror writing community, but for most of my life horror fiction was a straight, white, male dominated genre that praised (and paid) writers like Stephen King, Dean Koontz, Peter Straub, Clive Barker, Ramsey Campbell, Richard Matheson and, of course, H. P. Lovecraft. In fact, if you Google the term "horror writers", these are the names that pop up first, and then we get Shirley Jackson, Mary Shelley and Anne Rice, and then Tananarive Due, Linda Addison and Victor LaValle sneak in there eventually. Just a note for those of you who may wish to argue about Clive Barker being part of the LGBTQIA+ writing community, Barker closeted himself as a writer for many years until after he received notoriety and financial stability, when he felt safe enough to reveal the part of his identity he'd kept hidden. Women and BIPOC (Black, Indigenous, and People of Color) writers haven't always had access to the horror writing community, let alone publishers willing to feature and pay for their work. This reality has changed, and is getting better, but roadblocks and gatekeepers made access difficult for a long time and even called into question whether women and BIPOC writers were writing actual horror fiction.

If we look at some of the recent finalists and winners for the Bram Stoker Awards, it seems ridiculous to even think that women and BIPOC writers had nothing to contribute to the genre. However, when I began writing my own horror novel this question came up a lot. Was my supernatural slave narrative *really* a horror novel? Was I *really* a horror writer?

Being a new writer in any genre can be scary and difficult to navigate without the appropriate guidance and acceptance from a supportive community of like-minded writers. This can be a local writing group, fellow classmates, or an organization like the Horror Writers Association. Each of these groups can provide some level of support and guidance for new writers. But, first, your work needs to be recognized as fitting within the specific genre you write. I think that speculative fiction (horror, science fiction, fantasy) can be a bit more flexible than other genres, but there are still rules and expectations. Not only for the fiction itself, but traditionally, for who was writing it.

H.P. Lovecraft wrote, "The oldest and strongest emotion of mankind is fear, and the oldest and strongest kind of fear is fear of the unknown." He isn't wrong. This quote has served as a kind of definition or at the very least a starting point for how to talk about the horror genre. But is "fear of the unknown" enough of a definition to cover the spectrum and subgenres of horror fiction? If the only horror you write, watch, or read involves masked psychos wielding sharp objects for the sole purpose of stabbing scantily clad coeds, tentacled monsters who defy space and time, or the shambling undead in a post-apocalyptic landscape, then perhaps you aren't seeing the whole picture. I would argue that while Lovecraft's quote is an excellent starting point to open a discussion of horror fiction, one brand of horror, and therefore one brand of fear, does not fit all.

By expanding the definition of "fear" and "horror" you not only make space for a variety of diverse voices and unique stories, but you also open the genre to a wider and more diverse audience of readers. I think a lot of people who haven't explored the vast range of narratives within the genre often have a very narrow-minded and negative view of diverse voices within horror. Horror really is the genre of emotions, and because people sometimes have a hard time confronting their own feelings, it can be difficult to enjoy stories that focus on some of the more unpleasant and terrifying aspects of human nature. For some of us, the most terrifying thing you can do is confront the person staring back at you in the mirror. Horror fiction has a habit of holding up a mirror that reflects the tragic and unsettling aspects of our society as a whole back at us. Horror isn't the only speculative genre that does this, but I believe it takes the brunt of criticism for its social commentary on the human condition.

This process of reflection—of the self or society at large—is especially uncomfortable for readers or viewers when a narrative reveals parts of the past or present that we'd like to forget or pretend doesn't exist, such as racism, sexism, slavery, the Holocaust, the systematic rape of women in extremist cultures, child abuse, gay bashing, the murder of transgendered people, or the genocide of native cultures world-wide. For many people, fear is the strongest emotion because they are living a nightmare. There's no need to fear the unknown, because reality is terrifying enough.

When I was in my teens, I wanted to write like the horror writers I enjoyed reading and admired for their success, like Stephen King, Clive Barker, Whitley Strieber, Peter Straub, but especially, Anne Rice. The Vampire Chronicles created a strong desire in me to write about vampires even though I couldn't see myself in her fiction. Then I discovered Toni Morrison, Alice Walker, Octavia E. Butler and Jewelle Gomez, and realized I wanted to write like *them*. They were writing stories about people who looked like me, and even if their books weren't shelved with horror fiction, they were telling scary stories. I believe that good fiction—literary, genre, or anything in between—should not only entertain the reader, but also leave them with a sense of curiosity and wonder about the world around them. As a reader, I'm happiest when I can get inside the mind of a character who is different enough than me that I learn something new but written in a way I can relate to and empathize with their personal struggles.

Recently, a friend told me she had a dream in which Oprah declared me the Alice Walker of Horror. I laughed about it at first, but then started thinking about that as a concept. What genre do I write? Am I writing horror fiction? Toni Morrison's *Beloved* is a horror novel and, in my opinion, created a new subgenre, Black Southern Gothic Horror. I don't know if that's a recognized genre, but that's what came to mind when I read it. Morrison's novel affected me deeply and had a lasting impression. It's a ghost story set in the South after the Civil War and it is filled with powerful images that explore the idea that slavery had a lasting physical and psychological effect on the people who suffered under it. I wanted to achieve something like that and hopefully expand the subgenre of Black Southern Gothic Horror when I wrote *Invisible Chains*, which is a supernatural slave narrative with monsters.

While I enjoy reading stories about the Elder Gods, I don't fear Cthulhu. As a woman of color, I fear the many faces that hatred and oppression take in this world. I fear rape. I fear hate crimes. I fear poverty. I fear a lack of access to female reproductive health care. I fear institutionalized racism that prevents people from achieving their goals. I fear glass ceilings. I fear hunger and food insecurity. I fear global warming and ecological catastrophes. These are real things we should all be afraid of and they are excellent topics for horror fiction.

Our ever-changing sociopolitical climate is having, in my opinion, a positive effect on horror fiction. As more diverse voices emerge within the genre, I think we will have more stories that redefine horror on a very personal level. Stories that look at identity politics as well as horrific experiences that can only be told from the point of view of people who have experienced them.

I am a woman of color who grew up in a homogeneously white, rural community and dealt with varying degrees of bigotry and racism that masqueraded as acceptable social norms. I was born in the early 70s, which was a chaotic time of racially charged outrage and political protest. The historical events and social climate of that time helped to shape the person I am today, and they have had an influence on my voice as a writer and what I choose to write about.

Because I write dark speculative fiction about women of color confronting issues of identity while dealing with monsters, I was questioned on a regular basis about why I thought my debut novel fit within the horror genre. Which in turn, made me question and doubt my own claims of being a horror writer. Many of my first readers wanted to tell me I was writing a romance novel because there's a vampire in the story. As someone who reads a lot of romantic vampire fiction (no, like a lot), that feedback irritated me at first, but then inspired me to make my vampire as monstrous as possible so that people wouldn't confuse what I was writing as a romance novel. My novel is set in the Antebellum south, so people wanted to label it as historical fiction. And, because my protagonist is a young female slave, others wanted to categorize it as African American fiction. News flash: my novel is all of the above, but because of the violence and terror associated with slavery, it's also a horror novel. In fact, even though some of the characters are actual monsters, readers have told me they are the least terrifying aspects of the story.

While I was pitching the novel to agents and publishers, I received many rejections because people couldn't easily categorize what I had written. Therefore, they didn't know how to market it or where it fit within their existing catalog. There were many times during this process that I considered giving up and just accepting the fact that my book wasn't ever going to be published. So, what kept me motivated to keep trying? Remember when I mentioned the importance of finding your community? Well, I am very fortunate because my primary writing community is my MFA alma mater, Seton Hill University's Writing Popular Fiction (WPF) program. I couldn't have dreamed up a more diverse and supportive group of writers, mentors, and teachers. Deciding to apply to that MFA program was one of the best decisions I've ever made. In fact, it was during my first residency that I met Michael Knost. He had been invited as a guest to the In Your Write Mind writing retreat for alumni of the WPF program that is part of the summer residency each year. Meeting Michael made me conscious of how the program and my own social interaction would allow me to build and expand my community of writers.

That community supported and cheered me on each time I received a rejection and reminded me that I had written a good book. They kept me from giving up. Being part of that community also opened new doors for me in terms of being introduced to a larger community of horror writers and they helped me find the Horror Writers Association. I joined the HWA in 2014 and I've attended several StokerCons with fellow Seton Hill alums and mentors, and by doing so I broadened my community and finally pitched my book to the right publisher.

That publisher, John M. McIlveen at Haverhill House Publishing, not only gave my book a home but expanded my writing community by inviting me to attend NECON, which is another important event and group of people within the horror writing community. So, what if you don't have an MFA and access to a large community of alumni from a writing program? No worries. You can still find a community of writers by joining an organization like the HWA or attending StokerCon or NECON or other events that focus on the writing and publishing of horror fiction. I also recommend finding a writing group that is mainly comprised of people who write within the same or similar genres. Even if you have been writing for years, or have been published more than once, there is nothing more rewarding than being part of a community that supports your efforts, shares your goals, and understands what you're writing and why. If you're in a writing group and you have to keep explaining who you are and what you write, you should probably find another writing group. The same is true for organizations or events that you participate in.

Who you are and what you look like shouldn't determine the genre you write in; it's the subject matter and tone that determines your genre, even if you aren't writing a traditional narrative within that genre. For the longest time, I felt like I needed to prove or justify why my supernatural slave narrative, *Invisible Chains*, was a horror novel. As I mentioned, a lot of white writers, agents and publishers weren't "getting it." As if the experiences of slaves in America wasn't horrifying. But then, while watching the documentary, *Horror Noire: A History of Black Horror*, Tananarive Due said, "Black history is black horror," and I stopped wondering if my novel fit within the horror genre. And then, it was nominated for a Stoker, and I stopped doubting if I was a horror writer.

Stories about the experiences of women and BIPOC told from their point of view have a place in the genre whether white people understand those experiences or not. And, even though I've never met Tananarive Due, her influence as a writer and her work as a scholar have provided mentorship experiences from afar, and therefore, I believe I am part of a community of women of color writers who write horror fiction, along with other women I have actually met, like Linda Addison, L. Marie Wood, Jewelle Gomez, Rhonda Jackson Garcia, K. Ceres Wright and others I am getting to know, like Nicole Smith, Kanesha Williams, Denise Tapscott and Jessica Guess just to name a few. Knowing that you belong to a larger community of writers who look like you won't necessarily make you a better writer, but it just might give you the courage and support you need to keep working toward your goals.

Michelle Renee Lane writes dark speculative fiction about identity politics and women of color battling their inner demons while fighting/falling in love with monsters. Her work includes elements of fantasy, horror, romance, and erotica. Her short fiction has appeared in several anthologies, and has been featured on *The Wicked Library* podcast. Her Bram Stoker Award nominated debut novel, *Invisible Chains* (2019), is available from Haverhill House Publishing. Her nonfiction can be found at https://medium.com/@chellane and https://speculativechic.com/author/chellane72/

Living in Someone Else's World: Writing Tie-In Projects

Tim Lebbon

As this is an essay about writing tie-in novels and stories, I should probably address the elephant in the room before I really begin. It's an original elephant from my own imagination, not Dumbo or Nellie or any other pre-existing pachyderm franchise. Here it is: *there's sometimes a stigma attached to writing tie-in fiction.* I think that's less so now than when I started years ago, but it is occasionally still there. It can be viewed as a lesser form of writing, writing by numbers, and the term 'work for hire' carries its own weight. There are those who still see it as a less creative endeavour than writing your own novel/story, because some of your work—whether it be characters, landscape, situation, or universe—is already there waiting for you to use it or fill it.

But let me draw an analogy to see if this opinion holds up. If you're a screenwriter, and you're employed to be in *The Walking Dead* writers' room, you're creating work for hire. It's someone else's creation your working with. I'm not sure that would be stigmatised in the same way.

Before getting into talking about my experiences of writing tie-in novels, I'll lay my cards on the table—although

I almost always prefer writing my own original fiction, I don't feel that a tie-in project is a lesser task. I put as much effort into writing an original Firefly novel or a Star Wars novel as I do my own, and sometimes there's even more work involved, as I don't have to ensure my original novel fits into a pre-existing franchise. The editorial input is sometimes more intense. I'll often be working in a universe I'm not altogether familiar with (more about that later . . . it's not always a total labour of love!). And then there are the fans, who sometimes seem to be watching over my shoulder as I write. I'm conscious that I'm writing for the fans, for the readers, much more so with tie-in fiction that when I'm writing my own original work. With my own work I'm attempting mostly to write for myself, and I'm my own worst critic. With tie-in work, there's already a large and established fanbase eagerly awaiting my contribution to the canon they so love and revere. And these fans are often a) far more knowledgeable of their beloved franchise than I, and b) the owner of a dedicated website or message board. You see how accurate and careful I have to be!

So in many ways writing tie-in fiction is *harder* than creating original work. Why, then, do I do it? Is it simply for the cold hard cash? The love of it? Read on, and I'll try to shed some light from my own experiences. I'm going to talk about how I began, what I've worked on, the experiences I've had, and how it works for me as a professional writer.

And I'm pretty sure I'm done with elephants, for now.

Hellboy changed my life. Here's why.

Christopher Golden asked me to write a Hellboy story for the anthology he was editing, *Odder Jobs*. This was in 2002 or 2003. Chris and I didn't know each other then, but as he said in his invitation email, "We've probably passed each other in some convention corridor or room party". To begin with I said no, because I'd never read Hellboy and didn't think I could do it. As some of you reading this might know, Chris can be very persuasive, and he wouldn't take no for an answer. He just wouldn't. So I read all the Hellboy comics I could get my hands on—devoured them, in fact—and wrote a story called *The Glass Road* for the anthology. I loved doing it, and Chris loved the story, buying it for the anthology.

Pretty soon after this, we met on a hotel balcony during a New York convention. It might have been World Horror, or perhaps the Stokers, they tend to bleed into one-another in my memory after almost two decades. Oh, it was so romantic. We chatted, we clicked, and long story short . . . Chris has been one of my very best friends ever since. That Hellboy short story led to me writing a novel, *Hellboy: Unnatural Selection*, for a line Chris was editing at Simon & Schuster, and from that a second Hellboy novel *The Fire Wolves* for Dark Horse. It also resulted in me and Chris writing a load of original novels together (eight and counting, including the Hidden Cities novels and *The Secret Journeys of Jack London*), having the Jack London series optioned by 20th Century Fox and writing the screenplay, and to both of us making a lifelong friend. From little acorns. Or from short stories . . .

Some of the above isn't much to do with the subject of this essay, but a good portion of it actually is. Because something I've found with tie-in work is this—if you're known to deliver material that's good, faithful to the canon, and on time, you'll be asked to do other work, too. It can get you noticed. That first Hellboy novel led directly to me writing a Star Wars novel, *Into the Void,* when the editor moved from Simon & Schuster to LucasBooks, as well as the *30 Days of Night* novelisation and an original novel set in that universe, *Fear of the Dark* (which became my London vampire novel with a very loose connection to the source material ... lots of fun, and somehow I pulled it off!). And subsequent to those two Hellboy novels, Titan Books offered me the novelisation of the Joss Whedon movie *The Cabin in the Woods*. That resulted in me writing half a dozen (and counting) original novels for Titan, including *The Silence,* which went on to be a Netflix movie. And I also worked on a load of other exciting tie-in projects for them, including the novelisation of *Kong: Skull Island*, an original Firefly novel, *Generations*, and four Alien and Predator novels, which was a true labour of love.

So, I've done quite a bit of tie-in work. At last count, three novelisations of pretty big genre movies, and nine original novels set in established universes. Writing that down now even surprises me, but I've never regretted one of them. Right from the start of my professional writing career, I've always said that I'd never do a project that didn't excite me. There are those jobs like Hellboy, which I admit I didn't know an awful lot about when Chris asked me to write that first short story, and Firefly which, though I'd seen the series years ago, wasn't something I was necessaily passionate about. I got to know them more, and love them, and being asked to write these books actually introduced me to more terrific genre entertainment. But there were also projects like *Alien: Out of the Shadows,* my first Alien novel, which was a true labour of love. I've been an *Alien* fan my whole adult life, and having the opportunity to write this novel was wonderful. And a Ripley novel? Come on! Really? How could I say no?

I couldn't.

I'm a working, mid-list writer. I've been a professional full-time writer for fifteen years now, making my living exclusively from thinking things up and writing them down. I'm not a bestseller (not usually . . . but more on that soon). I guess I'm pretty established in the horror world, and that's a nice feeling, but I'm not often paid life-changing advances. I've been fortunate in Hollywood, with two movies based on my work (*The Silence* and *Pay The Ghost*), and a handful of options, a couple of which paid pretty decently. And I *love* writing. It's been a passion of mine since I was 9 or 10 years old, and working hard through my twenties and into my thirties, and eventually going full-time, I knew that I'd *continue* to work hard so that I could always be a writer. Taking on tie-in projects is part of that work. Yes, writing is art, and there's a constant weighing up of 'art vs commerce', and that's something I think about a talk about with friends all the time. But ultimately I write entertainments and want to continue doing so for as long as I can. I have no retirement plans . . . though I might slow down a little. Tie-in projects are entertainments, and I enjoy writing them and getting paid to do so. For me, it's all part of the job.

Would I stop writing tie-in novels if I was getting regular six or seven-figure deals for my novels? Honestly, I can't say, because sometimes they're so much fun (I'm looking at you Alien and Star Wars).

So, I do it partly for the money. These projects usually pay reasonably well for the time it takes me to write them. I pay myself a certain amount each month, and a tie-in project will usually pay for the time it takes me to write, edit and complete the novel. In that regard they're a decent turnover, but just occasionally one or two might earn me a little more, usually the more popular and bigger franchises.

It's also important not to forget how aspirational some of these projects are. More than once my wife has said to me, 'If twenty-year-old you knew what fifty-year-old you were working on now, you'd flip!' and she's right. I still remember my agent calling me and saying, 'So, do you want to write a Star Wars novel?' I had a good think about it for just under two seconds before saying yes, then had a few days waiting to hear from the editor, and wondering how many other Star Wars novels I'd have to read as research! Similarly with the first Alien novel. As I was writing I was thinking, *Wait, what? I'm writing a goddamn Alien novel!*

So as well as the money, and the considerations of a professional writer, there's an undeniable fanboy element when I take on some of these projects.

I hope what I've written above doesn't sound too mercenary, because it's not all about the payday. There's a creative challenge to these projects as well, and because I like pushing myself creatively, it's sometimes refreshing to take on something that takes me out of my comfort zone. I'd almost certainly have never written anything like Firefly if I hadn't agreed to write a tie-in and come up with *Generations*. And writing a Star Wars novel, with so much established canon and lore, and with the heavy weight of expectation from such a massive readership, was a huge and exciting pressure in itself.

There's also the career aspect to consider. To be honest it's not something I usually think about too much when I'm heading into a work-for-hire project, and I don't pick and choose them with strict regard to how they might further my career. But all these properties have established fanbases, and I've come to learn that getting my name out there on the cover of a Star Wars book can only help sales of my original novels. Star Wars especially sold amazingly well, somewhere way over 100,000 copies and counting. It got me on the New York Times-bestseller list, though I'm not for a moment believing that's because of who wrote it! But I still get plenty of emails about that novel, as well as many of the others (my Alien and Predator books especially), and often these readers will move onto my original fiction. True, a lot of Star Wars readers probably won't even notice who wrote the novel (unless something in there annoyed them and they take the trouble to contact me . . . I used the word 'bitch' in my Star Wars novel, my editor agreed it was in context, but I still had a lot of comments about that, not all positive). But I know for sure that plenty of readers first discovered me by reading my Alien or Hellboy novels, and they've since gone on to enjoy my original work. And that can only be a good thing.

That's what I've done and why, so I thought I'd write a little about the how. People have written whole books about 'how I write', but here's a very brief sketch of how I write a novel.

I have an idea. Sometimes it hangs around for years until another idea collides with it, and they start to grow. Sperm meet egg, if you like. So the growth continues, and then I'll eventually start making notes about the novel. That turns into a proposal or synopsis, and then I'll often start a novel with only a 5 or 6 page breakdown. The real planning and plotting comes when I'm doing the actual writing, when I'll make notes to myself at the end of the manuscript. These notes become more detailed for the forthcoming couple of chapters, so the actual construction of the novel happens as I'm going along. Writing a very detailed breakdown, scene by scene, feels almost like telling the story, and I like a bit of freedom to let the story and characters steer themselves.

That's not always the case with a tie-in novel, for various reasons that might involve licensor approval of a synopsis, editorial input at an early stage, or simply having to build a story around pre-existing situations.

I'm often asked how writing a tie-in works, and the honest answer is that it's different for virtually every project. So I'll talk a bit about several of the tie-ins I've written, and the ones that are perhaps most different in how the processes worked. And for this I'll split them down into the two main types of tie-in novels I've written—novelisations, and original novels.

Novelisations of movies involves turning a screenplay into a novel. Each time I've done this I've managed to get the screenplay emailed to me (whether it was 'officially' available or not . . . and usually I have to sign a non-disclosure agreement, and the physical screenplays sent to me are marked 'Tim Lebbon copy' so that if one finds its way onto eBay, the studio knows who to sue). I then cut and paste the screenplay into a document and write it scene by scene. This might sound horribly formulaic, but I learned the hard way that usually these projects require that you include all the scenes and dialogue—you can definitely add, but it's generally not well-received if you take stuff out. One of the novelisations I wrote had some pretty dodgy dialogue in the script which I omitted . . . and then had to add back in once the editor had seen it.

Formulaic maybe, but I still enjoy fleshing out and expanding scenes, and really getting inside the characters' heads. There's never any internal dialogue or thought processes in a script, and novelising it I can really get to know the characters some more, give them a background, and round them out.

Adding whole new scenes is something I also enjoy doing. And it can have surprising results. Whilst writing *30 Days of Night*, I wondered why an obvious scene had been missed—a Polar bear wanders into Barrow and the vampires toy with it, like cats with a mouse, before killing it. Confronting the world's most powerful land carnivore seemed to be a great way of communicating the power and strength of the vampires. So I wrote the scene and it ended up in the book, and a lot of readers told me how much they loved it. So much so that, over a Thai meal in Toronto at the World Horror Convention, I told this same story. Someone commented that a vampire Polar bear might be fun, and I agreed, and muttered 'White Fangs'. Chris Golden was sitting next to me. We caught each other's eye, smiled, and right after the meal confirmed that we'd had the same idea.

White Fangs. Jack London. So from that little scene came *The Secret Journeys of Jack London* trilogy, which sold in several countries around the world, as well as being optioned by 20th Century Fox, and me and Chris being hired to write the screenplay. I think you call that a result.

Little acorns . . .

Back to *30 Days of Night*, and a less-enjoyable aspect of writing a novelisation. By necessity you receive a script that's at least a couple of months old by the time the movie starts shooting. So it was with *30 Days of Night*. I spent my first two days as a full-time writer starting this novel, getting around 6,000 words down. I was very pleased with myself. Dare I say, smug. It was going very well.

Then my editor sent me the shooting script, which had changed significantly from the script I was using. I had to dump those 6,000 words and start again. Not such a result.

It's more interesting writing original tie-in novels. These are set in established universes, sometimes—but not always—using characters and places that are recognisible to fans of these franchises. I'll pick a couple of projects to talk about here, as the processes involved were very different. *Star Wars: Into the Void*, and my first Alien novel, *Out of the Shadows*. Both of these appealed to my fanboy instincts, and I commenced both projects with a literal smile on my face. I'd seen Star Wars in the cinema when I was 8 years old, and now I was being paid to create a story set in that universe! What's not to like?

As you know, Star Wars is a massive machine (much larger now than when I wrote my novel contribution to that far-away galaxy eight or nice years ago). There are scores of novels, as well as the comics and movies and animated series, but I was most relieved when my editor told me that my novel would be the earliest in the timeline, set some 25,000 years before the original trilogy. This meant I didn't have to read a load of other novels as research! It was also interesting as I had to tie into a comic series, *Dawn of the Jedi* by Jon Ostrander and Jan Duursema. I was asked to come up with a story and characters of my own, but it had to sit within this series of comics. So I had some calls with Jon and Jan, got sent all the comics, and I came up with four or five ideas based on what I'd read.

The responses from my publisher to these ideas were pretty much all: *Nope, you can't do that.* I guess because places I wanted to explore were going to be featured in future comics, or characters I wanted to write about were going to be killed or frozen in carbonite or something equally 'it's need-to-know, and . . .'. So instead, I came up with my own story featuring new characters, even new cities and moons (easier to destroy), but set in the same system as the *Dawn of the Jedi* comics. I included some of the comic characters in cameo appearances, but generally it was all my own work. In effect, this was a Lebbon space adventure story massaged and formed into *Dawn of the Jedi* shape! My editor approved the proposal and I was sent away to write. And what a great experience it was. I was a little worried about the edit, but that was a great experience too, and I had to change very little to bring it more in line with the comics. As I mentioned earlier, there was a tense moment or two when we talked about a couple of swearwords I'd included ('bastard' and 'bitch', from memory), but my editor agreed they were in context and they stayed in.

Alien: Out of the Shadows was a slightly different process. Part of a very loose trilogy of novels (the other two were written by Christopher Golden and James A Moore), the concept for all three was a one-page proposal from 20th Century Fox. Obviously there wasn't much detail there, but my novel was the first, and it had to be set between *Alien* and *Aliens* and feature Ripley in another adventure battling those pesky critters. Fox told us that the trilogy was canon, so it would have to tie in with all the other Alien canon stuff out there (I believe some of the comics weren't included in this). Now, there's an obvious problem here—in *Aliens*, and onward, Ripley doesn't remember whatever traumas I was going to put her through. She was asleep, with Jones the cat cuddled up in her cryo-pod dreaming of chasing their ship's mice (Jones, not Ripley).

But the allure of writing a Ripley novel was too great. *Aliens* especially is one of my top three movies of all time. Hell, it's probably my favourite. And Ripley is such a rich, deep, interesting and traumatised character that the chance to write her was a dream. So I dived into the novel with an idea of how I could make it work.

Apart from Fox's very scant one-page idea for the trilogy, I was given total freedom to make this story my own. My editor at Titan let me go with the flow, and I had a wonderful time visiting the Alien universe on my own terms. I got to create an exciting cast of characters . . . and then have a xenomorph rip their faces off.

Oh yes, this was what being a professional writer was all about!

The editorial process was quite intense, but that resulted in making what I thought was already a good novel even better. It was well received, and it went on to sell to a dozen countries, as well as being adapted into an award-winning audio drama by the legendary Dirk Maggs, starring Rutger Hauer! Its success also led on to me writing a trilogy of Alien/Predator novels, *The Rage War*. That was a big-scale project, set in the far future, and again it was something I'd probably have never written if I hadn't been asked—a vast military science fiction story. It featured such a huge cast of characters that I had to ask my Facebook friends if they'd like to feature (with the proviso that they would very probably die). It was heartening to see how many people craved to have their heads ripped off by a predator or their chest cavity smashed open by an infant xenomorph. Take a look. You might even find yourself immortalised—and killed horribly—in these canonical novels.

I mentioned earlier the balance between art and commerce. It's a delicate consideration that I talk about with writer friends all the time. Writers range from 'I'll write almost anything for money' to 'I can only write what I'm absolutely passionate and excited about and if it doesn't sell, so be it'. I think I'm somewhere in the middle, to be honest. I've had over 45 novels published now, and a dozen of them are tie-in projects. A large majority of what I write and have published is my own work, but the very fact that I was asked to write this essay shows that sometimes, the tie-in work has more of an impact. It's a balancing act I'm constantly conscious of, and if I was ever given a choice I'd usually prefer to be working on a project of my own rather than a licensed project.

But I've never regretted taking on any of these commissions. They've got me onto the New York Times Bestseller list twice (Star Wars, and 30 Days of Night), they bring readers to my writing who haven't heard of me before, they offer me different and interesting challenges as a writer, and sometimes they give me a real fanboy moment of delight. It's also great to be adaptable as a writer, and sometimes it's a refreshing change doing something different. If I've just emerged from a deep novel rewrite, it can almost be a palate cleanser writing a novelisation, when the bulk of the story structure and characters are there ready for me to build upon, flesh out, and elaborate.

I'm also always conscious of how lucky I am to be able to play in some of these worlds. I've written for some of the biggest and most-loved genre franchises, earned money and had fun doing it, and I'm sure there'll be more to come.

Even writing this essay, I've come up with an idea for a new Alien novel.

Tim Lebbon is a New York Times-bestselling writer from South Wales. He's had over forty novels published to date, as well as hundreds of novellas and short stories. His latest novel is the eco-horror *Eden*. Other recent releases include *The Edge, The Silence, The Family Man, The Rage War* trilogy, and *Blood of the Four* with Christopher Golden. He has won four British Fantasy Awards, a Bram Stoker Award, and a Scribe Award, and has been nominated for World Fantasy,

International Horror Guild and Shirley Jackson Awards. His work has appeared in many Year's Best anthologies. The movie of *The Silence*, starring Stanley Tucci and Kiernan Shipka, debuted on Netflix April 2019, and *Pay the Ghost*, starring Nicolas Cage, was released Hallowe'en 2015. Several other projects are currently in development for the big screen and TV. Find out more about Tim at his website www.timlebbon.net.

Chatterers and Dark Scribes
The Art of the Horror Interview

Lisa Morton

Whenever one of my writer friends bemoans a lack of recent sales, I ask if they've considered trying non-fiction. From the looks this question provokes, you'd think I might've suggested they grow more fingers to type faster.

I go on to explain why they should try non-fiction: because most magazine editors who are inundated with fiction submissions receive startlingly few non-fiction submissions; because non-fiction usually pays just as well as fiction; because, when done well, non-fiction is just as entertaining to read and artfully written as good fiction; because there are a lot of anthologies (like this one) that gather together non-fiction pieces; and because non-fiction sales can help a writer to grow their audience and keep their name out in the marketplace in between fiction sales.

By now, my writer friends are starting to perk up. "But," is usually the next question, "what exactly would I write?"

There are a number of non-fiction pieces that magazines, anthologies, and blogs usually buy. There's the article, in which you gather some facts and tell a story; this is the type of non-fiction that's closest to fiction, because a great article functions like a great short story, with a structure, a style, conflict, and a narrative that draws to a satisfying conclusion.

There's the op-ed piece, in which you present an idea and argue in favor of it.

You could try to write reviews of books, films, games, comics, or whatever.

Lastly, there's the interview.

This is possibly the most common non-fiction piece, but also the one that I see done poorly most often. Hey, believe me, I get it: if you're a blogger or podcaster or writer doing a lot of interviews, it's easy to stick to a template and hand all your subjects the same questions.

But the *best* interviews, the ones that will be praised and talked about and remembered, are the ones in which the interviewer has put in the work. You can spot these right away; they don't start with, "What was your childhood like?"

So how do you craft a great interview?

I've been on both sides of the interview table, and I've been interviewer/subject in print, on podcasts, on radio, and on television, so I've had a lot of experience with this interviewing stuff.

For the purposes of this article, we're going to put podcasts/television/radio aside for now and just focus on how you, the writer, craft and sell an interview intended to see print. And by the way, I would never suggest that my process of crafting an interview is the only workable one; this is just my method, and I hope it might work for some of you as well, but hey—use whatever *does* work!

The first step is identifying your market. If you've been hired by a particular editor to do an interview, you can skip this part; but for the rest of you, who might be wondering where to start, read on.

Pick a magazine, book, or blog you'd like to get into. Pick one that is both popular and pays decently, because you're about to put a *lot* of work into this interview; I'm not going to lie and tell you that putting together an interview is easy. Like anything else, if you do it well it's going to take a lot of hours, maybe even more than you typically put into a short story. You don't want to throw this interview away to some venue that won't pay you and where fifteen people will read your work.

Once you've picked your bucket list destination, familiarize yourself with them. Read other interviews to get a feel for what they want. Go over the list of who they've already interviewed so you don't embarrass yourself right off the bat pitching someone they've already covered.

After you go over the list of previous interviews, you should have a good feel for the types of subjects your chosen venue wants. For example: if you're pitching to a magazine that focuses more on contemporary horror literature, you probably shouldn't pitch a filmmaker or artist to them. Maybe your venue likes a particular type of horror. Read some editorials to find out if the editors seem to be most interested in a type of author or sub-genre.

Now you can give some thought to who you'd love to chat with. Has the magazine recently published something by an up-and-comer they haven't done an interview with? Have they published, say, a number of interviews with international authors? If you're not as knowledgeable about a type of horror they seem to focus on, you might read a few stories in that area and perhaps google a list of authors who write that type of fiction.

The next part can be a little tricky: should you query the magazine first, or an author you'd like to interview? If you check in with the magazine first, they might wholeheartedly approve your choice of author . . . and then you find out the author is unavailable. On the other hand, your chances of getting an author to agree to a lengthy interview are better if you can tell them that a certain editor has already agreed.

Here's what I'd suggest: look around at your subject's online presence. Do they post often to social media? Does their website make it easy to contact them? If you can answer "yes" to those questions, the chances are good that they'll agree to an interview. At this point you should be safe in querying the editor. Your query should be simple: suggest the author you'd like to interview, and perhaps mention what you find talk-worthy about their work. If you've done your homework right, there's a good chance the editor will be on board; however, if they're not, you might just come right out and ask the editor who they'd like to have an interview with.

Now you should approach your subject (provided you don't know them already—if you do, your job's a lot easier!). At this point, many of my writer friends have expressed trepidation: "But I don't know Big Author X— how am I going to get them to talk to me?"

Let me assure you: 99.9% of writers *love* to talk. It's why we're here in the first place, right? We want to communicate, and an interview request is also a little ego boost, especially to a newer writer. In other words, chances are very, very good that your chosen subject is going to say yes.

When you first contact your subject, you need to assure them of the market you've secured, so they know they're giving their valuable time away to a solid resource; and you should ask them their preferred method of conducting the interview. This question mattered more in the past, when interviews were likelier to take place over the phone or in person; nowadays, because of how busy we all are, most writers will opt for an e-mail interview. This will also make your life far easier, because transcribing even a short interview is a *looooong* process.

Now you've got your market, your subject, and the form of the interview lined up, so it's time to research. I like to know as much as I can about my subject before I start crafting questions, so I'll do the following:

- Read as much of the author's work as possible. Yes, you may have to spend a little money here to buy some books or magazines, but you are going to make back a lot more than you spend, so you're still ahead. Plus you'll be reading some great horror fiction! By the way, don't forget to look for anything that your subject may have written like an introduction or foreword to someone else's book; sometimes the most revealing bits can be discovered in those sorts of pieces.

- Read other interviews with your subject. Usually just googling will turn these up.

- Peruse your subject's social media and blogs.

- Look for bios of your subject. These can be found at their own website, their publishers' sites, their Wikipedia entry, etc.

- Look at your subject's website. Authors sometimes post interesting autobiographical essays or blogs at their websites.

By the time you've thoroughly immersed yourself in the subject's world, you'll probably have a lot of interview questions bubbling up. You may have read an interview in which you wish they'd discussed something in more depth, or maybe you're curious about how the author handled some element of one of their stories.

Let's discuss questions you should—and, perhaps more importantly, should *not*—ask.

First, the do's:

- 💀 Talk about the subject's work.

- 💀 Ask about their background in some area and how it led them to create an important part of one of their stories.

- 💀 Ask for further clarification on a subject just touched on in a previous interview.

- 💀 Query them on inspirations and influences, but try to be specific. In other words, don't just say, "What are your inspirations?", but rather ask, "What inspired you to create the character X in your last book?"

- 💀 Focus on their most recent releases, so they have a chance to promote their newest work.

Now, the don't's:

- 💀 Avoid questions that are too general. Sure, you can sneak a few of those in, but as I've already noted, too many generalized questions just feel lazy and aren't likely to be as involving to either the subject or the interview's readers.

- 💀 Avoid questions they've been asked a lot. If the author has written a beloved book or story they've already discussed frequently in interviews, your job will be to find an angle on that work that hasn't already been talked about.

- 💀 Don't antagonize your subject. Asking challenging questions is good, but goading or downright insulting your subject is not. For example, it's fine to ask, "Did you ever worry that readers of Story Z might be put off by the unusual style?", but don't ask, "What was it like getting all those bad reviews for Story Z?"

- Don't ask your subject non-writing questions, unless it's specific to either the market or the writer's work. What this means is: don't ask your writer what their favorite dessert is . . . unless one of their stories is about a dessert chef, or you're writing for a dessert magazine.

- Don't comment on your writer's appearance. Good grief, I really should not have to say this, but: If you are a male interviewer, it is not okay to comment on your female subject's appearance. It's beyond ken to me that anyone would ever do this, but I keep seeing women author friends comment on it, so it apparently happens fairly often. Even if you mean the comment as a simple compliment . . . just don't. Nothing is going to turn your subject off faster than you coming across as even remotely creepy. Be professional, and treat your subject as a peer.

- Pet peeve: don't ask, "What scares you?" It's the most over-used question in the field of horror interviews, and nearly every writer who gets it will roll their eyes, sigh, and come up with something caustic or silly.

Let's fast-forward now: you've compiled your questions, put them together in an order that makes sense, slapped it all into a nicely-formatted Word document, relayed that file to your subject, and gotten back the answers. The final question is: to edit or not to edit?

If you conducted the interview via phone or in-person, certainly you'll want to edit. Most of us speak in a broken rhythm punctuated by "uhhh" and "you know" and side tangents. There's no reason to include any of that in an interview.

However, if you're operating from an e-mail interview, you should need to do little to no editing. You already put the hard work as the interviewer into formulating the questions and laying them out in a logical order, so hopefully your subject has responded in kind. If anything, you may want to ask for clarification or additional information, but just be sure that you stay within the word count guidelines of your intended market. Correct any typos or errors, of course. If you do any serious editing beyond that, send the revised interview back to the subject for their final approval. We've all heard endless complaints from interview subjects whose words were quoted out of context, and there's really no reason for you to bring that kind of misery down on yourself. Just respect your subject and let them have the last word.

Now you can put the interview into the publisher/editor's preferred format, and write any introductory or framing material they may require. Then, that's it—you're ready to turn in your interview!

You'll have two final little jobs left: 1) make sure you are timely in completing any edits, contracts, and requests for your bio from your publisher/editor; and 2) keep your interview subject up to date on when the interview goes live.

In summing up: perhaps the most important word in regards to conducting a good interview is *respect*. Respect your subject and their work, respect your publisher/editor and their guidelines, and respect your readers by providing a fresh look at the interview subject. You'll accrue some respect in return (to say nothing of what you were paid), and that's never a bad way to advance your career.

Lisa Morton is a screenwriter, author of non-fiction books, and prose writer whose work was described by the American Library Association's *Readers' Advisory Guide to Horror* as "consistently dark, unsettling, and frightening." She is a six-time winner of the Bram Stoker Award®, the author of four novels and over 150 short stories, and a world-class Halloween expert. Her recent releases include the collection *Night Terrors & Other Tales*. Lisa lives in Los Angeles and online at www.lisamorton.com.

Finding the Story
Steve Rasnic Tem

How do you write a short story? It's a question I'm asked frequently, and to be honest even after 45 plus years doing this, I'm still figuring it out. Every writer develops a methodology that suits them. This is mine (at least for the time being).

When I first started writing fiction, I read all the craft books I could find. And I'm still reading them (most recently, Francine Prose's *Reading Like a Writer* and Steven Pinker's *The Sense of Style*). I took creative writing classes as an undergraduate and I went on to get a Master's in Creative Writing. I also read fiction voraciously, not just in the genres I wanted to work in. I read fantasy, science fiction, and horror, westerns and crime fiction, classics, slick magazines, comic books, and the latest issues of university literary journals. I studied how the stories began and ended, and how the authors structured the vast middle in between. My goal was to develop a large mental inventory of all the possible types of story and ways to tell them. I always advise writing students to read and study at least a thousand short stories, taking notes and building a repertoire of beginning, ending, and structural strategies.

In those early days the advice I heard, generally, was before you began writing you had to know both the beginning and the ending, and that all good stories followed a three-act structure. Later this three-act structure was elaborated, with act 2 becoming acts 2a and 2b, and with key dramatic scenes happening in specific parts of the narrative, usually based on the hero's journey.

There's nothing wrong with any of that. But I think it's important to emphasize our job is not to structure our stories in any prescribed way. Our job is to create interesting fiction which will engage the reader from beginning to end. Simply put, we're trying to cast a spell.

I do believe every writer should know the hero's journey and understand three-act (or four-act) structure. It's part of a good understanding of the craft. This structure is well-explained in such books as *Super Structure* by James Scott Bell and *Screenwriting Tricks for Authors* by Alexandra Sokoloff. One major plus of Sokoloff's book is she provides a catalog of key scene types and where they're likely to appear. This can be invaluable for writers stuck at a particular point in the narrative and needing to know what their options are.

But these structures are basically after-the-fact analyses of why good stories work. They're a way of reverse engineering the spell a good story casts on the reader. There are hundreds of different paths to take from beginning to end, and these vary depending on the length of the tale. I'm much more conscious of calls to action, "entering the adventure zone," dramatic reversals, etc. when I'm working on a novella or novel than when I'm writing a short story. Short stories require the reader's interest for a more limited period, typically one sitting. For me it changes everything.

It was the requirement to know the ending before I began writing I found the most limiting. I adhered to this advice, as I adhered to and abandoned the recommendation to produce a character sketch or questionnaire for all my major characters (Who has the time?). For the first few years of my professional career I only began stories I already had an ending for. I outlined each tale with a beginning, an ending, and the precise steps I needed to take to get from one to the other.

My real development as a short story writer began when I realized the parts I enjoyed writing most were the parts I hadn't planned out in advance. There were always question marks in my outlines, usually minor scenes involving the introduction of a secondary character or transitional scenes moving characters from one situation to another. I liked writing these ? scenes so much I tried to include more gaps in my outlines, until I reached the point where although I might know the beginning and the end and a couple of key points along the way, everything else about the story was still a mystery when I first sat down to write.

The other thing I determined was learning how to inhabit the protagonist or the narrator (they're not always the same person) was the most important part of the process, because this character was the key to everything else: the tone, the events, the settings, even the secondary characters he or she encountered. Sometimes I think of a story as a dream the protagonist had. How can I settle on an ending before the protagonist has had his/her say? Finding a process maximizing discovery and exploration became my priority.

I once read an interview with an author (I'm afraid I can't remember who) in which she talked about putting all her notes, research, and other materials for a story into a single word processing document. As she worked through the document each day, she added new notes, dialogue, scenes, exposition, research, and ideas, and began moving bits around and cutting anything which didn't belong. I liked this notion of writing using both building and cutting, finding the final shape of a story as if I were a sculptor, molding portions until they felt truer to the evolving creation, and removing anything which did not fit. The editing stage has always been a crucial part of the process for me—I usually cut at least 25% to 35% of my drafts—but this method elevated the editing process even further, by encouraging me to include items I knew in advance would never make the final, but whose temporary presence informed the narrative. Discovering the final text in this raw block of words added to the excitement of writing.

The ideas for my short stories come from a variety of inspirations. Some spring from a *What If?* question. What if I went to the movies wearing the wrong pair of glasses? What if there was a young man who could swallow anything? What if my bedroom closet was full of people?

Others are the result of self-inventory. What is the worst thing that could happen to me? What is my biggest regret? What am I most hesitant to write about? I don't write autobiography (with one possible exception), but I don't think twice about blending the details of my life with a fictional character's. Periodically I examine emotional issues, old traumas and fears, or subjects which make me uncomfortable. I believe there is potential story material in anything which provokes a strong personal reaction.

Frequently the seed is an overheard phrase or speculation (and sometimes it's a phrase I've heard coming out of my own mouth). *The longer we live, the more space we occupy. Does a heartbeat in France sound the same as a heartbeat in Japan?* Or maybe it's an image seen or spontaneously imagined: *Some days the dead drifted: the ones empty of viscera, whose skeletons had worn wafer-thin, whose remaining skin was like parchment.*

Often the spark is nothing more than a call for submissions received in an email or pulled off the internet. Stories about the wendigo. Stories on the theme of lost contact. Stories imagining an alternative take on Jack the Ripper. If the word rate offered is a good one I'll consider it, and if it's a topic that interests me I'll print out the guidelines, scribble the deadline at the top, and add it to the stack of possible short story projects on my desk. If it's a direct invitation I'll make an initial decision, either passing or promising I will attempt to write a story.

This stack is for projects I hope to tackle during the next twelve months. Depending on the source, the stack includes submission guidelines, notes for stories without a definite market in mind, and clipped together articles on a subject I've been studying which I feel compelled to write about. I have lots of other ideas scribbled down in two or three notebooks (boiled down from the dozens of notebooks I used to keep). Periodically I browse through these and if something grabs me, I copy the information onto a single sheet of paper and add it to the stack.

Sometimes a compelling idea comes to mind simply from reading the guidelines. More frequently, I haven't a clue. I may have a strong notion a story is in there. I just haven't found it yet.

Years ago, I called the stack of possible projects my "nagging pile." From time to time I'd stare at it, thumb through the pages, glancing at the deadline dates, looking for inspiration to jumpstart a story. Sometimes the timing would be right, I'd have an idea, and I'd pull out the guidelines and make a start on the piece.

Of course, deadlines would pass without sparking an idea and those guidelines went into the trash. I realized I wasn't capturing whatever enthusiasm or interest an idea, or a market had for me when I first read about it. I needed to find a more immediate approach to finding my way into stories.

Margaret Atwood once said she doesn't start her stories with ideas. She starts with the "living stuff": characters, overheard conversation, scenes. Recalling how I'd written my most satisfying fiction I found something similar. My best tales began with simply working with the materials I had, however slight. I've said this many times before—I don't know what I know until I've written it down. It's a discovery process I've fallen in love with.

Whatever sparks me to write—an urge, a phrase, an image, some dialog, a submission call—I begin a document file with some sort of title and start filling it with text. I write everything I can think of about the story or the topic I want to explore. If it's related to a submission call, I include the information from the call as well.

But I'm not just writing down information. I'm thinking about people and how the specific topic impacts them. As Atwood would say, I'm going for the "living stuff." Almost immediately I start probing for the emotional dimension. I write real or imagined dialogue related to the theme. People's internal thoughts and obsessions. I develop some sense of the kind of person who might say or think these lines. I try to find aspects of the idea reflected in natural or manufactured landscapes and I start building descriptive passages. I look for characters who I think personify different qualities of the theme and I start writing about them and their relationships.

By this point I usually have a fairly good idea who the main character will be, his or her drives and obsessions, and what the story is generally about. I may or may not have an ending in mind, and I may or may not have some notion how I want to begin.

I like to build my stories with "mirrors." I want key aspects of the protagonist's emotional conflict to be reflected in the setting, tone, events, and other characters. When the protagonist looks at the universe of the story, he should be seeing himself to some degree. This is one way I keep the storytelling concise.

When I run out of subjective inspiration at this level of brainstorming, I go online and do research on the topic. Anything I find that illuminates or stirs emotion during my research goes into the document. Sometimes I even include pictures. Basic research uncovers details I want to probe further. I don't worry about tangents; in fact, I welcome them.

Depending on my need for information, and whether I feel fully committed at this point, I may scour my reference library or order related books. Because of financial practicalities I try to restrict book buying to larger projects like novellas or novels, but I have been known to do this for short stories as well. I like to think the money isn't wasted—I may use these books for a later project.

If at some point I realize the necessary elements simply aren't coming together, I may go on to something else. That doesn't mean the effort was wasted. What I have now is a raw story package, a "starter" if you will (think sourdough). I name the file with identifying information and save it to a folder containing similarly stalled projects. Having worked on the story this far my subconscious often hasn't given up so over the next few days or weeks with increased clarity I may start adding additional elements to the document. Or maybe a few months or years later I review this material again and discover I now understand what to do with it. Some people consider me prolific. If I'm prolific it's because of my stockpile of "starters."

But if I have discovered my main character and have a handle on the story, I continue each day adding bits of scenes and dialogue, trying to nail down the story's emotional core. That's the essential piece for me. The main character's emotional involvement drives everything else, down to the vocabulary and the flavor of the language used. I'm an emotional writer. That's what I look for when I'm reading—to be moved, to have my emotions stirred—and that's what I like to do in the stories I produce.

Once I have the emotional thread established, I can understand what the story is about. I know my theme. I go back through the document rewriting dialogue and descriptions with tone and theme in mind. This is when I make my first real attempt to write a beginning (even though it's likely to change), and where I start designing the pacing as the emotional thread is hidden, then revealed throughout the story.

Sometimes when writing these trial segments in the document I'll test out different narrative attitudes or points of view, different openings, alternative scenes, etc. This is a quick and dirty method for assessing whether I've selected the correct point of view or if there's another approach which might work better. If I discover a more effective approach, I'll go back and rewrite accordingly. By the time I've completed this rough, out-of-order draft, these arguments should be settled and I'm working with consistent characters and a consistent point of view.

One of the last things I do in this early stage is rearrange the various passages into some sort of rough order, wrestling paragraphs to the front and paragraphs toward the end, composing transitions and creating new scenes based on vague notes and knitting bits of dialogue together. Some version of the final draft begins to make itself known. I start making the big cuts, deleting research, guideline materials, temporary scene drafts, and slashing through sections which no longer fit. Sometimes I know what a scene needs to do but I don't quite know enough to write it yet. But I can always capture my limited understanding and place the rough piece in its approximate position.

So, my writing progresses each day. Normally I work on two or three stories at a time, adding bits to each until one reaches the critical point where I can't let the story go and it becomes my priority until it is complete.

I usually allow three months to write an average length short story. The first 4-6 weeks are spent thinking about the story and building a rough version. The next 4-6 weeks are spent refining, rewriting, and creating the penultimate draft. The story is still percolating during this period, and each day

I'm making changes based on new realizations I'm having about my approach. My drafts became incremental once we entered the digital age. Each day begins with reviewing the writing from the day before and revising as needed.

Much of my time spent during the penultimate draft is about nailing down the beginning, finalizing the structure of the middle, and finding the ending that satisfies. Each has its challenges, which is why building an inventory of strategies through reading a variety of stories can be quite useful. Much has been written about these elements, perhaps nowhere better than in Nancy Kress's *Beginnings, Middles, & Ends.*

The beginning is important. It's there to grab the reader and keep them reading. It sets the tone and expectations for what follows (although both may be subverted later). If you're using the hero's journey, it's the start of the disturbance in the normal world, the launching pad for the hero into this strange other place. And on a practical level, it's where stories are frequently rejected by editors, so it needs to be as polished as you can make it.

You should also be aware when you establish a beginning you are making a kind of promise. There are questions posed and events and conflicts set into motion. If later, you don't answer those questions or resolve those conflicts the reader is likely to be dissatisfied.

If possible, I like to place an image somewhere near the beginning which embodies the theme or the emotional content. This image is revisited at the end, sometimes with alterations which reflect the journey.

During composition I'm likely to change the beginning multiple times, pushing bits of text up to the front of the story which I want to include. Sometimes the first paragraph is a combination of these ideas, and sometimes these become follow up paragraphs after the first few lines.

The middle is where writers seem to have the most difficulty. They've spent time making the opening as intriguing as possible. They have in mind a powerful ending. But getting from A to Z is a complete mystery, and it's not uncommon to read reviews of novels in which the chief complaint is "the middle lagged."

The length makes a huge difference. Truly short stories may not even have a true middle, the beginning turning into the ending with only a brief transition. The action line for many horror shorts is a steep, anxiety-driven rise (in many horror shorts the disturbance in the normal world has already occurred), followed by an even steeper fall into a "basement" sort of ending well below the character's beginning state.

A horror novel, on the other hand, might be mostly middle, with a brief opening followed by endless complications until the story ends. The longer the piece, the more difficult it is to sustain interest. When figuring out the plot of a horror short story I'm more focused on key scenes which raise the stakes while heightening emotion or advancing an obsession while revealing more of the story's hallucinogenic vision. When plotting a horror novella or novel I have to think of various structural elements I can use to vary the rhythm and keep the reader interested longer. Traditional patterns such as the hero's journey, three-act structure, and the use of subplots, reversals, and story "beats" can help. You can also plot the middle of a horror novel as a kind of "series of unfortunate events," raising the dangers and the stakes with each chapter until everything resolves in the end.

The basic task of the middle is to develop the implications and promise of the beginning. Sometimes it's about what happens when the character steps into this new otherworldly space. If a crisis is introduced in the opening, it's about the steps the character takes to get out of the crisis. If a journey is introduced in the opening, it's about the stops on the journey. If an image or pattern is introduced it's about altering or completing that image or pattern.

If you're not using some traditional structural pattern such as the hero's journey you can impose some other, artificial structure to get you through the middle and add dimension to the narrative. The movie *Seven* is a great example of an organic structure springing naturally from the storyline. A serial killer uses the seven deadly sins as a motif in his murders and the movie follows each murder in turn.

But the pattern you use doesn't have to come from the story itself. In fact, you may not need to reveal to the reader what the pattern is—it can work in the background. Some examples of artificial patterns used to create structure might include: the Stations of the Cross, cards in a deck (Tarot or Poker), ingredients in a recipe, rooms in a house, houses in a neighborhood, items in a catalog, items on a menu, travel directions, the first lines from the stanzas of a poem, the first sentence of each paragraph in a famous document, collections of aspects, colors, objects, instructions, in fact almost any list at all. I've written stories which were a series of improvisations based on words drawn from a hat. If set up properly you can make almost any pattern work for your narrative.

It's not uncommon to get stuck somewhere in the middle, and maybe more than once. You go to write the next scene and it isn't there. Sometimes the best thing is to enter a few quick notes about what you want the scene to do and move on to a later scene you know how to write. But it can be a signal telling you it's the wrong scene and you're trying to force yourself to write something which doesn't fit.

Usually when I hit that kind of blockage, I assume it's time to step away from the keyboard. If it's late at night I may go watch a movie or go to bed, but before I do either of those things, I tell myself I'll see something in the movie or I'll dream something to help me fill in the missing piece.

If it happens during the day, I'm likely to go for a walk or a drive and I tell myself I'll see or hear something or a series of things which will provide the answer. It sounds a bit looney, but it never ceases to amaze me how frequently this kind of self-hypnosis works.

One of the difficulties with endings is some readers have quite specific ideas about what makes a good ending. If the story doesn't end with a twist or a huge fight scene or with someone dying, they aren't satisfied. But for everyone else stories can end in hundreds of different ways. Reading a thousand stories will convince you.

For some stories the completion of the structure itself creates the ending. My old mentor the novelist Warren Fine liked to structure his books around a central image, such as a hand. The novel was complete when every aspect of the image was addressed. In this case, each finger folded in to make a fist.

You can also think of endings in terms of the classical climax and denouement, the final action tying things up thematically and emotionally. Sometimes the climax and denouement are the same event. You might also want to make sure the protagonist has a major reversal or "dark night of the soul" sometime before marshalling forces and entering the final event. But not all stories require these traditional elements.

Other ways to end stories include: a leap in time ("many years later"), a statement of hope or inertia, a description of a transformation, a character's change in belief, a final statement of feeling, a statement from the character he or she has learned something or is going to try a new path, a sudden change in camera focus, a realization a character can't do one thing but can do another, and a close examination of a work of art or other object and what it means in relationship to the story.

Writers develop their own preferences about what constitutes a satisfying ending. Charlie Grant wanted endings which "sounded like endings," and worked hard to write the killer last line which would give the reader either a moment of grace or a punch in the gut. My own belief is anything implied or promised in the beginning must be addressed in the ending, and it's not playing fair to introduce new elements.

I'm also a fan of the circular approach. If I introduce a unifying image at the beginning, I want to repeat or transform that image at the end.

Once I complete my penultimate draft, I set it aside for a period. Depending on the difficulty and length of the story this could be a minimum of a week, two weeks, a month, or longer in the case of a novella or novel. Admittedly this is a challenging thing to do when you're writing against a deadline and you're anxious to produce a finished product, but I try to plan accordingly. Getting distance from what I've written is essential. If I can wait long enough, I feel less attached as the author and can edit the story more objectively.

My focus at this stage is cutting: removing or rewriting awkward passages, rephrasing sentences to make them more concise, and deleting unnecessary sentences and descriptions. I've rarely encountered a manuscript which couldn't be improved by judicious trimming. I look for passages I've written out of distrust of the reader, because I was afraid the reader wouldn't "get it." In my experience these passages often overexplain and aren't needed. Sometimes paragraphs need to be moved or shuffled around, but this usually happens in the prior drafts. I also take another look at the ending to make sure it resonates and fulfills the expectations set at the beginning. Endings are a place where writers habitually overwrite, out of fear they haven't made their point. In fact, it's not uncommon to decide the last paragraph is unnecessary.

Once this draft is done, I go back to the beginning for a "finishing" draft. In the finishing draft I'm looking for punctuation, grammar and syntax issues, word choice, cliches, use of adverbs, dialog tags, unnecessary filler words such as "that," and distracting repetition of words and phrases. The best book I know covering these issues is Ken Rand's *The 10% Solution: Self-editing for the Modern Writer*. I've discovered I develop a unique tic particular to each story, a similar construction or phrasing used again and again. In the finishing draft I hunt down this tic and kill it.

Then, and only then, is the story done.

Steve Rasnic Tem, a past winner of the Bram Stoker, World Fantasy, and British Fantasy Awards, has published 470+ short stories. Recent collections include *The Night Doctor & Other Tales* and *The Harvest Child and Other Fantasies*. His novel *Ubo* is a dark science fictional tale about violence and its origins, featuring such viewpoint characters as Jack the Ripper and Stalin. *Yours to Tell: Dialogues on the Art & Practice of Writing*, written with his late wife Melanie, is available from Apex Books. Valancourt Books published *Figures Unseen*, his Selected Stories, and will follow up with *Thanatrauma: Stories* this Fall.

Interview with Anne Rice

Tina Ayres

Tina Ayres: What was it like growing up in New Orleans? What are some of your most fond memories of those days?

Anne Rice: I was born in 1941 and it was another world— before electric refrigerators, washing machines, vacuum cleaners, or air conditioning in homes. And my fond memories revolve around seeing the great changes that shaped the later Twentieth Century. I remember the first television introduced into our home with its tiny 6-inch screen and little black and white picture. I remember when the great screen porches on Southern houses were removed or glassed in as air conditioning took over. New Orleans is a city of 18th and 19th century architecture, and it has an extraordinary atmosphere for an American city, and feels in ways like a Caribbean port. All that filled me with delight.

Ayres: Can you tell us a little about Alice Allen? Did she leave a lasting impression on you in regards to being strong when faced with the challenges of the world?

Rice: My grandmother Alice Allen was a great role model, a strong elderly lady who worked tirelessly in the home squeezing oranges, preparing vegetables, sweeping, cleaning, cooking the daily meals, ironing the sheets and the clothes, and she was very refined and very proper. She wore only black, or black and white dresses, and usually a black straw hat with flowers when she went out. She was a staunch Catholic, and gentle and loving with children. She invited us to help with the chores, made it fun, and provided love and security. She was an anchor in the home, always there. Yes, her strength has influenced my entire life.

Ayres: What was it like when you first met Stan in High School? What did you love about him most?

Rice: He was handsome and brilliant, uncommonly brilliant. Unusual. He had elfin features and was very tall and had an athletic grace. He was a fine student. I found him enchanting. I think "unique" is the word that captures him perfectly. There simply was no one else like him, no one who spoke so fluidly and with such crisp articulation, who read interesting novels, who questioned traditional religious beliefs with such intellect. He was sixteen, you understand. He swept me off my feet.

Ayres: As someone who has lived through the death of both their soul mate and their child, what advice would offer others when it comes to dealing with such deep loss? Do you think love is the one thing we both leave behind and take with us when we go?

Rice: Losses are part of life, and we learn this more truly with each one. Seeing someone die is perhaps the only really supernatural event we witness in our lives. When life goes out of the person, it is truly all over in some unfathomable way. We have to be strengthened by this experience, and we have to let the grief flow. Modern life is too hard on the grieving. Grief is important. Yes, love is essential to a well lived life, but I do believe in an afterlife, and that it is a place of understanding and answers.

Ayres: Do you think love is a must when dealing with the hardness of the world today?

Rice: Without question. As W.H. Auden wrote in his poem, *September 1st, 1939*, "We must love one another or die." In the West we are now in an era where the dominant theme of life is love, and how to love effectively. Competition for resources, resolving political conflicts, all is now being tempered and tested by standards that involve love.

Ayres: What do you enjoy most about the act of writing?

Rice: I love most creating fictional worlds in which I can feel vital and work out all the problems of my life without thinking about them consciously.

Ayres: What does it take to bring worlds to life by using your words? Is that a difficult task to learn?

Rice: I never learned how to bring worlds to life with words. It's always been natural to me. I have a good ear for speech, for stories being told, a good "ear" for the prose I read, the storytelling in books, and when I write, it just pours out naturally. I fall into storytelling as if I was born to do it.

Ayres: *Are there any little-known things about yourself that your readers might be surprised hear?*

Rice: I am not sure. I tend to post about just about everything that interests me on Facebook. I think my readers are used to hearing me hold forth on my obsessions. They know I love hard rock music and TV shows like *The Waltons*. They accept me for who I am. My fiction is shocking. But they accept it too.

Ayres: *Your work touches on the occult and things that cannot be explained. Why do you think such things appeal to so many people?*

Rice: We ourselves are "occult" mysteries. We feel immortal though we are not; we sense that we have souls though we cannot prove that we have souls; we are witnesses to the process of a vast universe, yet we ourselves are so tiny as to be less than a nano particle in the universe. So "occult" literature is about us in symbolic ways. We are all vampires, ghosts, monsters.

Ayres: *What was it like to have Universal acquire to movie rights for* The Vampire Chronicles? *Any chance we will ever get to see the* Mayfair Witches *on screen?*

Rice: Any license of movie rights is exciting but involves risk. The readers are passionate and want any movie to be faithful to the books; they look to me to see that this is done; and that means I must not betray their trust. I must do my utmost to do what I can to see the films are faithful. I love film and I want to see great films made based on my work. There is interest in the *Mayfair Witches*. Perhaps something will happen soon.

Ayres: *Of all your series, do you have one you hold most dear or do you like them all equally?*

Rice: My two *Christ the Lord* novels contain the best writing I think I've ever done. But my *Vampire Chronicles* series is dear to my heart for its intensity, the long continuity of experience I've had with it, and my deep devotion to my hero Lestat.

Ayres: *How have you changed most as you have grown older? What words of wisdom would leave to others on the subject?*

Rice: I hope I've learned to be more patient with others, not to be so angry and irritable with those I don't understand. I am an optimist, and as I advance in age, I really do feel ever more strongly that most people, as Anne Frank said, are basically good. We have to allow our opponents their good intentions. We have to love. We have to acknowledge that kindness, no matter how hard or how mundane it seems, can save this world.

Ayres: *What was the best advice anyone ever gave you?*

Rice: My friend, novelist, Floyd Salas, told me as a writer to "Go where the pain is." This was the best writer's advice I ever received. As for life itself, my mother's advice, that pain could make you callous to the suffering of others, or highly sensitive to the suffering of others . . . this was an excellent and helpful observation. I believe with my whole heart she wanted me to be highly sensitive to the pain of others. And though I fail at this, I keep trying.

Ayres: What do you think is the key to a life well lived?

Rice: To love deeply and as Hemingway said, to know when you're getting your money's worth. Know how to be happy. Know how to recognize happiness when you are experiencing it. Know how to relax into love and into happiness. If you can't do that, you may miss the greatest experiences and rewards of your life.

Ayres: What are your personal feelings on ghosts and such? Do you believe the essence of a person lives on long after their body ceases to do so? What are your feelings on the afterlife?

Rice: I don't know the truth on any of it. This is what I believe. Yes, there are ghosts. So many have seen them and reported on them throughout history, that we can conclude, yes, there are ghosts. My personal belief is that we are body and spirit; and when we die, our spirit ascends to another realm. However, in some cases, the spirit may remain earthbound. It may remain earthbound as a ghost, and it may haunt or it may linger for any number of reasons, both positive and negative. But with most people, the spirit leaves the earthly realm. However, it can at times still communicate with those on earth, and this sometimes happens. But what really happens after death? I have no idea.

The Near-Death Experience research gives us very interesting clues into what may happen after death—that we pass into a realm where we learn new things, reunite with those we loved on Earth, learn answers to questions that tormented us, and have new opportunities to develop. The most interesting thing about the Near-Death Experience material worldwide is that it points to a "beyond" which is a place of change, and advancement. This is the opposite of the Christian Belief system, which sees all learning and advancement as finished at death.

Ayres: How do you hope to be remembered when your own time comes?

Rice: I hope I'm remembered for my novels, for writing books that had a strong impact on people, novels that transcended any genre and will live on in people's minds and hearts.

Ayres: Anything you'd like to say in closing?

Rice: Only that my appreciation of the Gift of Life increases every day. Once I heard a woman say on television, "Life is hard but life is worth it." I never forgot that. She is so right. I've lived an extraordinary life and I continue to have extraordinary experiences. I'm grateful for all of it.

New Orleans native **Anne Rice** has delighted fans with her erotic, gothic, and Christian writings. Selling over 100 million copies worldwide she has earned the position of one of the most prolific authors of our time. Her work has comforted and influenced writers of all genres for decades and continues to encourage others to seek solace in the written word. She is currently working alongside her son Christopher to, hopefully, develop *The Vampire Chronicles* and *Lives of the Mayfair Witches* into television series' reportedly for AMC.

Tina Faye Ayres operates the website *The Original Van Gogh's Ear* and considers interviews sacred as they allow one to capture a little of the subject's personality in written form. She lives in the middle of Nowhere East Tennessee.

Rejected! Ten Reasons Why and How to Avoid the Pitfalls of Rejection

Vince A. Liaguno

You're toggling between Facebook and Twitter. Somewhere between the cuteness overload of the latest video of goats frolicking in pajamas and the roiling anger of an uninformed political rant, you see the call for submissions for a horror magazine or anthology project that grabs you by the creative throat. You scan the guidelines; you get the gist and start working right away. You spend the next few weeks banging out your short story masterpiece with gleeful artistic abandon. By the time you hit the "send" button that whisks your story off to the editor, you're practically breathless with anticipation. With personal certainty, *this* is the best story you've written by far—a story no editor in his or her right mind would reject. *This* is the story that's going to put you on the map, the one that's going to garner agent interest in that short story collection of yours, the one that's going to win you accolades and awards.

A few weeks later, you receive an unceremonious rejection via email.

Dejected, you sit puzzling over the form rejection. How could this have happened? What didn't the editor see in your work? Why did your story get passed over?

Although the reasons for rejection—both subjective and objective—are countless, there are some common mistakes and omissions writers make when submitting to magazines and anthologies. Let's explore ten of the more common reasons that plague both fledgling scribes and even the more established players in the genre on occasion.

Rejection Reason #1:
Failure to follow the submission guidelines

Editors take the time to craft submission guidelines for a reason; it's therefore incumbent upon the writer to follow them. Submission guidelines generally incorporate the window of time during which writers can submit, the minimum and maximum word count range, how the editor wants manuscripts formatted, clarification on reprints, multiple submissions, and simultaneous submissions, and—if it's a specially-themed issue of a magazine or themed anthology—description of the project's subject and what the editor is looking for.

Of all the reasons for rejection, this one is probably the easiest to avoid if you take the time to *read* the submissions guidelines carefully—and then re-read a second and third time. Writers, especially those working within the short story market, are often juggling several projects at once. Keep a bulleted list of salient points from each project's submission guidelines to keep you on track and use that list as a final checklist before sending your story off to the editor.

I looked back at some of the stories I've rejected over the years for the various anthology projects I've helmed. Here are some of the more blatant examples of writers not following the submissions guidelines:

🕱 The submissions window opened on September 1st and closed on October 31st. Stories received on August 31st and November 1st were rejected outright. Don't think that getting your story in before anyone else's gives you a leg up in the process; conversely, don't procrastinate and send your story in late. This just shows the editor that the project wasn't priority enough for you to submit by the deadline.

🕱 Preferred story length was between 1,000 and 5,000 words. The submitted story clocked in at just under 10,000 words. When I rejected the story and pointed this out to the writer, I received a missive justifying the reasons why this story could not be told within the parameters I'd set as editor.

🕱 If it's a blind call for submissions, make sure any readily identifiable personal information is scrubbed from your manuscript. There is a reason why many editors prefer to have submissions blinded, and failure to do so will automatically disqualify your submission in those cases.

🕱 Understand what *reprints* are, what *no multiple submissions* means, and what *no simultaneous submissions* means. As I wrote this essay, I read an editor's social media post about a writer who pulled their story from his anthology with no explanation. The editor then saw on the writer's website that the story in question was accepted by another editor for another anthology. That editor's submission guidelines clearly stated that he wasn't allowing simultaneous submissions; this means that if you submitted a story to his anthology for consideration, you were expected to refrain from submitting that same story elsewhere until he had made his final editorial decision. The editor rightly pointed out how this writer just wasted the editor's time since three slush readers had already read the story and passed it up the editorial chain for further consideration. The story would have most likely been accepted. The irony here is that the writer took an acceptance in a book offering a penny per word. Had the writer followed the editor's submission guidelines and been accepted into his anthology, the writer would have been paid *eight times* that amount per word, had their story translated into Italian, and been included in the audiobook version. Time is money, and you should strive to get the highest rate for your time as possible. Submit your story to the market paying the most and then work your way down; otherwise, you may very well be—quite literally—selling yourself short.

☠ If the editor conveys that vampire or zombie stories are going to be hard sell for a particular anthology—or that they explicitly don't want them—do not submit those types of stories. Don't be that arrogant fool who thinks they possess the preternatural ability to deliver a vampire or zombie story that will blow the editor's socks off and change their mind.

Rejection Reason #2:
Failure to make a good first impression

Writers have one chance—and one chance only—to make a positive first impression. The first few pages of your story are going to have the greatest initial impact in accomplishing that. It's therefore imperative that you proofread your work. Go back to the submissions guidelines and double check that your submission is configured to the editor's specified format. Some editors will ask for specific indenting, line spacing, and handling of italics. In the absence of such specifics, default to Shunn's format.

Likewise, make sure the manuscript is visually appealing. Is your first-page header formatted correctly, with subsequent page headers different? Are you using an acceptable font? Times New Roman and Courier are the general defaults but, again, refer back to the submissions guidelines to make sure that the editor hasn't asked for a specific, less common font.

Similarly, when proofreading, look for consistency. When your main character starts off as "Michael" and becomes "Mark" a page later, it's not going to endear you to an editor. It's sloppy and amateurish.

Rejection Reason #3:
Failure to effectively bait the hook

The short story writer is much like a fisherman, and the opening paragraphs are your chance to lure the reader. But is your bait strong enough to get the reader to swallow the hook? The good news is that there are many techniques to craft effective story openings; but, like first impressions, there's only one shot to snag the reader with your literary hook. Choose wisely and avoid some of the more common pitfalls when opening your story.

Things to avoid in your opening paragraphs include: wordy, frontloaded exposition; the introduction of flavorless, featureless characters; lackluster writing or, conversely, language overload; flashbacks or backstory; and dream sequences or other generic or clichéd beginnings.

Conversely, strong opening paragraphs often present an inciting incident that pushes your protagonist into the story's central conflict or present a mystery element that will keep the reader turning the pages. A strong or provocative line of dialogue can also be a good kickoff point for your story.

Rejection Reason #4:
Failure to understand the definition of horror

Here's a trade secret, something largely unspoken and only whispered about at those cloak-and-dagger gatherings of editors that take place in hidden underground outposts every quarter century:

Editors and anthologists pulling together a horror project want horror stories.

Provocative and groundbreaking, right? Snark aside, you'd be surprised how common a reason for rejection this is. If you're submitting to a horror market, endeavor to understand the definition of horror. Above all, horror should evoke a sense of fear, dread, and/or unease. Failure to do this on some fundamental level will very likely relegate your story to an editor's "pass" pile.

When writing for horror markets, stick to the horror genre. If the editors say they don't want science fiction, chances are they're not going to like stories with flying taxis and dancing holograms. Unless an editor specifically mentions that genre hybrids are welcome, adhere to the K.I.S.S. principle: *Keep it scary, stupid.* And in those rare instances where horror and, say, science fiction harmonize beautifully—think *Alien* here versus *Jason X*—make sure that horror is the dominant force.

Likewise, don't fall into the bad habits of horror. Horror sometimes demands a suspension of belief, for example—not a suspension of logic. Stupid characters doing stupid things are not scary. Stories that reek of convention and cliché in the absence of originality won't pass muster with most editors either. Bring something inventive to the table. Show your mastery of the genre with your story.

Rejection Reason #5:
Failure to convey the theme

Some writers enjoy the challenge of writing for themed anthologies or magazines with themed issues; others prefer the unrestricted autonomy of the general, or non-themed, horror anthology or journal. If you choose the former, however, make certain that you *understand* the project's theme and are able to reflect that theme back to the editor in your work. The thematic requirements should be clearly outlined within the editor's submission guidelines; endeavor to read and re-read them.

If the call for submissions is posted to social media, follow the thread; often, others may ask questions or seek clarification from which you might glean some additional insight into what the editor is looking for without risk. Remember: Like writers, not all editors are created equal. Some may not take well to redundant questions in the public arena, especially if they feel their submissions guidelines clearly address the questions at hand. Others may even invite questions prior to their submission period opening; in those cases, take full advantage of their generosity with a well-worded query.

Otherwise, incorporate the project's theme into your story. During the open reading period for the first volume in the *Unspeakable Horror* series, which was clearly presented as an LGBTQ-themed horror anthology, I can't begin to tell you how many submissions I received that didn't have a single LGBTQ character or storyline. Similarly, there were countless others that clearly didn't understand LGBTQ characters or issues and appeared to be "winging it."

Write the story to fit the theme. Don't try to make the theme fit the story. Trust me: Editors can spot a trunk story from a mile away. During the open reading period for the *Other Terrors* (Houghton Mifflin Harcourt, 2022) anthology, my co-editor on the project, Rena Mason, and I would chuckle when stumbling upon a group of stories that seemed written for—and rejected by—another earlier anthology call. Save the previously-rejected trunk stories for those general, non-themed anthologies and magazines.

Rejection Reason #6:
Failure to remember that good grammar is still the golden rule

Editors want to experience terror from the story—not suffer nightmares from the grammar. Line edit, proofread, and then line edit some more. Proofread again. Repeat until verb tenses agree, the punctuation doesn't upstage your characters, and sentences enjoy self-actualization.

It's a common misconception—especially among newer writers—that an editor's job is to correct the writer's grammar. It is—and it isn't. Editors will polish a story before it's published, but that doesn't give the writer a free pass to submit something with egregious spelling and grammatical errors. The editor is there to catch something that might have made it past *your* half-dozen proofreads.

Reliance solely on spellcheck programs and grammar functions is a risky proposition, too. *You* are still the one who has to apply the thought process to catch those problematic homographs, decipher between those pesky apossessive adjectives and contractions, and properly fuse together the words that construct those killer sentences.

Rejection Reason #7:
Failure to avoid offensive stereotypes

We live in an era of heightened cultural sensitivity. Most of the fair-minded among us would agree that this is a positive societal turn. Gone are the days of lazy stereotypes. We recognize these for what they are: harmful and degrading to others. As such, in our efforts to convey respect and validation for the personhood of others in our writing, there comes increased responsibility to "get it right."

While there is much debate and public discourse on what to do with *older* works that contain these outdated and recognizably offensive stereotypes in the context of today, there is no room or reason to foster the same in *new* works. It is therefore compulsory for today's horror writer to eschew harmful depictions of other people and cultures in their writing. Editors are on watch for this.

I kept a blog during the reading period for *Unspeakable Horror: From the Shadows of the Closet* (Dark Scribe Press, 2008). I intended it as a communication tool with those who had submitted stories and those considering submitting to the project. In addition to the submissions guidelines, I used the blog to communicate monthly submissions statistics—number submitted, number accepted, number rejected. I also used it to communicate observations about trends that Chad [Helder], my co-editor on the anthology, and I were seeing in our slush pile readings. I remember being alternately disturbed and bemusedly incredulous over some of the submissions we received. Some outright equated the homosexuality of their characters with child abuse and—honest to God—bestiality. There were also an alarming number of stories about man-hating lesbians—story after story in which some poor guy's unmentionables got chopped, eaten, or otherwise lopped off.

Avoid these negative racial, gender, cultural, religious, sexual, and—yes—political stereotypes in your works at all costs. If you can't describe or depict a character in your story without resorting to some outdated stereotypical "observation," try harder. Chances are that if what you're incorporating into your story was once the butt of one of your grandfather's off-color jokes told around the Thanksgiving dinner table, it's not appropriate to be included in a story written in 2021 or later.

Rejection Reason #8:
Failure to remember that quality counts

Editors detest mediocrity. Whether they're looking to fill an anthology or the single issue of a magazine, they have a finite amount of space with which to work. They want the highest quality work to fill their word count.

Narratives that are little more than rambling, free-association generally don't make the grade. Think characters, plot, and conflict. Stories should have a beginning that grabs the reader's interest, a middle that builds and elicits an escalating feeling of fear, dread, and/or unease in the reader, and an ending that brings all that horror to a head. Characters need motives, and they need to act on those motives in a manner logical to the situation you've placed them in, to the time period and setting, and to themselves. Convey authenticity. Again, in the case of the *Unspeakable Horror* anthologies, it didn't take an authentic LGBTQ person to imbue a work with an authentic LGBTQ point of view; it took talent.

Similarly, when it comes to quality, nothing can drag the quality of a story down like bad dialogue. Read your dialogue aloud. If it sounds like something out of a poorly-scripted porn film, consider a screenwriting gig in the adult film industry. Likewise, refrain from writing dialogue phonetically when trying to capture an accent. It reads to an editor as lazy.

Rejection Reason #9:
Failure to save the preaching for the pulpit

There's a difference between seamlessly weaving keen political commentary into the fabric of a story (think: Jordan Peele) and dropping a political rant into the middle of it. Save the political speeches for <insert name of favorite political figure here>. Chances are they're better at them.

No fiction reader wants to be clobbered over the head by the author's political views, as brilliant and enlightened as said author may think they are. If the politics of the world figures into your story, fall back on that trusted truism of good writing: Show, don't tell. Instead of the political treatise being thrust at the reader through a character's impassioned oration or inner monologue, show the reader the effects of a particular political platform or agenda on the characters or the environment the characters are grappling with. Again, it should be central to the conflict and outcome of the story and not something dropped in arbitrarily.

Rejection Reason #10:
Failure to stick the landing

Don't blow the ending of your story. During my readings for numerous anthologies, there is always that handful of otherwise solid stories that were creative in concept and competent in execution but derailed in the final act from over-ambition or predictability.

Subtle endings are fine if executed well. Watch for endings that fall flat or take the action from 60 mph to a complete halt within the span of mere sentences. Pacing is everything in the horror genre. Many beginning writers think it appears cutting-edge to leave things nebulous, to fashion a more cerebral ending in a misguided attempt to leave readers deep in thought. Unless you're David Lynch, lose this approach. Respect your readers. They've invested time in you and the story you've crafted. They deserve a satisfying payoff, not some arthouse-clever muck of opacity that's going to leave them insatiate and feeling cheated. Twists—unpredictable but fair—are fine. Readers don't have to see the end coming, but they should be left feeling like they *should* have seen it coming because you planted enough hints along the way. Surprise them; don't trick them.

There are no shortcuts to writing good short stories. In many ways, the short story is a more challenging, more unforgiving form than those of longer works. While there may be room to go momentarily astray in a 100k-word novel and be forgiven, the short story has precious little room for such indulgences. It's a lean, mean format that carries heavy reader expectations. As with any form of writing, short stories—and their creators—can benefit greatly from a trusted beta reader or two. Objective feedback from a trusted friend or colleague can prove invaluable in helping you see beyond your own words.

Winning short stories (read: publishable) are the ones that grab the reader from the opening lines and hold them until the satisfying ending. They're the ones written with a good balance of technique and execution—not overwritten, not underwritten. They're the ones packaged properly, within an editor's guidelines, and presented polished. They avoid cliché and pastiche, instead gifting the reader with something inventive and engrossing. Such stories avoid the ten failures detailed above through the writer's engagement of a repetitive process of drafting, editing, and proofreading.

Vince A. Liaguno is a healthcare administrator by day, writer, editor/anthologist, and pop culture enthusiast by night, whose jam is books, slasher films, and Jamie Lee Curtis. He is the Bram Stoker Award-winning editor of Unspeakable Horror: From the Shadows of the Closet (Dark Scribe Press, 2008), Butcher Knives & Body Counts: Essays of the Formula, Frights, and Fun of the Slasher Film (Dark Scribe Press, 2011), Unspeakable Horror 2: Abominations of Desire (Evil Jester Press, 2017), and the upcoming Other Terrors: An Inclusive Anthology (Houghton Mifflin Harcourt, 2022). Visit him online at: www.VinceLiaguno.com.

Fearful Poetry

Linda D. Addison

"You have NOTHING
to fear from the poet
but the TRUTH"
—Ted Joans

Even poets started as readers of poetry, how else to discover and fall in love with the economic dance of words poems are made from? My earliest memory of poetry is nursery rhymes. Of course, no one called them poems, but I remember the sound of music weaved in the words of those fables.

Later, in elementary school, I came to understand the difference between stories and poetry. As these differences were taught, poetry became that scary, distant creation that many adults still fear to this day.

For me, that connection wasn't a choice—it was always there. When others in school had to fight to study poetry, I looked forward to it! In junior high and high school, libraries became my safe haven because I could choose to read more poetry and genre fiction not necessarily taught in school.

Today, in spite of society's fear of poetry, there are collections being published each year, and poetry in fiction magazines and anthologies. I never lost my love of prose, even through years of day jobs and life's changes. My journals—started in the 1970s to this day—are filled with bits and pieces of poetry. It is these journals that I farm for seeds to create my published poetry.

I have a special delight in teaching poetry workshops, but I gain extra joy when an attendee has never written a poem and professes apprehension of them as a reader or creator. Why? Because I know a secret. I know that person is possibly about to discover that poetry has been living inside them, whispering within the song of their life's joy and pain.

How to find that song? I begin the workshops with everyone creating writing seeds (inspired by reading Natalie Goldberg's books on writing). They are instructed to write whatever words come to them without stopping until a page is filled. These seeds/words are then used through the rest of the workshop to create work shaped by poetry forms (haiku, cinquain, etc.).

I do the exercises with them to show that even I write poetry that needs work. As we do each form, I also model the kind of edits that can be made to strengthen the images/messages/music. The real joy for me is reading the poetry created by the attendees—poetry that takes my breath away, poetry that many didn't know they had hiding under society's concept that poetry is inaccessible.

Getting Started

Like any kind of writing, it helps to read dark poetry written by others. In genre, there are so many wonderful poets. You'll find that poetry, like horror fiction, comes in all flavors—gothic, occult, slasher, post-apocalyptic, psychological, etc.

The Horror Writers Association website has a *Reading List* under the *For Horror Fans* menu available to the public.

The HWA Member-Recommended Reading List has different categories by year, the Poetry category for 2020 has more than 25 books listed. Or you can go to your online book buying site and search for "horror poetry books" (to my surprise *Moby Dick* by Herman Melville came up).

I also suggest reading and trying to write in different forms (sonnet, etc.) as a way to exercise your poetry muscles. You may not fall in love with different forms but they can bring something interesting out of your writing.

Writing horror poetry is about evoking an emotion that touches the reader in a way that may make them shudder. One way to do this is to write from places in you that shakes you up in some way, or as a reaction to something outside your personal life that you react to with aversion. Many of my poems begin this way.

Allow yourself to write as raw and messy as you want for the first draft. This allows the emotion to flow out without worrying about form or grammar, etc. because in the expression of authentic feelings is the roots to touching the reader. Journaling is an invaluable way to capture reactions to the world (inner or outer). Give yourself permission to write anything in any way you want because you don't have to show it to anyone at this point.

Yes, I Edit My Poetry

Editing begins when you've read a first draft and decide you want to shape it for others to read. I've added a list at the end of this piece that shows some of the books I've used (I have a lot more in my book case). Since this isn't an article about editing, I'll give you some of the tips I use to edit my work:

💀 Read the poem out loud, listening for anything awkward

☻ Look for words that I tend to use with first drafts & use the Thesaurus to try alternatives

☻ Try some opposite words/images to make the poem stronger (ex. instead of describing something as smooth, describe it as cutting/rough

☻ Remove words that make the lines read more like sentences, less is more. For example:
   Before: Each night felt like it would not end
   After: night would not end

☻ Change the shape of the poem adding breaks, indents to follow the breath when reading the poem out loud. Breaks can inform the reader when a new image/idea/concept is coming, indents can indicate a new line/image, but related to the previous

☻ See if changing the shape of the poem by following the breath/images begins to take on a form or pattern. For example, four-line stanza with line 2, 3 indented.

☻ Check for lines that stand out as extra long or short; is there a reason for that or should the long line be broken into two lines or re-written with less words?

Submitting Poetry and Other Stuff

Okay, the poem is in the best shape you can make it. Time to submit it. It's helpful to identify more than one possible market to send your work to, so if it is rejected, you can quickly send it back out (unless you see something obvious you can change to make it better, if not—out it goes). I like to pick three top markets and sent it to the top one first. Why not?

I listed some market listings below. Always go to the market site and check for their guidelines and follow them. If they only want poetry that is 50 lines or less, don't send 60 lines, no matter how great you think the poem is, there's a reason for the guidelines as written.

Some thoughts about creating a poetry collection. There are some advice I pass along that was given to me by Gordon Linzner (Space & Times Books) when I first talked to him years ago about publishing my first collection, *Animated Objects*. He suggested I try to publish some individual pieces in other magazines, anthologies first, then talk about a collection. This can be useful for a first time collection because it gets your name out and shows a publishing track record.

Once I'm ready to put a collection together, I don't always know what the pattern is going to be—it happens organically— which is how I write. I'm often inspired by the first poem in the book, then others follow. I know other poets are driven by a theme, which creates the foundation for the poems.

Collaborations often have some concept that two or more poets work with to write. When I did *The Place of Broken Things* with Alessandro Manzetti, we agreed up front that the poems would have some relationship to any combination of the six words in the title, which we had chosen. The first poem we wrote together was titled after the book and then we knew we were on a roll. That's pretty loose, but it worked out beautifully.

For me, collaborations have to be with someone where there's mutual respect and love for each others' work before writing together. We agreed to be able to give feedback on all the poetry created for the book, whether it's poetry written together or separately, without ego—with consideration to make the work the best it can be. We would send a starter stanza or two, if the other wanted to continue with it, then it became a collaboration, otherwise was a solo poem. It worked out that Alessandro and I each had 30% separate poems, and the last third we wrote together.

So what's left to do with poetry—other media! Award-winning Director and Screenwriter Jamal Hodge (and poet) released *Mourning Meal*, a film in 2020 inspired by a poem of mine (of the same name) which has been winning awards in film festivals. There's no reason for poetry to stay on a page, it can become interactive, part of collages, clothing, even tattoos; anything that can be imagined, can be made!

Resources

Some of the books I've use when writing/editing poetry:

- *The Art and Craft of Poetry* by Michael R. Collings; defines different forms

- *Writing Down the Bones* by Natalie Goldberg

- *The Haiku Handbook* by William J. Higginson

- *The 3 a.m. Epiphany* by Brian Kiteley

- *Poemcrazy: Freeing Your Life with Words* by Susan G. Wooldridge.

- *Ink Stained: on Creativity, Writing and Art* by John Urbancik

- *Writing in the Dark* by Tim Waggoner

Some Genre Poetry Market Listings Resources:

- The Grinder: https://thegrinder.diabolicalplots.com/Search/ByFilter?poetry=true

- 🕱 Ralan dot com:
  https://www.ralan.com/m.pay.htm

- 🕱 SFPA Speculative Poetry Markets:
  https://www.sfpoetry.com/markets.html

- 🕱 Horror Tree:
  https://horrortree.com/

- 🕱 HWA Markets for Horror Writers & Poets: https://
  horror.org/2016/06/trying-new/

- 🕱 Duotrope (paid subscription to use; $5/month, $50/
  year): https://duotrope.com/search/list/poetry/
  markets

Linda D. Addison is an award-winning author of five collections, including *The Place of Broken Things* written with Alessandro Manzetti, & *How To Recognize A Demon Has Become Your Friend,* recipient of the HWA Lifetime Achievement Award, HWA Mentor of the Year, and SFPA Grand Master. Addison has published over 370 poems, stories, and articles. Her site: www.LindaAddisonWriter.com.

The Ouroboros Bites Down

Laird Barron

1. The Provenance of Wandering Stars

Don't forget where you come from is an old admonishment that sounds more like a curse depending on how you hold your jaw: Provenance is a word of power, for good or ill. Elastic as the shadow hooked to your ankle, provenance follows wherever you may go. Mine was to be born in Alaska, grandson of a failed novelist, son of a quasi-survivalist. Spend the better part of ten winters pedaling behind the handlebars of a dogsled, and strange thoughts will percolate up from the hadalpelagic silt of your dreaming mind. At night, huddled near a barrel stove, I scribbled those fragments into a notebook. I'm still scribbling them as the calendar flips over into 2021.

Circa the latter 1980s, James Michener, Mary Stewart, and Robert Service rode with me as I mushed a team of huskies through the Southcentral Alaskan backcountry. Jack London, H. Rider Haggard, and Stephen King were there on fishing boats and in factory breakrooms. I didn't consciously seek to dissect or learn from the poets and novelists. They were company on a trek that, to the younger me, seemed purgatorial. To endure prolonged isolation and monotony, a person needs voices in his head besides his own. Hindsight reveals the truth: my favorite authors were mentors as much as they were entertainers. Philosophers and sages who appeared in my darkest hours. No matter their individual approaches, they were the Blind Ones describing the parts of the elephant. My personal elephants were life, death, and the great outdoors.

Biographical notes seldom interested me back when. Eventually, I reached a certain age and the interior lives of writers assumed newfound importance. It is said one shouldn't conflate art with artist, and that's solid advice. Yet it's merely advice. Provenance, upbringing, and preoccupations outside of setting pen to paper, offer a keyhole insight into an artist's world view. This insight can provide clues and context to frame the writer's body of work. Biographies and interviews are decoder keys.

Last I checked, Cormac McCarthy hangs out with fellow literary geniuses and nuclear physicists at the secluded Santa Fe Institute. Pulitzer-winning poet, Mary Oliver, allegedly hid pencils along the path of her nature walks. Lucius Shepard, renowned author of *A Handbook of American Prayer*, spent significant portions of his life abroad in the company of fighters, filmmakers, gamblers, and revolutionaries. Larry Brown (*Dirty Work* and *Big Bad Love*) wrote several novels and many, many short stories between shifts at the fire department. On the whole, neither Brown nor Shepard focused on the wilderness per se, yet the diminishment of civilization in its rural backwaters and ragged boundaries were cornerstones of their style and artistic temperament.

Master of the American western, Louis L'Amour; balladeer of the Goldrush Era, Robert Service; and Robert E. Howard, creator of Conan the Barbarian, depicted the wilderness as rugged, violent, and tempered by a primordial honor code. The natural world beyond urban walls was inarguably red of tooth and claw, yet blessed with purity and balance certain to ennoble men who survived its perils. These authors cast the wilderness as a Darwinist crucible that winnows weak animals, human or otherwise, and molds the survivors into its own majestic likeness.

McCarthy inverted that antiquated, humancentric paradigm. Peering at it through the lenses of *Blood Meridian* and *Child of God*, McCarthy's wilderness isn't a crucible, but rather a meatgrinder with a sluice that drains into an abyss. McCarthy's wilderness doesn't purify or ennoble the human tribes who thrive upon its alkaline mother's milk. Nor does it forgive the wretched few interlopers who escape its clutches and return to so-called civilization. McCarthy's wilderness is a deathscape of benighted provinces heated beneath the glare of a red sun, storm-wracked, and twisted and deformed over eons by the rotation of the planet. This is a wilderness where all principles are reduced to base impulses. True savagery rules here. Hunger, lust, and pain are the arbiters. Men revert to their animal characteristics. They are eaten by the good green earth and rendered to trace minerals.

Which of these wildernesses are closest to reality? As my friend and novelist, John Langan, would note, *A bit of Column A, and a bit of Column B.* The last time I saw a wolf at close range was almost thirty years ago on a bitter winter's dawn behind the Sheep Creek Lodge at Mile 88 of the Parks Highway. A large, grayish beast, yellow eyes colder than the icicle stalactites hanging from the eaves of the lodge. He was sniffing a dumpster and didn't hear me coming around the corner. We locked gazes. Pouncing distance for him. Near enough I watched the smoke of his breath rising. He took my measure, and then his leave. Two or three bounds and he was gone into the surrounding woods. A hundred-and-thirty-pound torpedo of fur and fang capable of tearing the ass end out of a bull moose with a couple of slashes. Neither the youthful spring in my legs nor the knife on my belt would have availed me had the wolf decided to try his luck with human prey.

My takeaway from a quarter of a century in Alaska is that you cannot encapsulate the essence of nature with an anecdote, or pages and pages of anecdotes. However, you may well be inspired to make the attempt. Any person who spent his or her youth driving a tractor in the heartland, or navigating the mean streets of a metropolis, would likely concur.

2. Look Back in Dread

Joyce Carol Oates once asked, *Where are you Going? Where have You Been?*

The Barrons moved from suburbia onto a remote homestead plot in the Matanuska Susitna Valley, Alaska. Our relocation coincided with the winddown of the Cold War as President Carter departed office and Reagan swaggered in. For a big chunk of the '80s (a shark-bite crescent of adolescence into my latter teens), we lived on a muddy little tributary creek a stone's throw from the Big Bend of the Yentna River. The property was isolated in the best horror-story fashion. Our ramshackle cabin occupied a hill bordered by open water and miles of mosquito-marsh, forest, alder thickets, and seas of devil's club. No roads anywhere, and no neighbors within a mile; you got there by riverboat and floatplane. In the deep winter after the river froze, we traveled by snowmobile or dog team. We communicated with the outside world via a CB radio that intermittently penetrated the static. On special occasions, a bush pilot friend of Dad's (a former National Basketball Association benchwarmer who also moonlighted as a strongarm for an Anchorage kingpin) buzzed the homestead and chucked a bundle of newspapers out the window for us kids to hunt down and retrieve. We thrived on old news and comic strips. Powdered milk, canned vegetables, rice, and whatever Dad could snag in a fishing net or wing with his rifle.

All of the preceding is to say that traditions of storytelling are strong among my kin. By dint of inherited characteristics and by blunt necessity. We exchanged stories to maintain our collective sanity. We passed them around the campfire: ancient mythology; fairytales; Dad's war stories of Vietnam and his father's accounts of service on a battleship during World War II; and Mom's often spooky anecdotes regarding her childhood in 1950s rural Alaska and Oregon. Moreover, ours was a rustic nuclear family who read voraciously and discussed books at length. Dad burnt through westerns. Mom loved historical romances and epic fantasy. I preferred planetary science fiction and sword and sorcery (as did my brothers).

When you live in a cabin, and your entertainment options are a portable black and white TV with spotty reception, a crappy AM radio tuned to a yeehaw country station, and a few stacks of novels that run the gamut from potboiler to highbrow lit . . . you'll read the covers off paperbacks of every genre. You'll recount the highlights. Sooner or later, you might even start writing your own. My brothers and I were the definition of indiscriminate. We treated every book with similar weight. That might be why I've never found genre infighting, or cross-genre wars, to be compelling. Eventually, we matured and acquired affinities for particular authors, but that was a secondary consideration to the simple act of consumption. Decades later, I frequently bump into a piece of writing and experience a jolt of recognition because it's something I encountered as an adolescent, uncritically absorbed, and moved on; always in quest of the next fix.

There were notable exceptions. Somewhere around 1980, I read *The Wolfen* by Whitley Strieber. Although the action is centered squarely in New York City, several sequences take place in parks, tenements, and junkyards where the occasional gunshot, or a sharp, truncated scream, is liable to go unremarked. The passage that chilled me to the core and has lingered in my mind, is an anecdotal musing by one of the creatures (the titular wolfen) who prey upon lesser beings such as humans, for food. The wolfen chuckles about his pack's origins as wilderness dwellers; how he and his packmates revealed themselves to hunters in lonely forests and pursued the hapless men to their cars, pouncing upon them as they struggled to lock doors and roll up windows . . . Strieber inverts the pleasure of the hunt with sly relish. As with David Morrell's *First Blood,* a pointed antiestablishment message powers the narrative. It says, in part, that monsters dwell among us and savagery will prevail.

I'm not sure whether Strieber got into my father's head, but here's an anecdote that occurred roughly around the time we initially read *The Wolfen.* The novel and the anecdote are enshrined in Barron lore and I'm aware both have nudged my own writing in a sinister direction.

Come winter, Dad packed his snowshoes and a rifle, hitched our huskies to an antiquated freight sled, and hunted for meat along a loop that encompassed a twenty to fifty mile stretch of river and seismic survey trails; crews slashed these "seis lines" across the wilderness during the 1960s. From the air they radiate like brutish imitations of Palpa and Nazca lines. Dad departed one morning on a routine circuit and returned as dusk blurred the panorama of snow and trees into hazy shadow. Usually, he kept his antique lever-action rifle in a scabbard or strapped over his shoulder. Not today—today he clutched it in his left hand, ready to aim.

I asked why he'd come back an hour ahead of schedule. Knocking ice from his beard, he grimly explained that he'd turned the team around in a swamp where the windblown snow barred further travel. While he untangled their traces and gave the dogs an encouraging pat, something odd occurred. One by one, the huskies left off rolling in the snow and socializing. Each glanced around nervously, sniffing the breeze, whining and growling at whatever they'd scented. Moments later, laughter erupted from somewhere beyond stands of birch and spruce. He figured it must be a raven or some other bird. But after a few moments, it pealed again, and closer. The timbre altered as it echoed through the trees. He described it as the deranged cackling of a lunatic. *Someone who was sick in the head*, were his words.

Dad whistled the team from an easy trot to a slow lope, eager to make it the four or five miles to the river. The dogs were of a similar mind. The cackler in the trees paced them for the next half an hour, shifting to either side of the trail until Dad and his team dropped down a steep bank and hit the river and booked it for home.

After dinner, our family gathered near the fire and discussed his close encounter with the weird. We'd seen plenty during our sojourn on the Big Bend. A lynx? A so-called cackling goose? Dad dismissed lynx based on prior experience. Cackling geese lived far to the south and migrated to California. *Wasn't a fucking goose,* he said. *Wasn't a raven or a martin.* Hunters indiscriminately murdered cow moose and black bear sows who were nursing cubs. One summer prior, a bear screamed in the darkness several nights running. Dad had taken a grave risk tramping out there, but never found her. Eventually those dreadful, sobbing cries of pain and horror ceased.

Daddy, maybe it was a wolfen, my youngest brother said. Too young to get his mitts on Strieber's novel, but little pitchers have big ears, as the saying goes, and he'd soaked in the conversations about the finer points of *The Wolfen.* Dad didn't scoff. He just frowned and sipped his tea. He wondered, as I found out later, where Strieber had gotten his own ideas. To whom had Strieber spoken? Hunters? Outdoorsmen? What had these folks heard in the woods? There's truth in jest. There's also a grain of truth in outlandish folklore.

Dad understood that what you fear will rise to meet you.

3. Ouroboros

My paternal grandparents came of age in the Dust Bowl era. Living through real hard times seems to have shaped the philosophy of their children—it created a gravity well of fatalism and poverty my parents would never escape. Dad didn't subscribe to modern medicine except for the rare life-threatening event such as the occasion the Elks Club sponsored my cancer surgery at the tender age of eighteen months. Mom hated the cold to the point of raving when the wood box got too low for her peace of mind. She wasn't the only resident of our homely abode who lived in shivering dread of the deepfreeze that typified January weather; she was just the only one who spoke her mind.

By adolescence, the brutalist ritualization of my existence manifested as a kind of trance. I think this semi-permanent hypnagogic state is more prevalent than we'd care to admit. Infant humans hit the scene, bellicose and struggling before decades of indoctrination pacify and sand our instincts to a reflective surface. People abuse sex and drugs to perfect their somnambulance. Others latch onto the arts or sports. In my case, writing was an act of lucid dreaming. To write was to gaze across the curve of the horizon, backward and forward simultaneously.

Because time is the Ouroboros, wishes and fears unerringly return to their sender. Naturally, a few days after my twenty-first birthday, I froze my right foot while stranded in a blizzard. Sure, it hurts to freeze one's toes, one's heel, but true suffering ensues when the doctor draws a lukewarm bath and that slab of blackened tissue begins to thaw. They held me in the tub, muttering soothing words, hands clamped on my bony shoulders. I tried not to scream; the sensation of nerves waking from the dead was of a vice crushing my bones. My long, unpleasant rehabilitation generally consisted of washing pain pills down with booze and staggering across the floor of a salmon processing factory while my foot sloshed around in its own juices in a rubber boot. I'd love to claim this changed me in some profound respect. Perhaps it was the pebble that started the avalanche.

Excepting a couple of pieces of poetry, I seldom wrote directly about Alaska, or my daily existence, while I lived there. I couldn't write about Alaska for almost twenty years *after* I left it behind. Instead, I moved to Washington State and set my stories in that region. Seattle and Olympia served as a different prism, a softer filter, for my imagination. Distance from the utter north allowed me to regroup mentally. Haphazard fragments crystallized into coherent narratives and I made a handful of professional sales.

Successful writing hinges upon translating one's inner landscape into a corresponding narrative. Potent imagery derives from a true memory or emotion and travels like a flung spear along an arc into the reader. In another life it might've been Jackie Collins or Agatha Christie who swung a lantern in the dark to guide me home. As a scarred survivor of rightwing Christian fundamentalism and backwoods poverty, my sympathies, and antipathies, are rooted in occult horror, westerns, pulps, and the variety of subversive noir that burrows under the placid façade of rural America, a la Jim Thompson. I identify with Michael Shea and Louis L'Amour more intimately than I do Herman Hesse or the genius Dorothy Parker whose black wit and sarcasm were admirable. Had my early life progressed along a divergent path, Shirley Jackson's tales of paranoia and social alienation might've steered me toward the horrors of suburbia a lot sooner.

Instead, Thompson, Robert B. Parker, Zane Grey and similar ilk are owed a bit of credit, or blame, for bookending those formative years. If I'm not grateful for everything I've endured or witnessed, I *am* thankful for the opportunity to reflect upon the big churning kaleidoscope of the past; thankful to forge those fragments into a spear I can cast forward. I'm thankful that spear will continue to arc after I've stopped.

Meanwhile, here's to never living in the woods again. Nor mushing a dog team up the Yukon in March, nor gutting another salmon in the hold of a trawler by the nauseating glamor of fluorescent lights. Here's to no more red and green waves of the aurora borealis squirming across the sky above Unalakleet on a night so bitter cold the snow grinds against my sled runners like I'm crossing dunes of iron. For years, my dreams were rooted in wind and cold and an endless plain of ice. I dreamed of inevitable death. In this dream of death, I set out across the waste. Plodding, one boot in front of the other, toward an ever-receding horizon that glinted like a dull knife. The wind kicked up and it grew darker and darker.

I didn't make a clean getaway from the wilderness. I didn't realize Alaska had frozen more than my foot; it had frozen all of me. Forging a new chapter in the Pacific Northwest was merely frostbite therapy on a larger scale.

4. Renoir is Dead

Van Gogh said, *we take death to reach a star*. Death is the chariot nobody wants to climb into. Many of us create art to fend off the charioteer's arrival. Not dissimilar to the biological imperative of producing offspring as a kind of limited immortality. Van Gogh's statement is beautiful and hopeful. I've wondered if that gulf beyond our terrestrial shores, the chasm that awaits us after our little biosystems fail and cease, is the same gulf we emerged from into this brief existence. Do we breach the surface of a black, bottomless expanse, roll, glittering and new in the light of a cooling star, and dive again?

Wild animals are imprinted with the pattern of their dams and sires repeating back and back unto the time of pea soup mists and room-temperature oceans. Genetic memory blazes within the veins of the fox and the wolf; the lizard and the owl. All creatures are born into the battle; ferocious, wary, and determined. Poets Mary Oliver and James Dickey described the micro and macro aspects of the physical universe in radiant detail. Robinson Jeffers meditated upon man and animals' connection to the raw, howling core of the natural world. He possessed scant charity for the human species.

Skin, blood, and bones—we are what we eat, what we absorb. This goes double for authors. Some declare, not incorrectly, that to write and write well, is to bleed. What is it that we bleed? We bleed memory. We bleed memories and reconstruct, or repurpose, those recollections; stories are the product of those small hours when we lie with one foot in the beyond, captivated by our inventory of regrets.

So, this is for the shear of gold and green of spring and summer in the Northeast. This is for the monarch butterfly whose wing won't unlatch, born with a clubfoot instead of a claw to catch the sweet autumn flowers. This is for the bull moose bleeding out in a field of flint-sharp snow after escaping a pack of wolves. This is for the flood of orange and red that crowns Mt. Denali at sunset in winter. She is a great fang of the Ouroboros. She is a drinker of blood and gatherer of bones.

Of these hauntings, the butterfly is most recent. Last autumn, my girl Jessica spied a caterpillar on the walkway and moved him to the safety of milkweed she'd planted to nurture the monarch population. We watched him retreat into his chrysalis; we watched him emerge, orange and black, with spotted wings. He could've inhabited a painting, so we named him after another master, Renoir. But his wing, his foot; alas, alack. Nights were cool and getting cooler. Jessica brought him in for safekeeping. She returned him the porch the next day. Renoir took wing across the yard and over a fence into the wild beyond. He wouldn't survive the long flight to Mexico, yet we'd given him a chance. Nature would take her course, as she does for each of us in our time. Rainstorms pelted the valley later in the afternoon and we worried for the poor little guy. At dusk the clouds rolled back and the air chilled. Weather reports called for sub-freezing temperatures. There was the monarch on the porch, bedraggled, exhausted. We sheltered him in a habitat with flowers. We fed him nectar and set his habitat in the sunlight and hoped he'd hang on until spring for a last hurrah. Every day, Renoir sipped his nectar and beat his wings and vainly battened against the mesh, struggling to fly south to Florida or Mexico where he belonged. Our butterfly remained with us for three months, until one morning he fluttered briefly, and stopped. Jessica laid him to rest in the roots of a potted plant on a sill with lovely afternoon exposure. I am uncertain why the loss of a butterfly has affected me, why it lingers the way it has, or engendered a powerful sense of defeat on my part.

We'll see Renoir again this summer in the whirling flights of monarchs who, at a distance, will resemble him completely. This knowledge is comforting—in the face of death, life persists. And the knowledge is bleak—life persists because it generates endless facsimiles of itself. We repeat and repeat. Eternal recurrence is a subject I continue to grapple: The Big Bang. The ultimate heat death of the universe. The Ouroboros with butterflies in its jaws. Even as I type this passage, a news item flickers on my media feed: two environmental activists were just slain in Mexico while protecting monarch breeding grounds. Such cosmic perversity will drive a man to drink, or write.

5. Chinook

Walk long enough and far enough, you'll meet yourself coming and going.

There are nights after a cold snap in January and February here in the Rondout Valley when a warm wind will roll out of the south. Shirtsleeve weather at 3A.M., and the snow will melt down to patches of bare lawn; rotten leaves will peel from graves beneath the sycamores and whirl across the yard and I smell the waking dirt. Real spring is still weeks off. In Southcentral Alaska we called balmy winds in the dead of winter a chinook.

That warm breeze and the scent of half-thawed dirt catapults me through time and space. I'm fourteen again, standing on a ridge overlooking the Yentna river just beyond a screen of spruce and alder. The wind is whipping those trees. My belly is grumbling, and in a couple of hours I'll be chopping a waterhole in the river ice. Later, my brothers and I will drag firewood from the woodlot on an ancient military sled with the help of a dog or two. Midday, I'll hitch the second string of Dad's huskies and take them out for a twenty or thirty-mile training run. I'll carry a rifle in case we get crosswise with one sort of predator or another. At night, by the glow of a kerosene lamp, I'll scratch a few more words of a fantasy novel that veers into horror and science fiction, depending upon whether I've committed a deep dive on Roger Zelazny, Andre Norton, or Poe of late. Later, staring at the rafters, I imagine there's something else, a wider world, and somewhere, a library shelf that holds a book with my name printed on the spine.

That kid sees his future as a veil of black thunderclouds shot through with slivers of golden possibility. He doesn't glimpse himself at the far end of the telescope, older, grayer, looking him in the eye. Maybe with encouragement, maybe not. Were I to hop a time machine and pay him a visit like the Ghost of Christmas Yet to Come, what would I say to the teenage Laird Barron? Damned if I know. Provenance holds on tight; I sincerely doubt any "wise" counsel of mine would change much.

Laird Barron spent his early years in Alaska. He is the author of several books, including *The Beautiful Thing That Awaits Us All; Swift to Chase;* and *Worse Angels.* His work has also appeared in many magazines and anthologies. Barron currently resides in the Rondout Valley writing stories about the evil that men do.

Creating Compelling Characters
Lucy A. Snyder

Characterization is something I consistently work on with my students. A few beginning writers have an instinctive knack for creating compelling people on the page; most aspiring authors, though, have to sweat over this a bit.

This article assumes that you've worked out the basics for your main characters. You know what they look like, where they're from, where they went to high school, what their profession is, what their mannerisms are, etc. You know if your character has any scars or old injuries, be they physical or psychological. You know if a character is a taciturn introvert or an extroverted chatterbox. Maybe you've gone so far as to do Tarot readings for your characters!

A common plea I hear from students who've done all that basic, essential character building is this: "I made my characters as realistic as I could . . . but the editor of the magazine I sent my story to said that my main character just wasn't engaging enough! What can I do?"

Realism is important, but a good character isn't just about realism. Real people are flawed and contradictory. It's possible to create a protagonist whose traits are pulled entirely from real life . . . but they're so boring or unpleasant that the reader just doesn't want to keep reading about them. The situation is complicated further because a character who is appropriate for one kind of story won't be right for another.

The biggest potential characterization chasm is between popular fiction—which covers most horror along with science fiction, fantasy, thrillers, mysteries, and romances—and literary fiction.

The core difference between popular fiction and literary fiction? Popular fiction focuses on the story, and therefore needs a strong plot. Literary fiction often isn't strongly plotted; its goal is to offer the reader beautiful writing and keen insights into the human condition.

Can a horror story be literary? Of course; there are a host of horror writers whose work contains gorgeous prose and profound insights alongside bone-deep chills. Joyce Carol Oates, Victor LaValle, Kelly Robson, Paul Tremblay, Gary A. Braunbeck, and Caitlín R. Kiernan are just a few. Writers who aspire to create literary horror have more room to play around with character conventions, but they do need to be aware of the expectations that different readers might have and the roles that characters play in terms of narrative mechanics.

In popular fiction, the absolute most important thing a main character needs to do is **drive the plot**. They need to have some kind of problem they're trying to solve, or some kind of goal they're trying to achieve. At first they won't succeed, so they try, try again: their struggles and the complications that arise from their initial attempts create the plot.

In literary fiction, the most important thing a main character does is to serve as **a vehicle for those keen insights into the human condition**. So, if the story is told from a first-person or close third person point of view, the character needs to be engaged with (and observant of/ insightful about) the world they inhabit. The character needs to be fundamentally believable to the reader. Some literary writers stock their fiction with closely-drawn, nuanced character portraits of everyday people; others write about colorful eccentrics.

Do literary characters have problems and goals? Sure. They have a complicated or difficult situation. But they might be too timid or too much of a mess to actually do much to improve their circumstances. They might just longingly dream about solving their problems . . . or be entirely oblivious to the true nature of their issues and blame the wrong circumstances or people for why they're unhappy. (Through subtext and/or secondary character commentary, the reader understands the truth of the situation by the end of the story, even if the protagonist remains tragically deluded.)

In a popular fiction narrative, there's the expectation that the protagonist will be changed as a result of the events of the story. Sometimes that change is emotional or psychological: they are galvanized or broken by what has happened, or they've learned something crucial about themselves or their world and are wiser/better skilled/more prepared as a result. (If it's a cosmic horror story, the protagonist usually learns something unimaginably horrible that has shattered their psyche.) Sometimes the change is literal: they've become a vampire or a werewolf or gained arcane powers. And sometimes they die. Death *is* a profound change, but if it doesn't fit the narrative arc, it can come across as a cop-out to the reader.

In a literary narrative, the protagonist often has some kind of epiphany or gains some insight into their life/situation at the climax of the story, and they are changed as a result. But sometimes, the whole point of the story is that in spite of everything they witness/experience, the protagonist is tragically unchanged/unenlightened; the reader might experience the epiphany that the protagonist missed.

Regardless of genre, a reader has to want to go on the narrative journey with the main character(s) in a piece of fiction. Often, this is because the viewpoint characters are sympathetic: the reader can relate to what they're going through if not actively like them and want to cheer them on. But there are plenty of successful narratives in horror that use viewpoint characters who aren't terribly sympathetic . . . but they are interesting! Or are in a compelling, interesting situation. Either way, the reader becomes invested in finding out what happens next.

Literary fiction especially is full of unlikable, difficult characters who are involved in situations that resonate with readers. My own take—and people may disagree with me here— is that literary readers have a higher tolerance for frustrating jerks than popular fiction readers do. There's the sense that literary fiction is good for your intellect and for developing your artistic sensibilities. It's *medicinal*, and we all know medicine often doesn't taste very good.

Popular fiction readers are largely reading for pleasure. They want a good story, and they want entertaining, relatable characters. It is possible to write a compelling-but-unsympathetic character, particularly in a thriller or a mystery where the focus is on solving a puzzle. Sherlock Holmes is an iconic character who has inspired a legion of clones, and in many ways he's a jerk. (Some modern retellings have notably re-drawn him to give him more sympathetic traits, but others have emphasized his arrogance.)

My own take on this is that if you're writing horror (or any other popular fiction genre), you're better off trying to add sympathy-inducing traits to characters, simply because the bar for making the character's situation unusually compelling is very, very high for people who've consumed a whole lot of narratives. Don't give your readers reasons to put down your story or novel if you can help it.

With all that in mind, here are some traits to consider when you're creating (or re-writing) a character with an eye to making them more sympathetic or interesting; you shouldn't attempt to build *all* of these into one character, because some traits are in conflict or are not genre-appropriate, but if you can't identify *some* of these in your character, you should do some rethinking:

1. They are **strong, assured,** and **act bravely** (if a hero) or **brazenly** (if a villain) in ways that the reader admires and which perhaps provide an element of wish fulfillment (or even a straight-up power fantasy). Horror fiction often has strong monsters and villains who are free to act out in ways some readers envy.

   - ☠ The flip side here is a bold character who acts without thinking things through. We can admire their confidence/bravery, but cringe at the likely consequences that we see coming but the character somehow doesn't. Handled well, this creates compelling plot tension; handled badly (for instance, because the character is unbelievably reckless) it can make the reader feel frustrated and less sympathetic towards the character.

   - ☠ Bravery isn't about being fearless; it's about taking action in the face of fears. Brave characters are almost always more compelling than those who either don't care if they die/get hurt/etc., or just lack the ability to imagine the consequences of their actions.

   - ☠ An overly confident, brash character is often annoying unless their brashness is tempered with humor; the evolving plot/situation needs to shake their confidence in some way to keep things interesting.

2. They are **competent.** The character has knowledge and skills and as a result does interesting or admirable things in the narrative. As with #1, this can tap into reader wish fulfillment. Sherlock Holmes and Thomas Carnacki are

supremely competent characters; so is Hannibal Lecter. If you're writing science fictional horror, keep in mind that competence is a hallmark feature of hard SF stories, which are well-stocked with characters who have PhDs in astrobiology but they also know small-unit military tactics as well as how to farm and knit and can repair a stardrive.

☠ The character's plot problems have to be proportional to their competence. The situation has to push them to the limits of their skills and knowledge and perhaps causes them to question themselves and their abilities; they have to struggle to overcome the situation, and the reader has to have some doubt that they'll succeed. Otherwise, if you have a character who is super-competent to the extent that there's no question as to whether they'll overcome a problem, then there's no real plot tension and you have an increasingly dull character on your hands.

3. **They're on a mission.** They've dedicated themselves to a worthy cause such as defending their city from zombies, caring for their terminally ill sister, curing a deadly disease, rescuing feral cats, etc. The reader sees value in what the character is doing, and admires them for their dedication and commitment.

☠ Plot tension #1: the character is dedicated to a cause . . . but either the cause itself or the methods used makes the reader cringe a bit. Perhaps they've dedicated themselves to a toxic religion. Perhaps their single-minded dedication to rescuing feral animals is ruining their marriage. Perhaps they're running a soup kitchen to feed the homeless (yay!) but they're serial killing and butchering wealthy suburbanites for soup meat (yikes!) The tension builds as the reader wonders: will this character wake up and realize what they're doing is hurting themselves or others? Or does the horror narrative take the reader by the hand and lead them to be increasingly sympathetic to the character's dangerous, transgressive situation?

- Plot tension #2: the character either isn't as dedicated to the cause as they think they should be, or they've begun to seriously doubt the worth of what they're doing, and they're having a crisis of faith as a result.

4. **If they don't have a mission, they're passionate about someone or something.** They have a new puppy they're crazy about. They have a girlfriend they adore. They're in a garage band and are preparing for a gig at a beloved venue. They love board gaming and are planning to compete in a tournament. Sometimes, these passions are plot-worthy, but sometimes, they're a matter of making a character more interesting, relatable, or well-rounded. Ultimately, if a viewpoint character doesn't care about anything, it's difficult for the reader to care about them and their fate.

- Plot tension: the character's passions are deep, but they're misplaced or unhealthy. The tension comes from the reader wondering if the character will realize what they're doing and change course.

5. **They have an inner ethical/moral compass**. This ties in with the character caring about their world. If their ethical values are something the reader identifies with, this builds sympathy. If the ethical values are quite different from the reader's, they can make the character more interesting. Villains, for instance, often see themselves as doing the right thing according to their own values. Hannibal Lecter is an interesting character in part because of his intelligence and competence, but also because he kills according to his inner convictions.

☠ Plot tension: the character knows what they *should* do, but they can't do it due to fear or lack of resources etc.

6. **They're relatable.** They're struggling with problems/situations that the reader can easily sympathize/empathize with. For instance, they're working low-paid jobs to provide for their family, or they're trying to help a brother who's addicted to pain pills, or they're having a conflict with their best friend.

☠ Risk: Creating a character who is a bit too mired in mundane problems can make them seem like a schlub, and a reader who is looking for an escape might be uncomfortably reminded of all that they're trying to forget.

7. **They're fun.** They enjoy life, and seek out creative entertainments for themselves and others. They're witty and talented. The party doesn't really start until this character shows up, and they unquestionably improve the atmosphere with storytelling, singing, dancing, jokes, merriment, etc. In addition to being interesting, this can very easily tie into wish fulfillment for the reader, because who doesn't want to have a great time being the life of a party?

☠ Plot tension/risk: a character has fun at someone else's expense. Will the character realize that they're being a jerk and stop being abusive? If it's not resolved/addressed in the plot fairly quickly, this can turn a fun character into a less likeable one.

☠ Plot risk: too much wisecracking can make it seem that a character isn't taking a situation seriously . . . and this can quickly sap the tension from what should be suspenseful or frightening scenes.

8. **They seem like people we'd want to be real-life friends with**. Who do we like as a friend? Aside from people who are beautiful/wealthy/powerful/fun, most people seek out friends who display traits of **agreeableness**:

☠ **Empathy** — they notice other people and other people's problems, and feel for them.

☠ **Altruism** — when they notice someone else has a problem, they try to be helpful without expecting something in return.

☠ **Cooperation** — they're aware of the social "cost" their needs put on others around them and try to mitigate how much trouble they put others to. They try to pull their weight in a situation and don't just sit back being waited on/tended to.

☠ **Modesty** — they don't have an overblown ego and have a realistic (or slightly self-deprecating) view of their own worthiness/skills/etc.

☠ **Straightforwardness** — they speak their mind and don't engage in subterfuge unless they have to.

☠ **Trust** — they're honest and trustworthy, and generally assume goodwill (or at least don't assume ill will) in others unless they have a specific reason to think otherwise.

☠ **Loyalty** — they honor commitments, and don't flake out when their friends and loved ones need help.

☠ But there's a risk here: too much "people pleasing" behavior can make a character seem passive, fearful, or manipulative, depending on the circumstances. Look more for ways in which characters can be aware of others' situations and responsive to them (engaging sympathy, empathy, and altruism) rather than just doing what they think others want them to do in order to avoid conflict (which displays passivity and possibly cowardice).

Ultimately, every character trait has potential positives and negatives. For instance, being high-energy is usually thought of as a good thing, right? Consider an energetic, intelligent character who can hunt zombies for 36 hours straight . . . but who also finds it difficult to sit still for long periods, and consequently he doesn't have much of a clue about technology and doesn't read books. He may have convinced himself that reading isn't that important . . . until the day he's desperately got to send a message to his team, and all he's got is a malfunctioning computer, and for the first time in his life he's got to comprehend a manual or he's dead.

The dark side of self-confidence is arrogance; for prudence, it's cowardice; for persistence, it's stubbornness, etc. It helps to think of characters as having traits that help them achieve their goals within a story along with traits that will complicate/hamper their efforts rather than thinking in terms of strengths and flaws.

Horror characters are often ordinary people simply trying to survive an awful situation, so it's perfectly fine to start with a passive character who's forced to take action to deal with the sudden intrusion of a terrifying threat into their life. Do they emerge a stronger, wiser, bolder character? Or are they broken on the wheel of their own flaws and bad decisions?

You're the author: it's up to you.

Lucy A. Snyder is the Shirley Jackson Award-nominated and five-time Bram Stoker Award-winning author of 15 books and over 100 published short stories. Her most recent books are the short story collection *Halloween Season* and the forthcoming novel *Apocalypse Apocrypha.* She lives in Columbus, Ohio with a small jungle of houseplants, a clowder of cats, and an insomnia of housemates. You can learn more about her at www.lucysnyder.com and you can follow her on Twitter at @LucyASnyder.

Interview with Robert McCammon
Brady Allen

Brady Allen: Swan Song *is a favorite novel of many, including me, and a popular short story of yours is "Pin." Speak to the biggest challenge, craft-wise, in writing each of these—one a sprawling epic, the other a narrow (pun intended) and tightly-focused short story.*

Robert McCammon: Well . . . there's really not a huge difference if you feel you have an interesting story to tell. The idea dictates the length of what you're writing . . . so I knew with *Swan Song* that it was going to be a long book because there were so many ideas, characters, and scenes in it. Whereas with a story like "Pin" it was a very specific idea with one character and one viewpoint, and again I knew it needed only a few pages to get the tale across.

Allen: *What's the trick to writing realistic characters? What's the trick to writing bizarre or grotesque characters? Were or are any of yours particularly fun or difficult to write? I*

179

think I recall hearing you say back in the early 2000s when I heard you talk at the Southern Festival of Books that the idea for Flint Murtaugh, the lone wolf and freak-show refugee who carries the body of his unformed twin brother Clint on his torso, came from a Civil War history book?

McCammon: Yes, that's correct about the genesis of Flint and Clint . . . a strange book I discovered about physical deformities that was published during the Civil War period. I do have fun with my characters, for sure. I enjoy trying to understand their motivations and what makes them "tick". Every character has a backstory—a life—that you can't always elaborate on when you're writing, but if I can't explore their backstories in depth, I do try to give some clue as to what I believe their history might have been. I suppose if there's any trick to writing realistic characters, it's imagining their life up to that point and attempting to understand what has gone before . . . and thus why they act as they presently do.

Allen: *How do you approach writing realistic dialogue? And, as a true Alabama gentleman, do you even think at all about writing a Southern dialect? Or better yet, do you even think about writing dialect at all?*

McCammon: I actually have written in Southern dialect for a couple of books and a few short stories. It's just a matter of remembering what I hear, particularly the dialects I heard growing up. This is a hard one to explain . . . I guess it's like an actor doing a dialect he or she is unfamiliar with . . . it's a matter of listening and remembering, is about all I can say.

Allen: *Research is a huge part of your writing, especially with your Matthew Corbett series of novels. Which comes first, the chicken or the egg: the research or the story? Do you do most of the research beforehand or during? Or even after?*

McCammon: The story definitely comes first. I do some research at the beginning but I continue to research all during the writing process. I recall something that caused me a bit of grief: I believe it was in *Mister Slaughter* that I presented the idea of a multi-barreled flintlock pistol. I hadn't done the proper research on this and thought I could simply "wing" it. When it got to the part where the pistol was supposed to be put into action, for the life of me I couldn't figure out how it would work. So I frantically turned to doing more research because the particular scene needed the pistol to be fired more than once . . . and lo and behold, I discovered all sorts of information on the multi-barreled pistols of that era, and the scene was saved. But again, I do research all through the writing process because you're going to come up against a lot of items (like a hundred different kinds of wagons and carriages) that you need to know about. All that information might not—and probably won't—make it into the book, but I like to know as much as possible.

Allen: Do you edit as you go (story by story or chapter by chapter), or do you just push through first. Why this way?

McCammon: I do a page at a time and don't go to the next page without feeling it's the best I can do. Then of course I do go back and make changes and corrections, but for the most part the editing is done page-by-page as I'm doing the actual writing.

Allen: Your settings are usually vivid and drip with atmosphere. Does most of this come from memory/imagination, or do you find yourself visiting and revisiting places and/or looking at photos?

McCammon: I guess it's mostly imagination, though I've based several locales on real places I remember. For the Matthew Corbett series, I've studied old (very old) maps of New York, Charles Town, and London. I've tried to imagine and describe New York as a relatively small but bustling and ambitious town surrounded by hills and forest. I have visited many of the places in New York City that I've described in the Corbett series and as I walked around, I tried to "see" what the town must've been like in 1703 or so. At least some of the hills are still there, though flattened a bit by concrete, and I found that though Trinity church has been rebuilt several times the original cemetery there has been pretty much untouched over the centuries. Very interesting to see the colonial-era gravestones there, just about all the names erased by time.

Allen: What's the best piece of writing advice, craft-wise, you've ever gotten?

McCammon: Don't be afraid to fail. Which means taking a risk with your writing, your ideas, and your characters.

Allen: What keeps you going and gets your shoulders over the keyboard after all these years and stories and books?

McCammon: I would say, the power of the story. I'm always working on something I'd like to read. I don't use an outline, so sometimes I don't know how things are going to turn out. That keeps me involved in finding out how the story will advance and what the conclusion will be. For me, it's fun that way.

Allen: *If you were secluded for several years—islands are cliché, so let's say in a shack on stilts in the swamp—what five books would you want to have with you to read over and over, so you wouldn't forget how good writing is done?*

McCammon: A shack in stilts in the swamp? I suppose the first book would be how to cook catfish a dozen ways and how to treat mosquito bites!

My pick of swamp-shack books would be: *Jonathan Strange & Mr Norrell* by Susanna Clarke, a book I've read several times and always find something new and wonderful in. There's an entire book in the footnotes she produces, and to me the world of magic in England that she's created is just simply magnificent. I think she's probably the only writer on the planet who could've written it!

Next up: the original Sherlock Holmes stories, which again I never get tired of reading. I enjoy the atmosphere as much as the mysteries and of course Holmes is a completely real and fascinating character.

Next: *The Constant Gardner* by John le Carre, a brilliantly-written book about medical politics in Africa, nefarious doings, and damaged characters . . . one of le Carre's finest works. I am a huge fan of his writing and am very sad we just lost him a few days ago. His research, his use of dialog, and his intellectual qualities were and are high achievements in literature.

And: anything by Ray Bradbury, whom I grew up reading and who I believe has had a major impact on my writing. I recall reading one of his short stories—"The Lake"—and being moved to tears, and at an early age thinking I'd wish to be able to communicate like that. Also I recall thinking that I hated to get to the end of anything he'd written because I enjoyed it so much, and that's something I try to do in my own work . . . leave the reader wanting more and feeling a bit wistful that the reading experience is over.

Last but certainly not least: *The Eyes of the Overworld* or *Quest at the End of Time* by Jack Vance. This is a series of linked stories in a fantasy world that might be another planet Earth eons past or eons in the future, and concerns the rascally varlet Cudgel the Clever in his attempt to gain revenge on a magician who has cast him into a far-flung territory of the world in search of lenses for the eyes that make all ugliness and poverty appear beautiful and enriched. Added to Cudgel's trouble is a scorpion-like creature called Firx that lives in his liver and gives him a pinch from time to time. It's great fun and Jack Vance was a master of description, atmosphere, and use of color. Yep, this would definitely be one of the swamp-shack books!

Robert McCammon is the author of 23 novels and two short story collections. Starting with his first novel, *Baal*, in 1978, McCammon quickly became one of the bestselling horror authors of the 1980s, with three consecutive novels hitting the *New York Times* Bestsellers List: *Swan Song, Stinger*, and *The Wolf's Hour*. During that time, he also won several Bram Stoker Awards for Best Novel and Best Short Story. As the '90s dawned, McCammon expanded his writing away from the horror genre, and his 1991 classic *Boy's Life* won the World Fantasy Award for Best Novel. After *Gone South* in 1992, McCammon decided to try historical fiction, which had always interested him. After clashing with a new publisher over the direction of his new books, McCammon retired from publishing for ten years. He returned in 2002 with *Speaks the Nightbird*, which became the first book in a planned nine-book series about Matthew Corbett. The Corbett books are set in the early 1700s, and each volume has explored different genres: mystery, adventure, chase, pulp, thriller, and more. In addition to the Corbett books, McCammon has also written contemporary novels, including *The Five*, *The Border*, and *The Listener*. *Cardinal Black*, book seven in the Matthew Corbett series, was published by Cemetery Dance on April 30, 2019. McCammon is currently finishing *King of Shadows*, the next book in the Matthew Corbett series. McCammon lives in Birmingham, AL. (Composed by Hunter Goatley).

Brady Allen grew up in a small rural town in southern Ohio and now resides in Dayton, Ohio. He has two daughters and a daughter-dog, and he teaches creative writing, Great Books, and composition at a local public college. Besides reading and his family, his loves are listening to Reds baseball on the transistor radio and Waylon Jennings. Former recipient of an Individual Artist Fellowship for fiction from the Ohio Arts Council, Brady is the author of the short-story collection *Back Roads & Frontal Lobes* and at work on a second collection, tentatively titled *Outliers & Inner Urges*.

Stories in Pieces:
Found Footage Storytelling, or Writing Epistolary Narratives for the 21st Century
Gemma Files

The thesis: In a media-literate and -saturated age (such as ours), using as many different streams of information as required or possible to tell a story simply serves to make it seem more real, as does tricking the reader into thinking they're an active participant in the story as it unfolds—forcing them to study it, to follow the clues. Creating a maze only you have the key to, but one they can *find* the key to, with your help. Using text, subtext and meta-text (text that comments on itself), each writer can decide on a strategy which makes sure readers get all the information they need in order to connect the dots along with you and feel as though they've helped "solve" the story by the time it ends, or at least stops.

The great part about epistolary/found footage storytelling is how surprisingly easy it can be to put a story like this together, much like building a collage, albeit one made out of images you yourself drew, then snipped apart for maximum impact. To tell a story from several different objective and subjective viewpoints, playing them off against each other to reveal a larger overall story, you can basically feel free to use every and/or any type of documentation you can think of, so long as it fits contextually: Website entries, Wiki-data, emails, snail-mail letters, newspaper articles, media outlet posts, chat logs, blog or diary entries, comment threads, text messages, tweets, official documents, press releases, transcripts of podcasts and interviews, descriptions of visual/aural data—films, videos, .jpgs, .mpgs, sound-files, etc.

In Paul Tremblay's short story "Notes for 'The Barn in the Wild,'" for example—reprinted in his collection *Growing Things*—he replicates the text of a notebook in which our main perspective character is jotting down research, memoirish fragments, doodles and various preliminary notes for an article he intends to write; as things become weirder, the protagonist finds notes he can't recall having made next to particular entries, and eventually whole pages in a degraded version of his own handwriting. But how different is this from, say, Bram Stoker's classic epistolary novel *Dracula*, stitched together as it is from diary entries, letters, clippings, telegrams and various other effluvia produced by several different characters undergoing the same linked set of supernatural events? Or, for that matter, how different are either of these tales from Cholderlos de Laclos's *Les Liaisons Dangereuses*, told as it is as a series of missives penned by two decadent aristocrats amusing themselves by manipulating and destroying various people they consider too naive or annoying to matter?

An argument could be made both that epistolary storytelling is one of the oldest types of fiction, and that the thing which makes it so innately fascinating both as a practice and a form of reading matter lies in exactly the same promise that attracts us to other sorts of metafiction, very much including found footage movies: The idea that by imitating the ways in which true-life events are documented (either during or after the fact), it allows writers to deliver on the most integral promise of storytelling itself, the impression of relating something that—while definitely *not* true—*could* be true.

Some of my favourite horror stories are epistolary narratives. "N," by Stephen King; the hypnagogic tales of podcaster Soren Narnia; "Pages from a Young Girl's Diary" by Robert Aickman; and on, and on, and on. At this point in my career, I've lost track of how many epistolary or semi-epistolary stories I've written, especially when you fold in the fact that any first-person narrative could be just as easily labelled epistolary—the text version of spoken testimony, or a piece of given evidence.

Like all classic hauntology (recordings, photos, film, etcetera produced during parapsychological inquiries), all found footage narratives—and, to some degree, creepypasta—spin on the basic assumption that technology can render reality (or, at the least, our perception of reality) objective. "Pics or it didn't happen" becomes "video tells the truth, film lies," even when we all know that both film and video are equally easy to fake. But since we really all start out knowing better, because all stories are fiction, found footage is also inherently creepy from the get-go. Documentaries are assumed to be educational, trustworthy, yet every cut and splice acts as directorial POV, nudging you towards a foregone conclusion the filmmaker has already decided upon. The fun lies in the way that these narratives dole out the necessary information, making you feel you're putting the pieces together yourself.

Although we think of found footage as mainly a visual medium (the name suggests as much), these are tactics used in sensation/thriller/horror storytelling at least since the 1880s, throughout what the Victorians referred to as Sensation Literature. "The Call of Cthulhu," by H.P. Lovecraft, essentially consists of someone describing a bunch of material a friend of his found in a box he inherited from a dead relative and how he put these items together to suggest a larger, interconnecting story. *A Mirror for Witches*, by Esther Forbes, is formatted like a pamphlet from 1600s Puritan New England chronicling the life and death of Doll Bilby, a woman accused of witchcraft. "Ghost Hunt," by H.R. Wakefield, is formatted as a taped monologue/radio broadcast delivered by a radio host who agrees to spend the night alone in a supposedly haunted house, climaxing with his own "live" suicide—it's also been adapted to "real" radio play format for various series, including *Suspense!*.

The key, I believe, lies that most classic of creepypasta lines: "Okay, so I know this sounds totally fake, but it's all true." By mixing and matching delivery systems, we create a net of suggestions which allow the reader to become a participant, essentially allowing them to trick themselves into believing in something they already know isn't real. It's just fiction to another level, but the suspension of disbelief required is even more gossamer-thin than usual and very easily punctuated, especially if you expand the story to include multiple POVs from very different character types.

On a purely practical level, the tricks of the trade may include:

- Interviews (transcribed), taken in studio or in field. These play a lot like radio scripts, so the podcast model is a good thing to study; scripts or transcriptions of many podcasts can be found online. I'd recommend *The Black Tapes* podcast as a good place to start.

- Research strings—tracing how someone researches something, using much the same format as an Internet browser history list, but slightly more expanded. This might include cited quotations from books, articles, back-and-forth comments on articles, etc.

- ☠ Official documentation—site entries, Wiki-data, newspaper articles/media outlet posts, chat logs, comment threads, text messages, tweets, official documents, press releases, etc. Format is important, but not to the point of making yourself insane; find something to model your version after, then check it for errors once you're done with first draft.

- ☠ Monologues—blog/diary entries, letters, emails, transcribed livestreaming or liveTweeting a la "#CONNOLLYHOUSE #WESHOULDN'TBEHERE" by Seannan Maguire. This last is an incredible challenge, especially since you have to run every section through Twitter to make sure it doesn't go over the character limit, but it's a wonderful way to make a story seem immediate, as if it's happening right before your eyes and your attention is part of the action. (More examples can be found here https://vampiresquid.co.uk/scary-in-under-280-characters-horror-fiction-on-twitter/) But on a slightly less technological tip, if you stick to physical documentation, you open yourself up to being able to move freely between time-periods in a way most found footage won't allow for, restricted as it is to eras after the motion picture camera was invented.

- ☠ Straight descriptions of visual/audio media—edited, unedited, collated, uncollated. Photos, film and video clips or footage, .jpgs, .mpgs, sound-files . . . but as you go back further, you also find works organized around descriptions of statues, carvings (A.C. Wise's "The Last Sailing of the Henry Charles Morgan in Six Pieces of Scrimshaw (1841)" http://pseudopod.org/2019/01/18/pp-631-six-pieces-of-scrimshaw/), mezzotints (cf. "The Mezzotint," by M.R. James), daguerrotypes, Polaroids, and on and on, ad infinitum. Supposedly unchangeable things that change, of seem to change, according to their viewer ("Did you see what I saw?" ". . . what did you see?") are the very heart of Uncanny Valley territory, as "wrong" and dreadful as the idea of looking into a mirror and seeing someone else's face.

@ Provenance—how did you get these documents? Where did you get these documents? Whose hands did they pass through? Have they been curated, overtly or inadvertently? Is anything missing, lost? What lens were the curators looking at this material through—what were their opinions/assumptions about their content? What are people choosing not to say/comment on, and why? (The lens of received wisdom can be fascinating to play with—ie, in A Mirror for Witches, the pamphleteers "know" that Doll Bilby is a witch because it's a commonly accepted fact, therefore everything they record "proves that she's a witch," whereas modern readers look at the same material and says "no, there's another possibility here—she might have just been driven crazy by everybody continually accusing her of witchcraft.") How can this information be reframed? How would you reframe it?

@ Annotations/Commentary—a wonderful example of this is Sarah Gailey's "STET", written as an article full of citations and editorial notes, all of which advance the overall story (https://firesidefiction.com/stet#one). Hard as hell to do, but possible! You can also put these in manually on the physical page as footnotes/endnotes or break to put the commentary in using a different font. See also Paul Tremblay's "The Blog at the End of the World," and *The Dionaea House* by Eric Heisserer, or "The Pine Arch Collection," by Michael Wehunt (http://thedarkmagazine.com/pine-arch-collection/#).

- 💀 Perspective—restricted or multiple? Single perspective is great for either total subjectivity or total objectivity, but multiple perspectives can be used to reveal information a single perspective might not have access to. It's also the difference between Adam LG Nevill's "dereliction" "Hippocampus" (http://pseudopod.org/2019/02/01/pseudopod-633-hippocampus/), in which literally nothing is explained (only described), and a version of the same scenario annotated/commented on by, say, experts in archaeology who might be able to explain where those weird mummies come from, or maritime disaster investigators who might be able to tell you what ship it was, who the crew were, etcetera. (Ask yourself if your story needs this sort of expansion.)

- 💀 Empathy vs sympathy—one primary complaint about found footage is that the characters tend to be overly simple or inherently unsympathetic. This may be because of the inherent difference between an audience member being asked to put themselves in the position of a character and a reader being asked to make the same leap. The reader's perspective will always be more intimate. Another really important thing that too few people play with, however, is complicity—making the audience member/reader feel as though their outside-the-narrative perspective allows them to understand things the characters don't, or make connections before the characters have enough information to do so. In found footage narratives we are often unable to alter the story's trajectory ("one year later, their footage was found"), usually because it's already fixed directionally before we even begin our journey through it, yet this last aspect can allow us to feel a bit more in control. The most control, however, would be if the narrative was formatted like a game, with multiple potential twists and endings. (Very Choose Your Own Adventure—"if this, then this." Possible in prose? Certainly, though it's a challenge.)

☠ Experimentation—there's always a new sort of delivery system to play with. Think about police/military body-cams and private security surveillance tapes, drone footage, GPS and Fit Bit readings uploaded automatically to the Cloud, downloading someone's voice-activated AI logs (Alexa recording a ghost's "voice" the same way a parrot might imitate the sound of someone being murdered). Anything and everything.

☠ Immediacy—is the story already done, or is it still happening? Is the narrator/editor part of it? Is the reader directly "threatened" by what goes on during the story they're reading?

Some other good things to keep in mind: Leave things to the imagination by considering framing—let stuff happen outside the frame of "the camera," as well as inside it. Noises in the dark count for a lot (which is why the invention of night-vision lenses has been a bad as well as a good thing for found footage). Maybe let the filming stop every once in a while, then rejoin your characters in progress, dropping readers back into the action without getting them up to speed. (The White Vault podcast uses an overall narrator to link sections of audio, thus skipping over—say—ten minutes of crawling through a tunnel, or eight hours of sleep.) Don't let the documentation be questioned (ie "why the hell are they still filming?"), perhaps by making at least one informational feed professional in nature—CCTV, news coverage, etc.

Switch perspectives to bring in new characters, which may in itself reframe the action (one of the best examples I've ever seen of this is in the novel *Security* by Gina Wohlsdorff, which is told entirely in CCTV feeds, one of which follows "the killer" doing things other characters can't see [and an overall narrator commenting on top of it, implying he may be the person employing said killer]). Part of the thrill of found footage is voyeurism, so use that. Also, bearing in mind frequent complaints that found footage horror protagonists often aren't "likeable," watching the horror unfold from the eyes of the person inflicting it could certainly both make for some uncomfortable reading and make us feel a lot more like rooting for the characters involved. And pay attention to dialogue, because when you reduce characters to speech and action, it's very easy for them to all sound the same. Try breaking straight description up with personal commentary/ monologue, to give an insight into the people involved.

As with all sorts of fiction, the idea is to work out both the story you want to tell and how you want to tell it, with an eye towards efficiency as well as effect. But because this is horror, part of that is figuring out what you want to be "scary" about the situation outlined—how you're going to build up and then undermine a sense of reality. If your reader doesn't believe in the reality of the situation when things are going as they should, they're sure not going to care once things start going off the rails. For me, this is where it helps to insert an element of your own emotional reality wrapped inside a pellet of something so dramatic that anybody might be affected by it, but your process may be different.

Say we begin with a story idea about a woman whose wife has vanished. The outline of such a piece could involve three types pf documentation: The first a newspaper article about the disappearance; the second a transcript of a wiretapped conversation (recorded by the police) between the woman and her brother-in-law; the third a series of entries from the woman's diary. The next step would involve figuring out a strategy of assemblage—how will you braid these streams of information together, and in what order? Where should you cut and/or paste? How will you find your narrative through-line, the information and events that move the plot forward most directly, let alone when and/or how to reveal these elements? Remember: At least one of your informational streams should always be from the POV of a main character, because character relationships are the primary mechanism that drives plot forward. We call this sort of stream the spine, and all the other streams orbit around it by necessity, interacting with it to produce a forward-moving story even if the story also contains information from the past (flashbacks told through older documentation), or information dropped in as a sort of sidebar (to elaborate on or inform the main text). Think of it like assembling a necklace out of three or more types of beads: Try to find, and make, a pattern.

I used to tell people that when you're writing something shorter than a novel, you sometimes have to make a choice between characterization and plot development ... ie, that the more detailed the plot is, the less deeply you can delve into the characters involved (and that it also helps to have fewer characters if you want to explore them more thoroughly). It's like the difference between inside action (thoughts, feelings, memories) and outside action (events, decisions, choices). But the fact is, even lightly characterized people mainly make decisions and choices because of their relationships with other people, and while you could call a lot of found footage narratives outside action-heavy, those relationships still need to exist in order to drive things along. It's the relationships that give us any type of sympathy with our protagonists, and plot without sympathy is just spectacle.

So how can you characterize people lightly and yet evoke sympathy? Well, it's a bit like knowing where to make the cuts when you're editing; in most cases, we skip the things we think can be taken for granted. Sometimes it's stuff like: "How did this character get from here to there?" "Well, we can probably assume they used a vehicle of some sort, and that it took a certain amount of time. If it was a car, it might take minutes; if a bus or a truck, it might take hours. If a plane, it might take half a day, depending on where they're going." But sometimes it can also be stuff like: "If people are members of a family, we *begin* by assuming they probably love each other, which means they'll be afraid for each other if they're in danger and mourn for each other if something goes wrong. If one or more of them don't, that's worth covering, because that's the exception to the rule. It's worth going into, because it's different."

We assume that making an assumption (as the old phrase goes) makes an ass out of "u and me." But the fact is, a lot of the assumptions we make are about things we generally understand. It's not a plot hole if someone tells somebody else they're coming to see them, and then a certain amount of narrative time later, they show up. You don't *have* to see the journey, unless something interesting happened along the way. And characterization can work a bit like that as well—if a mother hugs her son, that's pretty normal; if she tongue-kisses him and pulls him "offscreen," not so much. It makes us want to know more.

Figuring out your POV character and customizing one of the narrative streams—the spine—"for" them, if you haven't, is one of an epistolary narrative's most important challenges. Questions to ask in order to figure out the POV character might include: who is telling each section of the story, and why? What parts are and are not most important? Is any of the testimony involved subjective? Then maybe the person whose POV reveals that fact is "the real" main character, the person we should be most invested in. (And BTW, it's possible to have more than one main character, though seldom more than three.)

Try to also think about indirect methods by which to achieve characterization—what objective facts we can learn about the characters through their choices and actions, and how those might be integral to the plot. For example: if a person has a family background of mental instability and becomes a completely logical atheist/doubter because of it, putting them up against something supernatural may cause them to make the wrong decisions simply because in order to make the right ones, they'd have to change their entire outlook on life. Some people can, but it costs them. Both sides of that struggle create drama. And think about the relationships that drive your POV character's intersection with the plot. Who do they love? Who do they hate? Why? What will they do or not do, because of these relationships?

Finally, there's a certain liminality which comes with a first-person perspective—do we believe what we're being told, or not? Did our narrator see what they think they saw? Were they wrong in their assumptions? Is there, in fact, an alternative explanation lurking between the lines, the images, the roster of evidence?

First off, let's define liminality, as a concept. Derived from the Latin word "limen," meaning, threshold, it was originally applied only to the transitional period or phase of a rite of passage—adolescence, for example, or being a student or trainee, engaged but not yet married, someone who isn't quite one thing or another, but exists in a literal state of flux. (Historically, the concept has also been applied to people undergoing FTM or MTF gender transition, or even people who identify as intersex, agender, asexual or pansexual, as though these were negotiable states that haven't quite been "decided upon," but most people now understand that that's both inaccurate and potentially insulting. The term would, however, apply to those who identify as genderfluid.) In other words, state of liminality is one where the order of things has been suspended and is in flux, caught mid-transformation between fixed states.

The idea of liminality was first introduced into the field of anthropology in 1909 by Arnold Van Gennep, in his work *Les Rites de Passage*. Van Gennep described the rites of passage as having the following three-part structure: separation from the norm; a liminal period during which a new identity is decided upon; re-assimilation back into the norm. A person grieving a loss can be considered going through this pattern—she feels the loss, is inducted into a liminal transition period from grief to acceptance, then finally re-assimilates into society. It was not until the second half of the 20th Century, however—with the writings of Victor Turner, that the concept of liminality was explored fully. In *Liminality and Communitas*, Turner began by defining liminal individuals as "neither here nor there; they are betwixt and between the positions assigned and arrayed by law, custom, convention, and ceremony". But Turner gives hope by referring to "betwixt and between" through the concept of the "realm of pure possibility"—the idea that re-assimilation into a fixed state doesn't have to be the end of the story, and might not even be a happy one, if it is.

This reinterpretation leaves literal space for people—and narratives—which differ from the norm, horror stories very much amongst them.

Since my own inclinations are always to the dark, no matter what genre I'm dealing with, I tend to put things in horror terms. And luckily for me, horror is an inherently liminal genre, one whose central narrative convention as a whole may well be the realization—quick or slow, big or small, immediate or retroactive—that there is *something wrong*. This is one of the reasons why horror narratives so often tend to the conservative, or at least the predictable: because the discovery of wrongness means that there must have, originally, been a standard of innate rightness from which things can deviate. As such, you often feel you have only two choices: restore normalcy at the end of the narrative, or don't. Both choices can also seem utterly mundane, which is antithetical to the whole idea of horror and only half of the story when it comes to liminality.

So how do you get around this? In my opinion, first and foremost by playing with the delivery system:

experimenting with or combining various narrative structures and methodologies, the mechanics of mood and character perspective—whatever it takes, according to the challenge. You look at the content of the story you want to tell and then shape the way you're going to tell it accordingly. Sometimes you go where it seems most natural to, and sometimes you try to set up tension by going in exactly the opposite direction. Or a combination of both.

In other words, if horror is inherently liminal, then so is found footage/epistolary storytelling. The two are made for each other. The single perspective of classic found footage can't possibly show you everything at once about a situation, so its very limitations help you to imagine what it can't show you; expanded found footage/epistolary narrative allows for several perspectives (all equally limited on their own) crossing over and differing from each other, even contradicting each other, to create a composite, fragmentary picture of something impossible to describe directly.

Think of the central problem of adapting the works of HP Lovecraft, possibly the most liminal horror author of the whole classic horror canon. This quote from his story "The Unnameable" tells it best: "It was everywhere — a gelatin — a slime; a vapor; — yet it had shapes, a thousand shapes of horror beyond all memory. There were eyes — and a blemish. It was the pit — the maelstrom — the ultimate abomination. Carter, it was the unnamable!" Impossible to depict visually or through information-driven storytelling—but is it really? A thing that's all these things at once is liminal, wrong on every level...the only way you can come to it is through bits and snatches, at oblique angles, between the lines, liminally. By controlling not only what you choose to show, but what you choose not to.

I've often used the metaphor of an advent calendar—a series of doors covering a huge picture which we reveal part by part, by choosing what doors to open and in what order.

Sometime we do it from the bottom up or top down, from left to right or right to left; sometimes we open them in numerical order, and sometimes we just open them at random. It's up to us to figure out how best to do it, depending on our readers' powers of logic, analysis and imagination. When we tell them that something's wrong, how long do we want it to take for them to figure out exactly what that is? Do we choose to do that in linear order, moving fairly smoothly from point to point on the curve, or in non-linear order, sending them in directions which turn out to be thematic or emotional sidebars, increasing a sense of dread and disturbance with giving any sort of narrative reward?

So on the one hand, telling stories of liminality not only produces but defines the sense of unreliability that horror depends on, and on the other, it's also a position of pure creative potential—things could literally go in any direction you want. It's a terrifying sense of freedom.

To get just a tad more technical, these might be the primary questions we ask ourselves when starting to rough out a horror idea:

- ☠ What is wrong?

- ☠ How do we find out it's wrong?

- ☠ What's the fallout from that discovery?

- ☠ Is it fixable? (The horror impulse is to say "no," or "only at an almost equally intolerable price." Also, what value of "fixed" are you willing to settle for?)

This wrongness might be something familiar rendered unfamiliar— indeed, especially when dealing with a short story, this is often the place most people tend to start, choosing to skip the world-building element entirely, given they don't have a lot of time and space to play with to begin with, and just assume that the world of the story mimics their/their reader's own. They begin with characters like them doing the sort of stuff they usually do, then introduce a very domestic sort of wrongness into the familiar scenario. But sometimes the wrongness involved is on a level far larger than that of a simple haunted object or person you think you know who suddenly isn't behaving "like [themself]." In some cases, horror comes out of the reader's own realization that a story's characters inhabit a completely different world that they themselves do, and don't necessarily even notice is inherently wrong, until said wrongness rebounds on them. Shirley Jackson's "The Lottery" is a prime example of this trope, as is Robert W. Chambers's "The Repairer of Reputations," which also happens to have a POV character who we only gradually realize is ass-crazy.

So perhaps, rather than wrongness, what we're actually looking to fashion here is more like . . . a sense of unreliability. What's going to turn out to be unreliable in your story? The narrator? The world? The frame? Objects in the foreground? In the background? Other characters? Your protagonist's memories? Space and time? Logical consequences for certain actions? (In a universe where ghosts, monsters or dark gods exist, for example, evoking, mocking or just finding yourself in proximity with these creatures would not be a very good idea. In one where the Christian God is just a psychological construct, on the other hand, relying on Him for help would be a very *bad* idea, or at least a pointless one.)

One of the most wonderful (and difficult) things to make unreliable is the reader's own assumptions about what sort of story this is. I mean, *you* know you're writing horror, but your reader doesn't have to—until it's too late. Kelly Link, whose stories often begin like sweet, slightly twee magic-realistic fables and end by punching your heart out, is very good at this sort of thematic switcheroo. So is Jonathan Carroll, who once had his main character get out of a tight spot by suddenly just ceasing to pretend she *wasn't* actually the anthropomorphic embodiment of Death. Both their stories often start in one place and end in another, merely

202

through the simple yet integral trick of sudenly revealing their true nature/genre halfway through.

When I hit a block with my writing I tend to try a tense I've always avoided (I've done some surprisingly good work in second person present, ie "you are here, you do this," and I've secretly yearned to do something in the future, like Scott Edelman does with his brilliant story "What Will Come After"). Or I could do something all in dialogue, or get rid of dialogue entirely (Lovecraft!), which definitely works when it comes to framing something as an official document, or a diary entry, or a bunch of letters, articles, tweets. I might omit description, keep it all "offscreen," or go so deep into description almost nothing actually happens. I might tell the story backwards, or non-linearly—or even interstitially, by mainly talking about the things *around* the most important part of your story, thus forcing readers to try and figure out what it is that my characters won't address directly. I might even try to avoid explanation, or even exposition—shuck the usual trappings, embrace the uncanny, the numinous, the self-contradictory.

What we learn from crossing horror with liminality—much like we learn from crossing horror with fiction in general—is that the norm is not the same for everybody; the default is not the same for everybody. It can't be. So go to the opposite of your default and see what the world looks like from there. See what become abnormal, "wrong" and horrifying *then*.

Formerly a film critic, journalist, screenwriter and teacher, **Gemma Files** has been an award-winning horror author since 1999. She has published four collections of short work, three chap-books of speculative poetry, a Weird Western trilogy, a story-cycle and a stand-alone novel (*Experimental Film*, which won the 2016 Shirley Jackson Award for Best Novel and the 2016 Sunburst award for Best Adult Novel). She has a new story collection coming in February, 2021 (*In That Endlessness Our End*, Grimscribe Press) and one scheduled after that from Cemetery Dance (*Dark Is Better*). Her book *Spectral Evidence* (Trepidatio) won the 2018 This Is Horror Award for Best Collection.

Monstrous Matriculation
The Arguments for
and Against the MFA

Scott A. Johnson

The third most common type of question I get (after "Where do you get your ideas?" and "What are you doing in my house?") often fall along the same lines. "Where'd you learn how to write?" "How can I learn to be a writer?" "Do I have to get a degree to be a writer?" "Does a degree really help you that much?"

When it comes to almost every trade in the world, a person wishing to partake has somewhere to go to learn that trade. Welders, mechanics, teachers, doctors, lawyers, and even morticians wind up in a specialized program to get their bona fides and add a few fancy letters after their name. At the end of the program, you get a piece of paper stating that you are now a learned person and get to walk across a stage with a funny hat. And writing is no different.

Sort of.

There are programs all over the world that offer a Master of Fine Arts in creative writing, some more expensive than others. So the question becomes should you, or shouldn't you, go for the MFA. And the answer, of course, is complicated.

Full disclaimer: I teach in one such program (Seton Hill University's MFA in Writing Popular Fiction) and am an alumnus of another (Emerson College's Publishing and Writing Popular Fiction MFA program). This is not, however, a hard sell. Nor is this a klaxon warning you away. This may be the most frank and honest conversation you'll ever have about such programs, so I hope that's what you're looking for.

First and foremost, let's get this out of the way. Do you need an MFA to become a writer? Of course not. There have been plenty of writers who existed before the MFA was even a concept. There are hundreds of published and well-known writers who have little more than a high school diploma, and quite a few with even less than that.

In fact, to be completely honest, the only thing a person has to do to be a writer is write. To be a *good* writer, I suggest reading. Read everything you can get your hands on, whether in your chosen genre or not. But what happens if you find you've hit a wall and you just aren't improving? Or what happens if, despite the loving praise heaped upon you by friends and family, your writing isn't able to land an agent or get you published? What if you have a story in your head but can't figure out how to translate it to words on paper? In these cases, an MFA program might be a good place to start.

To begin with, not all creative writing MFA programs are created equal. For the most part, college MFA programs focus on so-called *literary* fiction. For most of these programs, the faculty seek to nurture the art of creative writing through dealing with the narrative of the human condition. Focus is given to literary pursuits, or the artistic value, of fiction, nonfiction, and poetry.

Let's assume that since you're reading a book called *Writer's Workshop of Horror 2*, that's not your bag. Mention that you'd prefer to write horror (or any one of a dozen other genres) and you're likely to be dismissed with the phrase "We don't do *genre* fiction here." The pooh-poohing of popular genres is a time-honored tradition in the hallowed halls of academia, and one that has only recently begun to fade.

In its wake, some colleges have created programs that are geared toward more commercial viability, and that appreciate horror, science fiction, mystery, romance, erotica, and every subgenre you can think of. These programs are few and far between, but they're out there. You just have to find them. And as more students enroll, chances are good the number of these programs will increase as well. Until they do, you have to do your research to find the program that will work for you.

But are they worth it? College is expensive and time-consuming, after all, not to mention stressful. And the last thing anyone wants is a case of buyer's remorse with such a large price tag. Well, their worth depends largely on you and what you hope to get out of them. For starters, let's look at what such a program *won't* do for you.

An MFA from any institute of higher learning is by no means a guarantee that you will become a rich and famous author. If it were, every student who ever tried his hand at angsty poetry would have a Netflix deal and a mansion in Malibu. In fact, there's no guarantee that you'll even get published. While some programs do post an impressive record of publications, the odds are simply not in your favor. Why? Because everyone else is sending manuscripts to those same publishers as well and the publishers have the ability to be very picky.

Moreover, there's no guarantee that you'll land an agent, a movie deal, the ability to quit your job slinging fast food, or even the proverbial suitcase full of money and promises of questionable morality. All of those things are *possible*, but they're unlikely. Walking into an MFA program with the mindset that it alone is your key to fortune, fame, and freedom from French fries is a recipe for disappointment and disillusionment.

Another thing that any MFA program worth its tuition won't give you: ass-pats. In every program, every term, there's at least one person who shows up with the mindset that they are the greatest writer since Hemingway and everyone in the program is going to tell them just how good they are. They believe they're going to turn the program on its ear and redefine the gold standard for what it is to be a successful student for years to come.

I'm sorry to burst your bubble, but that's not what these programs will do for you, and if they do, they're not doing their job. I'm not saying that a creative writing program is supposed to be a brutal stripping down of one's ego, but one goes into a creative writing program to improve. The faculty has one job: to make you better. And if all they ever tell you is how good you are, you're not going to improve.

For that matter, an MFA program will not make you the *perfect* writer. They can help you improve, sure. They can clean up bad habits and teach you those that are more effective. They can even make you better than you were when you enrolled. But a program can't make you "great." It can't hand you perfection with a silver quill. All it can do is point you in a direction.

Your dedication and perseverance to that direction doesn't even determine how far you'll go. In fact, no matter what program you go through, there's nothing that guarantees your success. Signing up for an MFA in a creative writing program is the same as enrolling in any other graduate program. Can you succeed? Absolutely. Is it a sure thing? Absolutely not.

So what will an MFA program give you? So glad you asked.

The first thing any MFA program should give you is an honest evaluation of your current skill level. The most important word in that sentence is "honest." Everyone's grandma thinks they're a genius, and you may very well be. But, as I said before, the single job that the faculty has is to make you better. They can't do that by heaping false praise on you. Ideally, the program should be able to tell you if you have shortcomings in point of view, characterization, mechanics, plotting, or a thousand other little things that make up a compelling narrative.

They should also be able to evaluate your strengths while still helping you identify areas where you could improve. It can be quite jarring for people who have never had this kind of feedback before, but it's a necessary part of growing as a writer. As areas of weakness are discovered, they're developed. As strengths are found, they're refined.

The goal of a good MFA program isn't to change you into the writer they want you to be, but to distill you down to the writer *you* want to be. To make your writing the best version of you that it can be. In order to do so, your writing has to go through the grinder of critique sessions and workshops to make you aware of not only shortcomings, but places where you excel.

Another invaluable thing an MFA program can help you do is develop good work habits. By giving you deadlines and assignments, they often force you to do what most writers recommend anyway: write every day. They get you into the habit of hitting a word count, of following submission guidelines, of putting yourself into the headspace where writing is expression. One of my favorite quotes is by an artist named Chuck Close:

Inspiration is for amateurs. The rest of us show up and get to work. If you wait around for the clouds to part and a bolt of lightning to strike you in the brain, you are not going to make an awful lot of work. All the best ideas come out of the process; they come out of the work itself.

Whether you agree or disagree, one thing isn't up for debate: writers need to develop good writing habits, and a good MFA program can help.

Another important function of MFA programs is to expose you to a variety of genres, techniques, styles, and voices to help you grow into a well-rounded author. Many young writers show up with a particular genre in mind, and have only ever read in that one genre. But because you have to read assigned books that may or may not be in your chosen genre, you wind up learning that, no matter the genre, good storytelling principles apply.

You learn the tropes of any particular genre, the "rules," and how to apply them to your own work. In many cases, the student discovers an affinity, or even a love, for another genre. They develop their own voice, their own style, and it comes out of broadening the perspective.

Perhaps the most important part of what an MFA program can provide is the human element, an environment of your peers. We all know the frustration of needing honest, knowledgeable feedback on a piece and finding either feedback that isn't honest or feedback that isn't knowledgeable. MFA creative writing programs were designed to fix that through peer and instructor critiques. Getting feedback from someone whose life goal is similar to your own is a valuable tool, especially if that feedback is reciprocal.

In one MFA program, for example, students are teamed with groups from all levels of the program for critiques, and they work with these critique groups through the thesis, which is, in most cases, a market-ready complete manuscript. They're also assigned a mentor, someone with actual professional writing experience, who gives tips and criticism of their work.

Of equal importance is the networking that occurs in the program. Not everyone who gets an MFA in creative writing wants to be a novelist. Many go on to be editors, agents, even publishers and publicists. That old saying of "it's not *what* you know, it's *who* you know"? Whether it's true or not, it never hurts to have friends in the business. Also, classmates aren't the only networking possibilities. Take a look at the curriculum of any given program to see who their guest speakers are. Find out if they offer pitch sessions with agents or publishers. Chances are they do, and that's an important opportunity that shouldn't be passed up.

Moreover, not everyone who is in an MFA creative writing program comes from a creative writing background. The program in which I teach has an unusual constituency of filmmakers, doctors, soldiers, and even the odd rocket scientist or two. What's incredible about such programs is that most everyone in the program is willing to lend their life experience to your writing project.

Writing about a law firm? Chances are there's someone who has at least worked as a paralegal in the program, if not a full-fledged lawyer with dreams of being the next John Grisham. Need to know about deadly poisons? Better than even odds that someone in your group knows more about them than they should. Alternative religions? Don't get me started. And because these people are in the same program you are in, they are willing to share their knowledge with you.

But one of the biggest intangibles of any MFA program can be summed up in one word: support. When joining a program, you are immediately thrown in with a group of people who will prompt you, challenge you, commiserate with you, and who genuinely understand what it means to have writer's block when a deadline is looming and can help keep you motivated.

It's pretty common for the bonds forged in such a program to last long after graduation. In fact, one such program's alumni stuck together so well that a writers retreat was born out of it. And it's not just the students. The faculty should also encourage and offer praise where it is due and lend support to their students.

Perhaps the most important thing that an MFA program has the potential to give you is confidence. Hear me out. I'm aware that this career, as well as any form of artistic academic program, comes with a healthy dose of impostor syndrome. I'm also aware that the moment you get accepted and start reading your classmates' work, there will be people that make you question every life choice you've made because there's no way you believe you'll be half the writer they are. But here's the thing: these programs make you apply. You have to hand in a writing sample. The fact that you got in means that you're capable of telling a decent story. And the longer you stay with the program, the more you realize that *everyone* has some form of impostor syndrome, and that for every person you think is better than you, someone else believes you're better than them.

It's a vicious circle, to be sure, but the point is this: you walk into that program raw and unrefined. You come out of that program confident with the knowledge that you were good enough to graduate, and you not only have those three little letters after your name, you also have the entire history of the program holding you up. If that's not a confidence booster, I'm not sure what is.

And let's not forget the other thing an MFA program can give you: a terminal degree. What good is that? Most colleges and high schools require a terminal degree to teach. It gives you the pedigree that *may* sway an agent to give your piece a chance. And it gives you a *potential* career path to pay the rent until that suitcase full of cash and a movie deal shows up.

So, if you choose to enroll in an MFA program, how does one choose which one? There are a lot of factors to consider. First off, are you looking for a regular, low-residency, or fully online program? Some programs teach only face-to-face, and would require close proximity to the campus. A low-residency program typically does the lion's share of the work remotely with a brief residency period (usually about a week) in which all the students in the program are actually on campus for intensive study and in-person workshops. This tends to work well with people who have careers, families, and other responsibilities, but who don't mind traveling for a week every so often.

Then there are the completely online programs with courses that can be done from anywhere in the world. An advantage is that the courses are largely done at your own pace. A disadvantage is that your own pace may vary. Some courses grade pass/fail, while others go a more traditional four-point grading system.

Another thing to consider is the emphasis of the program in question. As I've stated before, some programs focus only on literary fiction and poetry. In the popular fiction programs, some focus on the writing only. Others focus on the writing, but throw in a bit of the business end as well. One program gives an even split of writing as well as layout, marketing, and editing for those who want to go into the publishing world, but not necessarily as a writer only.

Some programs focus on traditional publishing while others embrace independent or self-publishing. Take a good look at the curriculum and see what is offered, what is required, and what are considered electives. Then examine your goals and find the program that aligns with them.

The location of the program may seem to be linked to the question about residency, but it presents its own set of challenges. For example, if you live in the United States, but the program you want to attend is in Edinburgh, Scotland, you'll need to apply for a student visa. There also comes the question of where you'll live, and how you'll afford to, if you choose a program that is face-to-face only and in another country. While most schools have programs to assist, you'll need to start getting paperwork together well in advance if that's where you want to go.

One way to choose a program is to simply look at the faculty list. How many people on the list are professional writers? How many are lifelong academics who have no publishing credits to their names? And if everyone on the list has at least one or two professional credits, have you heard of those books? Have you heard of any of the teachers? Check out their book reviews, snoop on their blogs and websites. You're a writer, so research should be part of your routine by now.

You should also check out sample syllabi and course descriptions, as well as a guest speaker list, to see what works well with your expectations. Are you looking for a nuts-and-bolts approach to writing where you study grammar and mechanics? Or do you prefer classes with names like "Abracadabra! Using Magic in Popular Fiction"? The point is that although the programs work toward a similar goal, the approaches are vastly different and one may work better for you than another.

Of equal importance to your decision-making process is to check their list of alumni. Colleges love to tell you who went there and what they accomplished, so most of them will have a list of their notable former students so people like you can see how successful they are. And, if all else fails, run a search on your favorite author and find out if they went to college, and if so, where. It's also not unheard of to reach out to a particular alumni to ask opinions on the program. Most, if not all, are willing to share their experiences with their alma mater.

Of course, the overreaching question here is whether or not an MFA program is worth the money, stress, and time. And the answer to that comes in the form of two questions. First, what is your reasoning for going into it? Are you going into it because you feel it's expected of you to reach a terminal degree? Then maybe pick a different program or path.

Second, what do you expect to get out of it. Are you going into it to expand your skillset and improve as a writer? An MFA can help. Do you expect instant fame and a fresh fanbase? An MFA program may not be for you. Do you expect your ego to take a beating as your skillset is forged in the fires of honest criticism? You're in the right place.

With MFA programs, the old saying of "you get out of it what you put into it" certainly applies. If you take an MFA program seriously, put some real effort into it, and work to improve, it's likely worth every dime and then some. If not, it may be a waste of your time and money.

The most important part of any kind of decision-making process, however, is keeping your expectations realistic. It is in your best interest to make the most informed decision, whether you decide to enroll or not.

Scott A. Johnson is the author of eleven novels, three true ghost story guides, a chapbook, and a short story collection. In his free time, he 3-D prints, teaches martial arts classes, and rides his motorcycle through the Texas backroads with his pug. For more information, visit his website at www.creepylittlebastard.com.

Magazines 101

Monica S. Kuebler

If you want to understand the world of magazines, it helps to start by acknowledging two inarguable truths: magazine editors are busy people, and they get a lot of email. No matter in what capacity you end up dealing with a magazine, never forget these two facts, they might just save your life—or at least your coverage/byline.

Moving right along . . . if we accept that magazine editors are busy people who get a lot of mail, it's not a difficult leap to a third key truth: magazine editors like authors, publishers, and publicists who make their lives easier. They may be willing to jump through hoops to land an interview with a best-selling writer, but why take risks when you can approach them in a manner that makes them want to cover you? Because—yes, the truths keep coming fast and furious here—as much as authors need reviews and interviews, magazines need content. In a perfect world, this relationship can achieve a fruitful symbiosis.

In order to form such a relationship, however, it's important to make note of the fact that magazines, digital-only editions aside, are still physical media, having to go through all the rigors of editing, layout, proofing, and printing, meaning the concept of "lead time" remains important, despite the instant gratification of the internet age. Lead time, in this instance, means how long in advance of your release date a publication needs a review copy in order to ensure that coverage can be timed to the same month your book lands in stores (as magazines prefer to do). If we're back in that aforementioned perfect world, you should be approaching magazines at least three months ahead of your release date. Magazines prefer to cover things when they are fresh, so if you're reaching out thirty days before your book hits store shelves, it's too late. The corresponding print edition has already gone to press.

So now that you know *when* to reach out, *how* do you do it? Let's refer back to that second truth: Magazine editors get a lot of email and a lot of review copies. In my tenure at *Rue Morgue*, I've seen everything from one-line emails with an Amazon link at the end (don't do this) to pages-long treatises about the story, the author's life and writing process, the book's journey to print, etc. (don't do this either). If you don't have a publisher or publicist reaching out to media on your behalf, that's okay, but you need to view this process as a pitch of sorts. Keeping this in mind, the information provided should be relevant, succinct, and complete. It's far easier for you to supply the pertinent info in an email than it is for the editor to hunt it down after the fact.

Any request for coverage *must* include:

- Title of book, author name, release date, and publisher.

- Some form of plot synopsis or teaser.

- Information on how a free review copy can be acquired (digital or physical).

Extras, in case you want that coveted gold star:

- Link to the release on Amazon and/or the publisher's website.

- A brief note introducing yourself and calling attention to anything interesting/timely about your book aside from its release. For instance, have you or it been nominated for an award, have you sold the screen rights, or does it tie into current events? Or is there a cool story about its writing? (Keep this to a couple paragraphs if possible.)

- Make yourself available for interviews.

You've now crafted an email packed with helpful information about your release that will assist an editor in making an informed decision about coverage.

You take a deep breath and hit send, and within twenty-four hours that familiar impatience kicks up.

This seems like a good place to remind you that editors are busy people who get a lot of email, and also that print is not the internet. Magazines have limited space between their covers and depending on where a publication is in its production cycle, it may not be assigning stories or reviews the week your email hits an inbox. Or they are waiting to see if a writer expresses interest in your book. Or they may have it/you pegged for coverage as part of a bigger feature later. Or . . . or . . . or . . . You get the picture. There are a lot of gears turning, and while it's likely that you're not privy to any of them, don't—for the love of all things unholy—*nag the editor*, and definitely don't repeatedly send your email/press release hoping for a different response.

Don't get me wrong, either of those things *will* guarantee that you and your release get attention, only it will be the wrong kind. It's entirely possible to annoy your way out of coverage, because—here comes another of those cold hard truths—that magazine editor owes you nothing; magazine editors are a rare few and authors are many. If you are difficult to deal with before you land coverage, an editor is going to assume that you'll be equally difficult during any coverage given.

That said, you don't have to hit send and forget it. In fact, you shouldn't. There's a wide chasm between nagging and touching base. Reach out a week or two after your initial email (longer if you send a review copy by mail, especially internationally) and check in to make sure they received the info/review copy, inquire about coverage plans, and give any pertinent updates about the title (any awards/accolades since the first email, changes to release date, etc.). Be useful, not a nuisance.

If your book doesn't get selected for coverage, don't give up. There are lots of writers both traditionally published and otherwise vying for attention each month—far more than *any* print publication has space for—and very hard decisions are constantly being made. But while magazines have limited pages, the good news is they are always publishing more issues. So, if you don't get a review for one release, keep letting editors know about subsequent ones.

Which brings me to a final point about supplying complete, succinct information along with interview availability. Sometimes things in magazine-land are far from that picturesque perfect world we dream of, and a feature will fall through at the eleventh hour and require a replacement that can be subbed in quickly. If you've done your job correctly, dear author, it's now your email's chance to shine, giving that frazzled editor everything they need to save the day and make their print deadline.

Congratulations! You're the hero. You've landed the big interview. This is the part you usually get to control. If you have a preference for email or phone or Zoom, speak up. Choose the one you are most comfortable with. Same goes for scheduling a time. Do your best to plan for a time/place free of noise and interruptions (e.g. barking dogs, needy youngsters, etc.). This not only ensures that everything starts and ends on time, but that you won't be mis-transcribed. Don't be surprised if you are asked for some images to accompany the article. These need to be high resolution, print quality (300 dpi), and if the editor or art director sends along any special instructions, do your best to follow them.

One more thing, if you ever receive a disappointing review from a publication, never write the editor or reviewer to complain or argue about the review. That's just bad form. Not everyone will like your work, and that holds true for reviewers too.

Got all that? Good. The wonderful world of magazines awaits you. And if all you want from print media can be summed up with "Review my book! Interview me!" then you can jump on ahead to the next chapter. However, if you've ever considered contributing content to a magazine, please read on . . .

Still here? Okay, let's grab a favorite beverage and pull in close for a wee chat. You remember those truths from the opening paragraph? Skim back if you need to because they still apply—and now we're going to throw a new one into the mix. Chances are, you've heard it before. Probably way, way too many times. Here goes: *You never get a second chance to make a first impression.* That tired cliché is here to say that when you reach out to a magazine with either a specific pitch or an interest in writing or reviewing, you need to treat it as a job interview of sorts, and you wouldn't walk into a job interview with mustard down the front of your shirt, would you? So, make sure you're not sending a mustard-stained email. This means proofread not only the body of your message, but also make sure that your subject line, links, and attachments are correct and complete. If you're introducing yourself to an editor for the first time, a bit of background is reasonable:

who you are, who you've written for, and two or three relevant writing samples. All that said, if you send a message with the subject line "I want to writ for your magazine" (an actual email I once received), certain assumptions are going to be made about your attention to detail.

Speaking of attention to detail, before you send a magazine anything, do your homework on the publication. Like publishers, many magazines have submission guidelines posted on their website. Read them. Learn them. Adhere to them. No matter how above the guidelines you feel you may be, be assured that you are not that special. Guidelines help us all, as does targeting your email to one or two relevant people at the publication (again, check the website), rather than carpet-bombing the entire staff.

Questions to consider concerning your pitch:

- Is this pitch appropriate for the publication? (i.e. Do they publish stuff like this regularly/ever?)

- Is the pitch complete? Not just in subject matter you want to cover, but it should have a proposed length, who you'll be interviewing, and maybe even some sidebar ideas.

- Is it relevant? Most magazines prefer timely content, so pitches should be linked to new releases, special anniversaries, and other noteworthy events. Some pieces are evergreen (retrospectives, for instance), but a timely pitch is an attention-grabbing pitch.

- Has the magazine covered this release already?

An addendum here: Pitching something that recently appeared in a mag is a dead giveaway that you didn't do your homework.

Much like addressing a female editor as "Dear Sir." Don't be that human. Let Google empower you.

Now that your pitch is in, you need to practice some patience. As with coverage requests, follow up after a week or two; don't be obnoxious. And if you do wow the editor and land the story, respect the deadline. Magazines are put together by a team and if you are late or sloppy, it delays every single department and risks delaying the entire publication—a dire predicament because on-sale dates are non-negotiable. Perhaps this is a good spot to drop a final pair of truths: editors have long memories, and organized writers who get their copy in on time get pitches picked up more often.

Of course, your work's not entirely done when you file your piece. Once the magazine hits newsstands, don't forget to promote it on social media. That's important too. It's still a rough landscape for print publications out there, so every eyeball and social media share counts.

Adopt these best practices, and you may soon see your name/book in the glossy pages of your favorite magazine. It's as easy as remembering a few simple truths.

Monica S. Kuebler has spent the last eighteen years wearing a variety of editorial hats at *Rue Morgue* magazine, for whom she penned *Rue Morgue Library #3: Weird Stats and Morbid Facts*. She also writes poetry and monster stories; her young adult vampire serial—which began with *Bleeder (Blood Magic, Book 1)*—can be read at Wattpad.com. She completed her first novel for adult readers during the pandemic lockdown.

Interview with Stephen King and Richard Chizmar, co-authors of the novella "Gwendy's Button Box"

Bev Vincent

I've known Richard "Rich" Chizmar for twenty years. He and I have frequently shared information we couldn't divulge to anyone else. So, when Rich got the chance to collaborate on the novella "Gwendy's Button Box" with Stephen King, I was one of a few people who knew while it was under development.

He didn't come right out and tell me what he was working. Instead, he sent me a few text messages in January 2017 asking for Castle Rock details. After I responded, he sent me an email that began, "Wanna hear the coolest news that you can't share with anyone else in the world?" He responded to my enthusiastic "Of course!" with a screenshot of the first page of the first draft of "Gwendy's Button Box."

I read an early draft of the novella that February and, subsequently, got to interview Rich and Steve prior to the book's launch, to discuss how the project came into being. King has co-written stories and novels with his sons, Joe Hill and Owen King, as well as with Peter Straub and Stewart O'Nan, and Rich has been involved in collaborations of his own. Each experience is different. Here, King and Chizmar reveal how "Gwendy's Button Box" was co-written.

Bev Vincent: *Steve, what can you tell us about the genesis of "Gwendy's Button Box"?*

Stephen King: I had the idea for the story last July [2016], and thought it was a little like Richard Matheson's "Button, Button," but could be its own special thing. I liked it because it basically postulates putting the fate of the world in the hands of a child (like Trump).

Vincent: *At what point in the writing process did you seek out a collaborator?*

King: I didn't know how to finish it. So it just sat there until this January. I didn't seek out a collaborator; one kind of fell into my lap. I've corresponded via email with Rich Chizmar for years. I sent him "Gwendy," and basically said, "Do what you want, or it will stay unfinished."

Vincent: *So, set the stage for us, Rich. You're sitting at your computer one day and you get an email from Stephen King asking if you'd like to work on a story with him?*

Richard Chizmar: Steve and I email and text pretty regularly about a wide variety of subjects. On that particular day, we started talking about round-robins (multi author projects) and collaborations. He mentioned that he had a short story he couldn't finish and I told him I'd love to read it if he ever wanted to send it over. The next evening, I remember it was a Friday and I was on my way to my son's hockey game, "Gwendy's Button Box" showed up with a note that read: "Do what you want with it."

Vincent: When you picked yourself up off the floor, how did you respond?

Chizmar: I sat in the parking lot and read the manuscript, and emailed Steve back right away. My response that Friday night was "Absolutely! Yes! I'd love to finish it!"—but I was also moderately terrified. I let the idea settle over the weekend and when I sat down to write my story notes on Monday morning, moderate fear blossomed into full-blown terror for about an hour or so. How in the hell was I going to collaborate with Stephen King? Right?! Thankfully, the feeling didn't last, and the story just sort of took over and stole me away. The nerves disappeared, and before I knew it, I found myself in Castle Rock.

Vincent: Given that he's been rereading all of your books and stories for his Stephen King Revisited project, Rich seems like an obvious choice—he'd be familiar with Castle Rock and its history and geography. What was it like working with him?

King: Working with Rich was very easy. For one thing, he knows my stuff, backward and forward—probably better than I do. I didn't give him any direction (that I remember), just let him run with the ball. He did a terrific job of bringing it home. My confidence in him came from reading his short fiction. And he's good with suburban family life. Terrific, actually; very loving, which gives the scary stuff extra bite. He wrote the middle and the end. I did some work on the end, expanding it, and there it was. Tout finis.

Vincent: Did you discuss story possibilities externally or did you just write and see where the story took you?

Chizmar: The unfinished story that Steve initially sent clocked in at just over 7,000 words. I sat down and blazed through a lot of pages in the next three or four days and quickly sent them to Steve before I had a chance to chicken out. He did a pass of his own, and sent it back to me for another run at it. Then, we did the whole thing all over again—one more draft each. We did discuss some possibilities via email, but mostly we just ran with it. We each tweaked things the other had written and went off in our own directions. The whole process was fascinating and so much damn fun. That's what I kept telling Steve: this is fun!

Vincent: *I was impressed by how seamless the writing was in the finished product. I couldn't tell who wrote what.*

King: If it seems seamless . . . well, that's always the goal, isn't it? You don't want the reader to be jarred by one voice giving way to another. (It may have helped that we were men writing from a girl's POV.) The secret ingredient is that we both went over the story, giving it additional layers—you'll see the same thing, I think, in *Sleeping Beauties*, the collaboration with Owen.

Vincent: *There must be a temptation to try to imitate Steve, but nothing in the story felt like imitation. How did you approach this?*

Chizmar: I truly never gave it a moment's consideration. I just sat down and started writing and let the story take me where it wanted to take me. I didn't try to do anything different stylistically than I would have had the entire story been my own. And, somehow, it worked. When we were finished and I read over the completed story, I was astonished to find that there were times when I couldn't immediately recall who wrote what.

Vincent: *What was it like to work in someone else's well-established universe? How did you make sure you were* *"playing by the rules"? Is this something you've done before with another writer—working in an established setting?*

Chizmar: I've collaborated a handful of times before, but never in someone else's specific universe. Fortunately, I know Steve's work very well, and I also have some good friends walking around with a wealth of King-related knowledge in their heads (Bev Vincent and Brian Freeman are two that come to mind), so playing by the rules wasn't an issue at all. I didn't find working within an established universe the least bit confining or restrictive either. I honestly just kept thinking "I'm in Castle Rock," and tried my best to honor the ground I was walking on. I felt a very real responsibility to that.

Vincent: Steve, why did you decide to return to Castle Rock? And does "Gwendy" tie in to the newly announced Castle Rock *series on Hulu?*

King: I went back to Castle Rock with this one before JJ [Abrams] sold the series to Hulu, so that didn't play a part. Mostly, I just . . . well . . . missed the place!

Vincent: When commenting about your recent collection, A Long December, *Steve said that you set your tales "in no-nonsense, middle-class neighborhoods I can relate to." How do you envision Castle Rock? Is it a bad place, a place that attracts bad people, or is it just an ordinary town with a history?*

Chizmar: I think Castle Rock is a pretty ordinary town with a colorful history, like a lot of small towns tucked away in New England. Now, Derry . . . there's a bad place that attracts an awful lot of bad people. I think Castle Rock makes perfect sense for the story of "Gwendy's Button Box." It fits.

Vincent: *You've had a long and productive writing career, not to mention an illustrious publishing career where you continue to publish many terrific authors. How does this experience rank in terms of your career to date? Do you have future collaboration plans?*

Chizmar: It's the cherry on top, no question. I've always been a big dreamer, but I never dreamed this big. Not even close. As for future collaboration plans, I'm actually writing a story right now with my 18-year-son, Billy. It's about a haunted lighthouse in Canada and will appear this summer in an anthology called *Fearful Fathoms*. We're having a wonderful time with it.

Vincent: *Steve, do you plan to work with Rich again, or with other writers in the future?*

King: I don't have any plans to collaborate again, but no plans NOT to, if you dig.

Almost exactly two years after I received that first text from Rich asking for Castle Rock details, I received another. "What's the name of the river in 'The Body' where they found the body?" And just like that, I knew Rich was back in Gwendy-land again. This time, as it turned out, he was flying solo, having been given the opportunity, with King's blessing, to create a follow-up to "Gwendy's Button Box." He is the first author permitted to write a book set in one of King's fictional towns. As King says in the introduction to "Gwendy's Magic Feather," Gwendy likely wouldn't exist without Rich Chizmar. She and her story would have lingered in limbo in an incomplete manuscript on Steve's computer. So, in a very real sense, Gwendy is as much Rich's creation as she is Steve's. It took a collaboration to bring her to life. In 2022, we will see the two authors collaborating again with the final installment of the trilogy with *Gwendy's Final Task*.

Stephen King's books have sold more than 350 million copies, and many have been adapted into films, television series, miniseries, and comic books. King has published 62 novels, including seven under the pen name Richard Bachman, and five non-fiction books. He has also written approximately 200 short stories, most of which have been published in book collections. He has received Bram Stoker Awards, World Fantasy Awards, and British Fantasy Society Awards. In 2003, the National Book Foundation awarded him the Medal for Distinguished Contribution to American Letters. He has also received awards for his contribution to literature for his entire bibliography, such as the 2004 World Fantasy Award for Life Achievement and the 2007 Grand Master Award from the Mystery Writers of America. In 2015, he was awarded with a National Medal of Arts from the U.S. National Endowment for the Arts for his contributions to literature.

Richard Chizmar is a *New York Times, USA Today, Wall Street Journal, Washington Post, Amazon,* and *Publishers Weekly* bestselling author. He is the co-author (with Stephen King) of the bestselling novella, *Gwendy's Button Box* and the founder/publisher of *Cemetery Dance* magazine and the Cemetery Dance Publications book imprint. He has edited more than 35 anthologies and his short fiction has appeared in dozens of publications, including multiple editions of *Ellery Queen's Mystery Magazine* and *The Year's 25 Finest Crime and Mystery Stories.* He has won two World Fantasy awards, four International Horror Guild awards, and the HWA's Board of Trustee's award.

Bev Vincent is the author of The Dark Tower Companion, *The Road to the Dark Tower*, the Bram Stoker Award nominated companion to Stephen King's Dark Tower series, and *The Stephen King Illustrated Companion*, which was nominated for a 2010 Edgar® Award and a 2009 Bram Stoker Award. In 2018, he co-edited the anthology *Flight or Fright* with Stephen King.

Riding the Rollercoaster

Donna J. W. Munro

I just released my first novel in 2021.

I'm fifty years old.

By this point in their writing lives, most successful authors have a deep backlog of books out in the world. By the time they're in their fifties, they've become the wise people on the hill that the unpublished writers flock around, touching the hems of their garments, hoping the success will rub off on them.

I am not hacking on those fantastic established writers who offer a hand up. I think they'd read what I'm about to say and agree 100%.

No amount of hands up or flying in the right circles or wishing or hoping gets you to the top of the mountain.

I'm not at the top of mine, though I'm proud of the heights I've reached.

How did I get here? Why haven't I gotten further?

Life is what happens when you are making plans. John Lennon said that before his life was ended when he was ten years younger than I am.

My life almost ended around that time too.

Let me go back and give you the whole story, because this isn't a cautionary tale. It's my rollercoaster and I've loved the ride.

When I was in fourth grade, I could read at the same level as a high schooler. I was also one of those latchkey kids who had hours of alone time waiting for my parents to get home from work. My family is blue collar, but both of my parents were readers, thankfully. They couldn't afford to buy enough kiddie chapter books to keep me happy, so they started handing me their books.

Both read horror.

Stephen King's *Salem's Lot* was my gateway drug. Then I read the short story collections. I learned to love good short stories from the hum and whispers of King's incredible stories in *Skeleton Crew* and *Night Shift*. I tried many times to write like King. The sweet dark dreams and the slimy trails he left in my imagination weren't easy to emulate. But very early on I knew what I wanted. I wanted to write my way through the dark.

Then in high school I got lost in my own angst, though I did manage to graduate and wrote a whole lot of bad poetry and sad broken stories that limped and wobbled. I married my soul mate at twenty and had my kids at twenty-one and twenty-two.

Those years were all struggle and scrabble. I went to college to get a career while my husband worked three jobs at a time. Our kids did homework at the same table I did. We were always tired. I became a social studies teacher. We were movin' on up.

I wrote between all of my jobs (teacher, mom, household manager, etc.) and my short stories didn't suck as bad. That's when my hubbie and I decided I could afford to chase the dream. After researching for a program that would let me write all the horror and darkness without trying to make me into something I'm not—a literary writer—I hit the jackpot. I found Seton Hill's WPA program. I flew into Pittsburg with one publishing credit to my name and a folder full of violent little stories that had nothing much to recommend them. A serial killer who murdered for god. An abused wife who turns into a pigeon. A boy who kills himself and his goldfish in a chest freezer. And the idea for a novel.

It was glorious. Up to that point I'd nursed this secret little dream. I was thirty something and feeling my age. My kids were busy all the time doing the things that we fill our lives with–dance, softball, karate, scouts–but I only felt my own growth when I was writing that problematic first novel. I was lifted up by my gifted teachers.

I graduated with a Masters of Arts in Writing Popular Fiction, a shiny novel signed by my incredible mentors, and all the confidence that an agent was going to grab me and carry me off to fame.

Then nothing happened.

Reality is a bitch, isn't it? I sent out my novel to publishers, starting at the top and working down, and queried agents who handled work like mine. I did all the things you are supposed to do, but nothing happened. Until, DAW sent me the WORST rejection I've ever gotten in my life. It didn't just take the wind out of my sail. It sank my boat.

"Though the ideas are engaging, the writing doesn't interest me."

I didn't write again for years.

I went to writing events feeling like an imposter. The comment they made emblazoned itself on my heart like a brand. I bought my friends' and classmates' books with pride, knowing that I wasn't good enough to be where they were. I don't know how I even muscled up the bravery to go to my alumni events other than wanting to be near success, wanting to hear about success that I believed I'd never have again.

My friends tried to get me to write with them. I remembered that I like to write short stories in my late thirties when my SHUmates started a little writing group. It fell apart pretty quickly, but I managed to write a few short stories. I was mending. I was thirty-nine.

Then my dad got sick. I can't express how it broke me to watch him die from cancer of the lung and brain. He'd been my greatest supporter in life. My best friend in my darkest years. He'd always believed I was a writer. I remember reading him my stories in his last few weeks and him telling me that I had to keep climbing. That life is a rollercoaster and you have to lean in.

He died on Christmas with me, my husband, and his wife by his side. It wasn't pretty, but he knew he was loved.

I was totaled by his death.

I never wanted to read or write horror again. My life was horror. I slid into the darkest hole I'd ever been in. Depression hadn't ever been insurmountable for me, but after losing Dad it's become my constant companion.

A couple of years later, my doctor found the cancer in my breast. Interductal breast cancer with lymph node involvement. Stage IIB.

It's funny, right before my diagnosis I'd almost convinced myself that I could start trying to publish again. Forty-two wasn't too late. I'd met Mike Knost, the best horror writer's fairygod friend, and learned about the HWA and had pitched my book to one of my favorite horror publishing couples. It was a comeback. I felt it in my bones, but . . .

Chemo, radiation, double mastectomy, rebuild surgery, many small adjustment surgeries. Scars. So many scars.

I cried myself to sleep almost every night. I couldn't eat and lost all my hair. I couldn't climb the steps to sleep next to my husband. My life was horror. Each day was full of indignities and pain and small kindnesses that I sorted and held close.

The writing community lifted me up. They sent gifts and money and messages. They reminded me that there is life on the other side. And they reminded me that I was a writer.

I think I was forty-five when I went to Imaginarium Convention. That's where I met Steven Saus and Anton Cancre, who got me involved in writing flash fiction. It was one of those moments when the sky opens up and the angels sing, and suddenly your life makes sense. A short story that could be anything based on an image. I went from having a D.O.A. novel, some good NANOWRIMO starts, and about ten viable short stories to, at the time of this writing, over 300 short stories.

It's the Ray Bradbury method of writing. Write one short story a week. In a year you'll have 52 short stories and they can't all be bad. Ray Bradbury became my seat mate on this crazy writing rollercoaster.

Here's what I learned.

- ☠ If you write a story a week, you build up a nice catalog of stories to submit.

- ☠ If you have lots of stories, then you don't take any one rejection or critique to heart (ala my DAW rejection).

- ☠ If you write a story a week, you become a master of the elements of storytelling. You can focus on certain skills. For example, I wrote nothing but first person for six months until my writing partners really felt I'd broken through with that close voice.

- ☠ You pay your dues. They say you have to write a million words to get really good at it. I agree.

But most importantly, I remembered that I'm a horror writer. Sure, I like the ick factor and creeping my readers out. But writing my dark fantasy and cozy horror stories week after week taught me that horror is essential to our quality of life. Horror is actually a celebration of survival. Horror is a recognition of the human spirit. It's the breathtaking, clickity clack of the uphill climb of a coaster where you can't see what's next. It's the moment of terror when you see over that hill and look into the abyss you are about to fall into. It's the feeling of the car leaving the tracks and your stomach rebelling as you scream into the wind. It's even that jerky stop and stepping out onto solid ground.

Since Imaginarium, I've published over sixty short stories. When I get a rejection, it's usually personal because the quality of my writing is better. But even when I don't get a "good" rejection or sale, it doesn't hurt. It's just another hill to climb.

At forty-seven, I attended my first Stoker Con. I've been to so many conventions where Sci-Fi dudes dismiss my experience, and cosplay kids don't care about writing. They are fun. I love going and getting my nerd on, but Stoker Con was a revelation. I met Linda Addison and Lisa Morton and Lee Murray, incredible examples of women with some years kicking ass and taking names. They encouraged me. Lifted me up. Horror writers are a family. They'll walk through the darkness with you.

The folks at Stoker Con told me to take my novel fragments to a place called Borderland Boot Camp. I met my one of my dad's favorite authors there, F. Paul Wilson, and my manuscript got the shit kicked out of it. But Tom Monteleone, Douglas E. Winter, and Ginjer Buchanan all pushed me up the hill. Write again, keep going, they told me.

My second Stoker Con, I pitched an old NANO project I had rattling around in my hard drive to Johnny Worthen of Omnium Gatherum. It had been so long since I'd thought about the project, I couldn't even remember the main character's name. It's Ellie, by the way. Zombies were so last year when I pitched it, but Johnny heard something that charmed him. He requested a full manuscript, a real vote of confidence for a forty-eight-year-old pitching a YA series.

Then the wait.

Seven months went by. Honestly, I'd given up and was working on a new novel.

My son and I were at Windy Con, hosting a "For the Love of Comics" party and doing panels. I saw the email from Johnny in my inbox and said to my son, "It's a rejection." As I went to open it, he came up behind me and watched. It wasn't a rejection at all. We both squealed and started calling people even though it was late and most of them were in bed.

The next year was editing. Round after round until I turned it in and . . . Covid hit.

Fuck covid. I wrote the next book anyway. Book 2 called Runaway should be out in late 2021. Then I wrote book 3 as my Nano for 2020. It's called Revolution. I hope it will be out in early 2022. The point is, I'm at the top of this awesome hill, a three-book deal *finally* and with such good people (seriously, Omnium Gatherum are great folks), then covid kicked my launch in the ass.

But you know what? I'm fifty. I can take anything this damned rollercoaster can dish out. I've lived hard, seen the world and looked death right in the eyes, and I still keep writing.

That's the point of the rollercoaster, you know? It scares you, takes your breath, makes you wish you were dead, but then you hop the line and get back in that metal bucket that's aimed for the sky. You close your eyes and scream, but you love every second.

Keep writing, my friends. That's the real secret. Write because it's who you are and it's your truth. Write up the hill every time you climb out of the deep depths. Write to the edge and throw your arms up and scream at the time ticking away and the opportunities you think are lost.

The ride isn't over until they throw your ass out of the park. I dare 'em to try to catch me.

Donna J. W. Munro's pieces are published in Dark Moon Digest # 34, Flash Fiction Magazine, Astounding Outpost, Nothing's Sacred Magazine IV and V, Corvid Queen, *Hazard Yet Forward* (2012), *Enter the Apocalypse* (2017), *Beautiful Lies, Painful Truths II* (2018), *Terror Politico* (2019), *It Calls from the Forest* (2020), Borderlands 7 (2020), *Gray Sisters Vol 1*(2020), *Borderlands Vol 7 (2020)*, and others. Check out her first novel, *Revelations: Poppet Cycle Book 1*. Contact her at www.donnajwmunro.com or @DonnaJWMunro on Twitter.

Way Down South in the Dark of Dixie
Writing Southern Horror Fiction
Ronald Kelly

What is it about the American South that makes you uneasy and creeps you out? Is it the terrain? The dark woods and lonesome hollows? The Appalachian Mountains shrouded with mist or the Spanish moss laced bayous of Louisiana? Maybe it's the isolated stretch of rural highway with no streetlights to speak of or the abandoned farmhouse down the road, that in your mind, is most certainly haunted? It could be the people. Not the good, decent folks that practice Southern hospitality, but the other kind. The ones you saw in movies like *Deliverance*, *Southern Comfort,* or *The Texas Chainsaw Massacre*. Maybe it is some of the more sordid and unforgivable events of Southern history that bother you; slavery, the Klan, racial injustice, or Martin Luther King falling to a gunshot on the second-floor balcony of the Lorraine Motel in Memphis.

Yes, there certainly seem to be plenty of things to unsettle and potentially frighten you about the states south of the

Mason-Dixon Line. I reckon that is why I've spent thirty-five years of my writing career spinning tales of Southern-fried horror. For some of you, it's a place of potential danger and disaster. For me, well, it's simply . . . home.

The sub-genre of Southern horror is a specialized one and there are only a

few of us in dark fiction who devote ourselves to it wholeheartedly. Those authors who write the stuff and do it damn good include Robert McCammon, Joe R. Lansdale, Elizabeth Massie, James Newman, and John Quick, as well as storytellers of past generations like Manly Wade Wellman, Michael McDowell, and Karl Edward Wagner. In his 1991 anthology *Borderlands 3*, Thomas F. Monteleone had this to say about it: *"There is a sub-genre that seems to have come to life on its own—a kind of spontaneous generation once ascribed to maggots on dead meat or that coiling swirl of dust balls in the corner of an abandoned house. It's called Southern Horror, and it's marked largely by a preying upon the natural urban paranoia of the rest of us, i.e. those of us who don't live in places called "vales" or "corners" or "hollows". It is marked by a strong regional flavor, a familiarity with custom and superstition, and a style that can't be faked."*

So, you might ask, what region constitutes the territory of Southern Horror?

Generally, the states considered to make up "The South" are Alabama, Arkansas, Florida, Georgia, Louisiana, Mississippi, North Carolina, South Carolina, Tennessee, Texas, and Virginia. I tend to include Kentucky and West Virginia because, in my opinion, they are just as Southern in custom and tradition as the others are. After all, any place that features a life-sized statue of the Mothman prominently on its town square has to be Southern in nature . . . and, if it isn't, it certainly ought to be.

The two main ingredients that make Southern horror work best are characterization and setting. If you have engaging, flesh-and-blood characters and credible locales that readers can step comfortably (or, better yet, uncomfortably) into and walk around, the writer has won half the battle. Add a dark and credible plot to the mix—one that the reader feels they are personally involved and invested in—and the short story or novel is on its way to being solid and memorable.

There has always been a moral chasm between light and darkness in Southern culture; one that is as divisive as a line drawn in the sand, or as we like to say, " being on the right or wrong side of the tracks". On one side lies the get-up-and-get-ready-for-church crowd; those who relish normalcy and embrace family heritage . . . the kind who enjoy sitting on their front porches on a warm, sunny afternoon, spinning tall tales and indulging in a cold glass of sweet tea and a slice of Mama's pecan pie. On the other, lies the wild bunch; midnight drag racers and hellacious honky-tonk patrons. Drinkers of rotgut whiskey and home-brewed moonshine, barroom brawlers, and backwoods "yokels" with an unhealthy fascination for honed steel and firearms.

Traditionally in Southern horror, the former group is the protagonists and the latter the antagonists, although lately there has been more of a gray area surfacing between the two . . . a blurring of that long-standing line. Often in current fiction, the religious right, particularly the more fanatical factions, are depicted as the evil threat, while those once considered to be "heathens" and "no-account rednecks" have become the acceptable "everyman" protagonist, in a gritty, anti-hero sort of way. Personally, I tend to be old school in my characterizations, relying on past folks that I've known or known of, to build my cast of characters. I do, however, shuffle the deck sometimes and go against the grain. There is nothing more satisfying than to have the small town outcast—the one that folks despise and consider to be utterly useless to society—come out of nowhere and save the day.

In my own writing, I have discovered that coming-of-age tales meld very well with the dynamics of Southern horror. Jeb Sweeny in *Fear,* Cindy Ann in *Hindsight,* and Keith and the gang in *Hell Hollow* . . . all are ordinary kids battling the worse kinds of rural evil, be it a slithering snake-critter from a hellish county, a transient mass murderer in a pickup truck, or the spirit of a soul-stealing traveling medicine show man inhabiting the body of a serial killer. One of my all-time favorite coming-of-age novels set in the South is Robert McCammon's *Boy's Life,* which depicts rural life in Alabama with incredible heart and versatility. The wasp attack during the church service is truly a classic. Another is Joe Lansdale's *The Bottoms,* a Depression-era murder mystery set in a small Texas town, in which a young boy and his sister discover the body of a black woman in the bottoms of the Sabine River, brutally murdered by an apparent serial killer. It is tense, atmospheric, and thought provoking, and, along with *Boy's Life,* one of my favorite coming-of-age novels of the Deep South.

Setting also has a great deal to do with the mood and believability of tales of Southern horror. Lonesome backroads, particularly those winding through dense forest or stretching across acre upon acre of deserted pastureland, can practically lead to anywhere and spawn terror and dread for the reader. After all, in such places of isolation, there is no one around to hear you scream. In turn, the hills and hollows, peaks and valleys, of the Appalachian Mountains are steeped heavily in superstition and dark folklore. The legends and mythos of Appalachia, from Virginia clear down to Georgia, serve as useful fodder for the Southern-fried story mill. In fact, Appalachia is known to have more sightings of mysterious cryptids than anywhere else in the United States. These include all manner of legendary mountain monsters such as the Tennessee Wildman, Ol' Orange Eyes, Phantom Cats, Sheepquatch, Devil Monkeys, the Wampus Beast, and the Grassman, just to name a few.

One location that's rarely explored in Southern storytelling, but can be used to great effect, is the fetid swamps and dark bayous of Louisiana. That region is one of my personal favorites to explore. I have penned several Cajun and Creole horror tales over the years, including *The Web of La Sanguinaire, Beneath Black Bayou, Mojo Mama,* and *Suckers!* I particularly love to write Cajun dialogue. The rhythm of speech is quirky, unique, and fun to depict on the written page. Also, there are numerous creepy-crawlers and swamp critters to make bayou stories entertaining and cringe-inducing; creatures such as alligators, snakes, spiders, lizards, gars, and leeches . . . all sufficiently dreadful and icky in nature.

Texas is a state that most folks don't immediately consider to be Southern, but actually is. Joe Lansdale has written much about the more temperate and wooded area of East Texas, but West Texas should also be included in the Southern horror canon. I've explored the Lone Star State many times, in such short stories as "Dust Devils", "Thinning the Herd", and "Flesh-Welder", and in my second Zebra novel, *Pitfall,* in which a brood of hungry Tasmanian devils invade a sleepy, West Texas town.

Like many regional writers, those who specialize in Southern horror tend to focus the lion's share of their work on territory that is intimately familiar to them. Although I have written stories that encompass all the states of Dixie, most of them take place in my home state of Tennessee. Basing your fiction in a community or small town similar to the one you grew up in, or amid a dark and isolated stretch of woods that you once played in as a child, give your story a tone of authenticity that is difficult to accomplish if you are writing about a place you have never actually seen or experienced before. Furthermore, physical senses can kick in, triggering a mutual connection in the mind of the reader. The smell of wood smoke in the air or the dry, musky odor of an old house that has sat unoccupied for far too long. Or maybe the roar of a distant freight train and the mournful wailing of its whistle, or the lonesome call of a whippoorwill, the chirring of crickets in dewy grass, and the monotonous peeping of toads along a backwoods creek bed.

Inspiration for rural horror tales can come from numerous sources. Regional legends and ghost stories, family and local history, mysterious happenings and unsolved crimes can all spark engaging storylines. Many of my early short stories and novels were inspired by tales told to me by my grandmother and mother. Stories of local hauntings and true folks you'd not want to run into in the dead of night, as well as ancestors who had fought in the Civil War, both for the Blue and the Gray, including others who had headed out west, either to seek fortune ahead of them or flee from trouble dogging their heels from behind. In fact, I absorbed so many family stories that took place during the Great Depression or during and after World War II, that I discovered I could write effectively in those time periods with very little or no research whatsoever. I mostly attribute that skill to my grandmother and her engaging way with spinning a tale. A good storyteller—be it vocally or through prose—can impart an infectious sense of time and place that transcends the mind and sinks directly into the soul.

In the world of horror fiction, regionalism gives the reader an opportunity to break the bounds of their mundane life and take a journey beyond the confines of the armchair, however distressing and frightening it might be, into a realm beyond their own. Tales of Southern horror have much to offer in the way of chills and nightmarish tableaus, as well as a welcome reprieve from various horror locations and tropes that have been greatly overused in the past.

Born and bred in Tennessee, **Ronald Kelly** has been an author of Southern-fried horror fiction for nearly 35 years, with fifteen novels, twelve short story collections, and a Grammy-nominated audio collection to his credit. Influenced by such writers as Stephen King, Robert McCammon, Joe R. Lansdale, and Manly Wade Wellman, Kelly sets his tales of rural darkness in the hills and hollows of his native state and other locales of the American South. His published works include *Fear,*

Undertaker's Moon, Blood Kin, Hell Hollow, Hindsight, The Buzzard Zone, After the Burn, Midnight Grinding & Other Twilight Terrors, The Essential Sick Stuff, The Halloween Store and Other Tales of All Hallows' Eve, Season's Creepings: Tales of Holiday Horror, and Irish Gothic: Tales of Celtic Horror. He lives in a backwoods hollow in Brush Creek, Tennessee with his wife and young'uns, and a psychopathic Jack Russell Terrier named Toby.

The Cities That Never Sleep: Telling Stories in Urban Landscapes

John Palisano

The city never sleeps. There is always someone awake—always something happening. Throughout the world, lights burn through the night. Traffic may wane or there may be traffic jams out on the 101 freeway at 3:00 o'clock in the morning. Cities don't shut down at certain times as they often do in the suburbs. Things are always busy, busy, busy. There's barely time to breath or recharge. Other than the feeling of being overwhelmed and never fully recharged, how can we tell stories set in urban landscapes? Specifically, how can we tell genuine, suspenseful tales of the weird and horrific?

In this examination, we're going to touch upon several aspects of what differentiates stories set in urban landscapes from those set elsewhere. We'll dive into settings, the author's voice, the characters and their dialogue, the conflicts, problems and solutions, and possible themes.

Most fans of horror would have come across Urban Horror first through movies such as *Candyman, Tales from the Hood,*

Spawn, and *Blade.* Going back earlier, films such as *Sugar Hill, Scream, Blacula Scream* and *Michael Jackson's Thriller.*

Since the mid-twentieth century a good deal of horror examined the fears of people moving out of the cities and either returning to a life in the suburbs, or beginning a new one. Often these stories centered upon a new family eager to leave the hustle and bustle—and dangers—of city life behind, only to discover even worse unmentionable things in their new homes.

But what about those who did not leave the big city? What of those who chose not to? Or who are not able to due to their economic situations? Traditionally, the suburban horror stories starred middle-class white families with the means, while urban horror stories starred black characters in the city. These stories gained popularity in the 60s and 70s blaxploitation films, but soon became mirrored in fiction, as well.

SETTING

In contrast to the haunted suburban houses so popular throughout the 60s, 70s, and 80s, stories set in urban landscapes feature popular cities throughout the world. Instead of a family being cut off and isolated, characters in cities are often navigating indifferent crowds, heavy traffic, and busy destinations.

Noise is a constant in the background of urban stories. Even (and especially) at night, the city does not sleep. There are sirens. Ambulances. Traffic. Arguments. Fights. It all blends into a blanket of sound the characters become numb toward.

On the flip side of the normal life of a city used as a setting for urban horror stories are post-apocalyptic tales. With the complete absence of the normal city soundscape, they become places of fear. It just doesn't feel right. The comfort of knowing there are people everywhere, and resources readily available vanishes. The scope of the city becomes a threat. Many obstacles crop up. Unforeseen enemies have many places to hide. Signs of life in a post-apocalyptic environment can become a calling card for any number of bad things just looking for something.

Urban landscapes may also take the form of cities in history. In horror, there are many prime examples. Modern stories that explore historical times in cities include Anne Rice's New Orleans in *Interview with the Vampire*, Alan Moore's London in *From Hell*, and even future cities in works from Philip K. Dick. Each of these are prominent examples of how authors can defy reader expectations. Stories set in cities can choose either path and tell an effective, suspenseful story. Finding a unique urban setting will allow your writing to blossom while offering a rich and detailed world for your characters to inhabit.

VOICE

The author's voice can be quite different when reflecting an environment set in an urban landscape. Maybe it's a little grittier. Harsher. Less patient and mellow. Or maybe it's poetic and vast, like the city itself? Choosing how you tell your story is as important as any other element. Will you choose to inhabit the mind of a character and tell it all in first person, such as Paul Tremblay's *Survivor Song*? Or maybe third person would feel more appropriate? Maybe your story would be even scarier if told in an epistolary format using news clippings, text-message transcriptions, or other means. How you choose to tell your story can and will make a big difference in how you build suspense. The big question is in how you will immerse your reader within the story.

First person can certainly work. It will put the reader into the mind and shoes of a character. They'll see the story through the perspective of the character. This can be heart wrenching and terrifying on many levels.

Third person offers the ability to use multiple character points of view. It may be easier to tell a more epic and scope-filled story.

Maybe you'll discover blending these formats can be best. In Max Brooks's *World War Z* novel, each chapter is told from the point of view of distinct characters in cities around the world as an undead plague spreads.

On the flip side, we see most of the story in Richard Matheson's *I Am Legend* through one man's perspective: Neville, the last man on earth.

Both pathways are effective and riveting. You can ask yourself how the story would change if you switched from one voice to another. Think about how a classic work may be less effective . . . or more effective . . . if they were told from another point of view. It can also be a great exercise to write a few chapters of your story in either format to see which one seems to truly gain traction and feel right for you.

CHARACTERS

Living and surviving in the big city takes a certain type of individual. It's much harder—but not impossible—to get by as a quiet or shrinking violet type. On the flip side? Some of the most fascinating city stories center upon previously quiet or seemingly invisible people. Something gets triggered inside, causing them to act. Is it a Bernhard Goetz type, tired of the constant subway robberies, who becomes a vigilante? Could there be a person so tired of being crushed under the corporate heels they finally snap? The possibilities are endless.

We can also learn a lot about a character from where they live in a city. What does Patrick Bateman's penthouse and high-class living style say about him in Brett Easton Ellis's *American Psycho*? There's a duality there that brings out a great inner conflict between the character and the reader. What is it that made someone at the top of the world snap and become a serial killer? These are interesting ideas to explore when developing your characters.

To contrast, what happens when hell comes to a more average, apartment-dwelling city person? Struggles like paying the bills and just catching the right train to work or getting groceries can seem insurmountable for many characters. What happens to these folks who are just hanging on and getting by when their normal routines crack? These types of characters can be as equally nuanced and fascinating. Just check out novels such as Ira Levin's *Rosemary's Baby* for an outstanding example.

DIALOGUE

It may be tempting to think city folks all talk and speak rough and tumble, but that's far from the reality. It would be obvious to jump right into a pseudo-Brooklyn accent for a story set in New York City, or a Valley Girl accent for something set in Los Angeles. These are long-standing cliches that may best be avoided in favor of something more genuine. So, how does a writer capture the truth in the way characters might speak in the city? It would be ideal to actually go to a city and observe. Of course, that may not be possible or even practical. What about movies? Television? Streaming shows? While those can be good overall gauges, they may be stereotypical in their portrayals. Use your best judgement. Other great resources for dialogue could be interviews and non-fiction articles. Places that are not fiction can offer a more realistic depiction of how people actually speak.

Most importantly, though? In our connected world, there's often not the disparities between dialects and regional speaking there once was. As a creator, you can also have a lot of fun with shaking things up, as well. What if someone from rural Texas moves to New York? Surely, their accent would travel along with them. What if your principal character went to finishing school as a teenager and the instructors have hammered all traces of their Brooklyn accent out of them? Meanwhile, their friends are highly steeped in their dialect. That alone can cause some tension, humor, and a more realistic portrayal of groups of people. After all, in actual life, how many people all talk the same when they're hanging out?

One of a writer's biggest jobs is to draw characters that are distinct and individualized. A large part of creating unique characters is knowing how they speak. A suggested technique might be to think about how well you know your favorite movie or television stars. Can you 'think' in their voice? Do you know what they'd do in lots of different situations? Probably. Developing your own characters . . . especially your principal characters . . . to this point of realism will only make your storytelling that much better and more immersive and 'real' to your readers.

PROBLEMS & SOLUTIONS

There are entirely unique problems for our characters to navigate in an urban landscape. Immediately coming to mind, transportation differs from in the suburbs. Mass transit is ubiquitous. In most major cities, underground subways cart people from destination to destination. It's a far cry from the SUVs and glossy pickup trucks in the 'burbs. Having and owning a car in the city isn't practical or useful for most people. Finding parking can be its own horror show, after all! In the 70s and 80s, New York City's subway system was notorious and seemingly dangerous. This was seen in many era-specific films such as *The Warriors* and in fiction such as Clive Barker's *The Midnight Meat Train* and Whitley Strieber's *The Wolfen*. Worldwide, subway systems have also been used to great effect as horror set pieces in London's tube from Sarah Pinborough's *Breeding Ground* as well as James Herbert's *The Rats*.

Streets bring obstacles on many fronts. In the normal world, city streets are filled with traffic. Cars stopped bumper to bumper at red lights. Either that or they are racing at top speed, only inches from the curb and pedestrians. Imagine trying to cross the street to safety if an enemy is in fast pursuit. Where to go? And as city dwellers have an attitude that they've seen everything, many might not even realize what they're seeing is even real, or just another hoax, or someone filming a guerilla style video. There's also the phenomenon of people just walking by and ignoring crimes. People don't want to get drawn into a dangerous conflict. They don't want to put themselves at risk. At their most cynical, some may simply not want to be bothered, and to hell with the victims.

Sidewalks and streets can also become serious problems. Lurkers can hide in alleyways. Our characters can even go down alleyways in search of something offbeat, only to find themselves inside a new, hidden, and equally dangerous world. Only steps away from the main sidewalks and streets, alleyways seem like safe zones for criminals and other ill-intentioned things to operate under cover and out of the view of law enforcement or those who might report them.

In a post-apocalyptic scenario, streets can pose different types of problems for your characters. The streets that were filled with moving cars may be overrun with dead vehicles. Not only do they make travelling more difficult, but they also offer a terrific hiding place for stray zombies, or werewolves, or just plain old desperate people. Just crossing the street can be a suspense filled challenge for your characters. What would seem so simple in normal times becomes a serious issue.

Of course, alleyways in a post-apocalyptic city can be enormous threats, but that danger can be flipped. Alleyways can become shelters for your protagonists, offering them an escape route off the primary route if they're being pursued by any number of threats. What once was a potential trap and problem for your character flip-flops and becomes a solution.

Apartment buildings can be immense problems for characters in an urban landscape. The sheer number of occupants can be psychologically overwhelming for them. Being compacted and living in close quarters can be daunting. Similar to how people don't react to crimes on the street, many neighbors may not be inclined to get involved in any crimes going on right next door, especially if they can't hear them. If things get noisy, maybe they'd bang on the wall and holler to keep it down, or call the landlord. Maybe in your story the neighbors eschew the stereotypical ideas and are close, banding together to build a small community within the big city. If bad things go down, they'd be the first to notice and act.

In a post-apocalyptic scenario, an apartment building can be a safe refuge. Many of the comforts people are used to would still be available, with minor adjustments. They become armored forts against outside threats. Designed to be self-sufficient, with many being able to operate on solar power, apartment buildings may be a great refuge, especially if their inhabitants band together to form a makeshift crew or army against any looming threats. Their higher levels and roofs have the added benefit of acting as lookout towers to spot anything amiss before it gets close, and sometimes to be able to notify any search and rescue teams. We've seen just this scenario in countless zombie films and novels at this point. So, an apartment building can be a great solution to the problem of where to go and how to survive a post-apocalyptic world.

To turn the situation around once more, the building that offered refuge can quickly become a deathtrap if the threat breaches it. A horde of zombies is just that much more effective and overwhelming if they have your characters trapped in a hallway. It'd be like shooting fish in a barrel for the hordes. That being said? Any number of creative escapes may be had. Ducking into an apartment would provide momentary shelter. Or finding a stairwell. Or down the laundry or trash chutes! What may have appeared to be an end game may actually not be if the characters are brave and clever enough. Although, once breached and overrun, the apartment building would be uninhabitable, which would force your characters back out onto the streets and in search of another safe zone.

Out on the city streets, bridges are ways out of the city, or pathways to other places believed to be safer. They can be destinations for your characters—ways for them to escape the overall threat of the city that's been decimated and overrun.

Some may feel safer with the space of the suburbs or rural landscapes. Of course, those offer problems of their own. As often happens in horror stories with characters attempting to cross bridges, bad things happen. There are unforeseen threats once they get to the bridge. There is another zombie horde on the other side they hadn't expected. The villain has beaten them there and forces a showdown. The bridge may be unpassable because it's been reclaimed by nature, or blasted and destroyed by those not wanting to allow such a simple escape. Bridges are highly metaphorical, as well. They can act as significant moments to add a climax to an act of the story, or even as a finale.

We can use bridges as a solution for characters to escape the city, but can also become a tremendous problem of their own. As a creator, maybe you can even play on these expectations and use a bridge in an entirely novel way.

Tunnels have also been used effectively as set pieces in urban landscapes. Who would ever forget the crossing in the dark sequence from Stephen King's *The Stand*? The protagonists needed to cross the Hudson River, and with the George Washington Bridge too far or too inaccessible, the Holland Tunnel seemed a natural solution. Once there, navigating through the dark with so many dead at their fingertips became a worse problem. Again, a simple solution that quickly turns into a worse problem.

Can tunnels be solutions, as well? What if your characters make it to Grand Central Station in New York City? Many of the tracks lead out of the city and out to the suburbs. It's possible to escape the city using them. Of course, there are likely many hurdles. Others would think the same thing. Some may use that to set up traps. Maybe there are good stations along the way who have used the cover to make way stations to help shelter people out? We can explore similar situations and setups around the world. It's a method of transportation filled with many unique and rich potential ideas for telling your story.

THEMES

Usually, themes develop in the background as stories are being developed and written. Often, they aren't clear to the author until much later in the process. Of course, most are specific to the story being written. When you are working in a world of urban landscapes, though, there are often themes that are built in. One of the more common themes centers upon humankind vs the industrial, civilized world. What does living and working in a city mean for people? Are they giving up their connection to nature? Are they evolving into something different? Is there a way to find a balance between the two? Many cities have parks and other natural preserves. There are rooftop gardens and pools. We built many cities next to rivers and have extensive water lifestyles.

Another theme might be finding humanity within a sea of seemingly faceless, uncaring crowds. Used in horror, finding the humanity may even be found among the crowds of the undead or vampires or other inhuman, supernatural threats. There are many twists and possibilities along those lines.

What is your theme? How do you know what it is? Can there be more than one? These are questions that will probably be answered after we complete the first draft and allow the work time to simmer in the metaphorical back drawer for a while. It's upon reflection that any possible themes might become apparent to the author. At that point, you can choose to amplify them during rewrites by maybe adding subtle elements to the story. It can also be a good idea to lower the intensity of any elements you may feel may be too obvious. If something is a cliche, it may make the reader disengage with the story. We don't want that—not even for a moment. Instead? See if there are any elements that may be able to be less intense. That goes back to one of our first points of discussion: the author's voice in telling their story. It's all connected.

SUMMARY

The recipe for telling and writing stories in urban landscapes covers several key areas. Setting immediately comes to mind and in most cases will involve a city, either in full swing, or possibly one struggling through a post-apocalyptic disaster. The author's voice plays a vital part in really bringing a reader into the story. What Point of View they choose can often make or break a story. With richly developed characters that defy cliché and stereotypes, readers will have anchors on which to see themselves within your story. Problems and solutions unique to these stories can include many urban elements like streets, sidewalks, alleyways, apartment buildings, subways, and bridges, to name a few. These can really make the landscape come alive with their unique pros and cons. Last? Themes will naturally evolve as you develop, tell, and find your story. Connecting all these elements can result in a truly three-dimensional and immersive story—one that will haunt your readers for years or decades to come.

One big caveat I always advise to other writers is to take what works for you and leave the rest behind. While I hope you've enjoyed this exploration of writing stories in urban landscapes, what you do with this is entirely up to you. Remember that there are rules, but there aren't any rules. I hope you got some excellent information, tips, and further understanding of storytelling using urban landscapes, even if it's saying, "Forget all of this!" and chuck everything to the wind. Regardless? I wish you the best with your work and most importantly? Go write!

John Palisano's nonfiction, short fiction, poetry and novels have appeared in literary anthologies and magazines such as *Cemetery Dance*, Fangoria, *Weird Tales*, *Space & Time*, *Shmoop University*, and many more. He won the Bram Stoker Award for excellence in short fiction and is currently serving as President of the Horror Writers Association.

Interview with R.L. Stine

JG Faherty

JG Faherty: *I'd like to start off by saying thank you for speaking with us. I'm glad to be catching up with you, it's been almost four years since the last time we go to chat.*

R.L. Stine: I'm very happy to be included. Nice to talk with you.

Faherty: *You write for both the Middle Grade and Young Adult markets. What are the most important thigs a writer needs to consider when writing horror for each of these reading levels?*

Stine: If you are writing horror for a middle grade audience, you have to make sure that the readers know your story isn't real; it couldn't really happen. Once the readers know that, you can go pretty far with the scares. With an older audience, you have to do just the opposite. Every detail has to seem real or the readers won't be scared or get into the story.

Faherty: *You're famous for your dedication to writing a detailed outline for every book. Was this something you did before you got started in horror, or only after you began writing novels?*

Stine: Everyone hates to do an outline, but I can't write without one. I started outlining because my editors demanded an outline to approve before I started writing the books. With an outline, I know everything that's going to happen in the book when I sit down to write it. Then I can just have fun with the writing since I've already done the hard part. And if you do a complete outline, there's no way you'll ever have writer's block.

Faherty: *Aside from outlining, what is your process when it comes to writing a book? For instance, do you have a notebook that you keep ideas in and go to them later? Do you ever work on more than one book at a time, or perhaps be writing one and outlining another?*

Stine: I just write. I'm pretty much a machine. I have no writing rituals. I do one book at a time. I'd get too confused if I worked on two books at once. I already forget my characters' names halfway through the book. (That's the problem with having written over 300 books!) I have no list of ideas. I don't really try to think of ideas anymore. I try to think of good titles. I get a good title first, then it leads me to the story idea.

Faherty: *After so many years of writing, how do you still stay in touch with that inner child that is universally identifiable to kids each generation? After all, kids today are different— different technologies, different experiences, a very different world they grew up—than they were in the 80s or 90s.*

Stine: Kids stay the same. The technology changes. Kids don't walk around with Walkmen anymore and they don't go to their MySpace page. But kids' fears stay the same. They're still afraid of the dark, afraid of strange new places, afraid of something lurking under the bed. I honestly think the *Goosebumps* books could have been written in the 50s when I was a kid. You just have to get rid of the cell phones!

Faherty: There are certain things you won't include in your books, such as real-world violence, divorce, etc. because you don't want to frighten the children. But you don't mind scaring them with fantastical monsters. What is the difference between the types of fear (real and imaginary)?

Stine: It's the difference between witnessing a car crash and witnessing a giant monster stepping on your car. Kids are very smart, and they know the difference between real horror and fantasy horror. That's why I think parents and others who want to take away kids' TV shows or video games because they're too violent are misguided. Fantasy violence is good for kids, I think. It gets out a lot of natural aggression. And kids don't confuse it with real violence that is disturbing.

Faherty: You got your start writing humor, and you've said in the past that humor is important to set up or complement horror. How do you know when you've achieved the right balance, so that you increase the scare factor rather than minimizing it?

Stine: It's a fine line. Too much horror and your story isn't believable. Too much humor and you've lost the horror. There's no way to describe the right balance. You just have to learn it by writing.

Faherty: Goosebumps *and* Fear Street *are pretty much all standalone books, with certain monsters occasionally being used more than once. Why is that?*

Stine: I make everything as hard as I can for myself. I start all over with a new set of characters and a new location in every book. I think it would be so much easier to have a continuing character and continuing stories, but I'm not smart enough to ever try that.

Faherty: *You've said in the past that Slappy (from the* Goosebumps *books) is one of your favorite characters, and you've probably written more books with him as the big bad than any other type of monster. What is it about him you love so much?*

Stine: Honest truth: I don't love Slappy. And I don't get Slappy. Why are people afraid of a wooden dummy that comes to life? I really don't understand why he's scary. But I have to keep writing Slappy books because he's my most popular creation. I gave a talk recently in Toronto at Halloween time, and forty people in the audience came dressed as Slappy!

Faherty: *What do you do differently for the* Goosebumps *books and* Fear Street *books? How much farther will you go with the* Fear Street *stories, and why? Do you have a certain age cutoff for violence, or blood?*

Stine: No one ever dies in *Goosebumps*. If there's a ghost, he/she died long before the book started. In *Fear Street*, however, lots of teenagers bite the dust in every book. The *Fear Street* books are realistic, believable murder thrillers. The *Goosebumps* books are fantasy novels.

Faherty: When I write, I often think of new things while working on the actual manuscript that are very different from my original outline. Does that ever happen to you, or do you go over the outline multiple times until you've worked out all the possible plot deviations/idea changes?

Stine: I generally stick to my outline. My outlines are very complete. Of course, I have ideas while I'm writing. I incorporate them. But I always make sure my outline is complete enough so that I don't have to be creating a new story while I'm writing.

Faherty: Some writers prefer music in the background, others prefer silence when they're working. For instance, I like silence when I'm writing but music when I'm editing. Some people like a bright office, others prefer dim light. What is your atmosphere or environment like?

Stine: I had a friend who wrote YA horror. She wrote on a haunted desk and had to have a dark room and deep organ music playing while she wrote. I don't have anything like that. But I do need quiet. I don't understand authors who write in coffee shops or diners. I'd be way too distracted.

Faherty: You once mentioned that you purposely don't give your characters a lot of depth because you want the reader to fill in all the gaps in their heads, that this makes them relatable to everyone. What is your level of characterization so that they seem like real people instead of caricatures or stereotypes, but still remain purposely vague? Do you think this is something that is particularly important for young readers, while adult readers identify better with fully-fleshed characters?

Stine: I'm criticized often for the lack of characterization in my books. But I think the books are a LOT scarier if the readers put themselves in the place of the protagonists. Since most of my books are written first-person, that means the reader is experiencing all the frights and horrors. The whole trick to these books is close point of view. So I don't describe the protagonist in any depth.

Faherty: *Tell me about your writing style. Do you try to put down a certain number of words per day? Do you work better when under a deadline than not?*

Stine: It seems I'm *always* under a deadline. I write seven to eight books a year. I treat it like factory work. I write 2,000 words every day. I sit down to write at about ten every morning, and I don't get up till I've reached my 2,000 words. That's about ten pages.

Faherty: *Plot, dialog, and setting. How are these different when writing for MG or YA audiences? For instance, when writing for middle graders, how do you determine the amount of detail you include when describing a scene, or a setting?*

Stine: My books are all plot-driven. They are all dialogue, all story, not much description. It makes them fast and easy to read.

Faherty: *You've said that nothing really scares you—especially horror. So how do you know what will scare your audience?*

Stine: There are a lot of safe bets. Lots of people are afraid of the dark . . . afraid of spiders . . . afraid of being in a new place. There are so many horror tropes. If you make the readers feel they are inside the scene, you can make anything scary. I once wrote a scary *Goosebumps* book about a sponge found under a sink!

Faherty: *How do you keep pace with the newest technology and social media advances that are so vital to kids' social lives, and how do you decide how much of that to work into the story (or get around not using it)?*

Stine: I try to keep out as much technology as possible. Mainly because it changes every ten minutes. Cell phones can ruin any mystery story. It's too easy for a character to call for help. I try to get rid of the cell phones as early as I can in every story.

Faherty: *One final question: What words of advice would you give to someone who's looking to write specifically for the MG or YA readers?*

Stine: Keep reminding yourself to *enjoy* the writing. Don't ever listen to people who say that writing is hard. Writing isn't hard. Creating your own world is fun and rewarding and enjoyable. If you keep remembering that, if you look forward to writing instead of dreading it, your writing will go smoothly and you will be a lot more productive. And happy.

Faherty: *Thanks again for taking the time to do this. It's been a real pleasure, as always!*

Stine: Stay scary, everyone.

R.L. Stine has written hundreds of horror fiction novels, including the *Fear Street, Goosebumps, Rotten School, Mostly Ghostly,* and *The Nightmare Room* series for Middle Grade (MG) and Young Adult (YA) audiences. He is the best-selling children's book series author of all time, and a recipient of the Horror Writers Association's Lifetime Achievement Award. He has also won three Disney Adventures Kids' Choice awards, three Nickelodeon Kids' Choice awards, an Inkpot Award, and the Thriller Writers of Thriller Master Award. You can follow him on Twitter (@RL_Stine) and Instagram (@RL_Stine1), and at RLStine.com.

A life-long resident of New York's haunted Hudson Valley, **JG Faherty** is the author of 7 novels, 10 novellas, and more than 75 short stories. He's been a finalist for both the Bram Stoker Award® (*The Cure, Ghosts of Coronado Bay*) and ITW Thriller Award (*The Burning Time*). His most recent novel is *Sins of the Father*, a Lovecraftian tale of love and revenge set in 1800s Innsmouth. He grew up enthralled with the horror movies and books of the 1950s, 60s, 70s, and 80s, which explains a lot. Follow him at www.twitter.com/jgfaherty, www.facebook.com/jgfaherty, and www.jgfaherty.com.

You've Got No Fiction if You Don't Have Fact

Rena Mason

The title of this piece sort of came from a song lyric I'd heard over the radio one day. At first, I thought I'd misheard it. After all, fiction is the work of the imagination, right? Then the lyric repeated, and I stopped and thought about what the songwriter might've meant by it. Was he trying to be ironic? The more I mulled it over, the more the lyric made perfect sense. In every piece of fiction, there must be some instance of fact making the work of fiction "real" to readers. Something relatable to ground the story, allowing the reader to feel at ease in suspending their disbelief.

Most writers learn to accept guidance with caution early on in their careers, especially when it comes to writing. Something that works for someone else may not work for me, or you, but the fun part is trying out all the different techniques as we learn our craft. From the novice to the pro, it's difficult not to be close to our work, but if you're newer to writing fiction you might also be seeking direction from other writers, instructors, handbooks, workshops, retreats, and the like. You'll twist the information you acquire and shape it and make it your own as you gain experience, figuring out what to use and what to let go. One phrase I often hear as advice to early writers is: "It's fiction, you can write whatever you want."

Well yes, and no.

Think of a story or two you've read with a premise that seemed outlandish, even improbable, but as silly as whatever aspect of it might've seemed bizarre to you at the time, you read it until the end. There are authors who are masters at not only writing an excellent story, but making the fantastically impossible plausible enough to hold your attention as well, and I'm sure you can guess many of those I'm referring to without my listing them here.

Not everyone stops and analyzes why they enjoyed a particular story or how they related to it after reading it, but through my own observations, I've realized I'm able to immerse myself in stories more if I can relate to something early on. It might be a familiar setting, a character trait, a behavior, or a bit of verity—scientific, historical, or other—that supports the fiction.

But as a newer writer, where does one begin with that? Early in any career, I think it's natural for people to imitate their career heroes, and it's no different for authors. There's nothing wrong with it and in part, it's how we learn. But eventually, in order to tell "your" story, you'll branch off on your own as you establish your unique voice and style.

I read a lot of fiction for entertainment, but I also read a healthy dose of nonfiction to learn, and if I learn something from fiction I picked up for entertainment, or am entertained by a work of nonfiction, it's a pleasant bonus and I'm more apt to purchase something else from the author or subscribe to the magazine or journal.

Because I'm an author and also a Registered Nurse, I tend to scrutinize fiction I'm reading if there's anything medical-related in it; I can't help it. And when I'm writing anything medical-related, I either use what I know or do a quick search depending on how much information I think I need to buttress my fiction without overwhelming my readers. It's important to weave that information throughout the story on a need-to-know basis rather than dumping it in chunks for convenience. If you've ever hurried through a story to find out what happens next and find yourself reading ahead and passing over paragraphs then you know what I mean. As readers, our brains learn to hone in on info dumps and skip over them.

We all have experiences we either consciously or subconsciously work into our writing, the same way our views on culture, politics, society, mores, etc. find their way into our fiction. We are storytellers after all, and even if it's not readily apparent, we have something to say when we write these stories. This is why I think it's important to strengthen any fiction with some fact or true experiences if we want readers to relate to our stories, invest their time and money, read our stories through to the end, and then (hopefully) leave a review.

For a scientific factual example, let's say a main character in a story uses a drug to paralyze their victims. It's easy enough to make a drug up, but there may already be one available that does what the main character needs it to do. If it's a fictional drug, it has to make sense or at least have some facts around it to boost it up to make it believable to readers who may have a little bit of knowledge on the subject. This may not seem like a big deal, but nothing throws me out of suspending my disbelief faster than reading a vital component of a story that I know the author got completely wrong and could've easily fixed with a little Internet search. That's just lazy writing, unless the author got it wrong on purpose. After all, the general public doesn't need to know actual dosages or formulas. That might be seen as irresponsible writing.

Now back to the character with the paralyzing drug I'm using as a scientific factual example. Keep in mind paralytic agents do what their name suggests—they paralyze. What does that mean exactly? Well, look it up is what I'd normally say. You don't have to be a doctor or a scientist to get the gist of it. They block neuromuscular transmission and cause paralysis of the muscle, which means *all* muscle. The diaphragm, which we all use to breathe, is a muscle. If the character is paralyzing their victims for any length of time using a paralytic agent, he or she may have to "breathe" for their victims to avoid them going into respiratory arrest and dying. As a reader, reading this in a story, I'd be visualizing the character dragging their victim down a dark hall while stopping intermittently to do CPR.

Wouldn't it have been easier just to clobber the victim on the head and then physically immobilize them? Or maybe make the main character a pharmaceutical scientist or a chemist, or a lab technician in a clinical study for a new paralytic agent that targets specific muscle groups. That's still currently fiction, but it's strengthened by the facts the author chooses to weave into the story. If an author decides to go this route, I hope they do an Internet search and give their readers some accurate details about what a clinical study might entail, or what a lab technician does. They can take the information and mold it to what the story needs, to build up and support their fiction. The search may even take the story in a different direction than originally intended, but that's not always a bad thing.

Medical diagnoses are another example of scientific information I notice authors using incorrectly, particularly in regards to cancer. For instance, the main character in a story has been "coughing" for months. They finally go to a doctor's appointment (most likely a general practitioner) and then the doctor steps out of the room and then returns moments later and tells the character they have cancer and only have a specific number of days or months to live. This then sends our character on their rushed journey to right all their wrongs, seek revenge, or go on a killing spree for no apparent reason other than they have cancer, they're dying soon, and others probably should too, or their brain tumor also gave them psychopathy, anti-social personality disorder, and other personality disorders. Yikes. That may happen on TV but most people who have ever gone to the doctor for a checkup or physical know that lab results of any kind take forever. This character would be referred to an oncologist and then there would be a bevy of tests to identify the condition. It's a process. This may also seem obvious, but I've read it.

There are over 100 types of cancer and numerous treatments including radiation therapy, surgical implants, chemotherapy, excision, and more. Most readers have family members and friends who have had some type of cancer and have likely spent time on the Internet and WebMD for information. It's so easy with all of the technology at our disposal nowadays, and it's inexcusable not to find some facts when writing fiction to back up the subject. Specific diseases, conditions, and injuries and their signs and symptoms are more difficult to make up without readers noticing, and it may not bother some readers, but it wouldn't be an issue with an Internet search or reaching out to peers in the medical and/or writing fields. Using mental illness incorrectly or as a kind of deus ex machina in fiction is something else authors should either investigate and get right or avoid.

For an author experience example, I'll use myself and something that I recently wrote. I open the story with a chaotic scene in a lab (using some real science facts as well), but my main character, a genome editing lab technician, is standing off to the side observing the chaos and is disturbed by something she sees being done to an infant. Soon after the incident, she picks up this newborn and cradles it even though she's uncomfortable doing so. Although she's female, she doesn't have a lot of experience with babies, and holding the baby feels awkward to her. Then adding to the anxiety of her inexperience, she notices something off about the baby in her arms.

I believe this is a relatable experience for many men and women. When I was a teen, I used to babysit, but the children were always older, and I didn't have a baby sister or other babies around me growing up. For some reason I'd had it in my mind I wouldn't hold a baby right and might drop it, which of course would've been one of my worst nightmares at the time. One night in my early 20s, I was working as operating room nurse on call doing pediatrics. The anesthesiologist asked me to go and get the baby from its parents in preoperative holding and carry it back to the OR room. I couldn't move. I just stared at him like I didn't understand what he was saying. Then he asked me what was wrong. I told him I didn't feel comfortable carrying a baby back and briefly explained why. Needless to say, he wasn't too happy with me, but he went and got the baby himself. Fortunately, I didn't do a lot of pediatrics, and most of the time newborns stayed in their bassinets, and I'd roll the whole thing back and let the doctors and assistants handle the baby. I never got comfortable with holding infants until I had my own, and to be honest, I'm still uncomfortable holding other people's babies. My hope with adding a real and personal experience like this into a story is that readers might relate to it and that it might resonate with them and keep them reading. Especially after they read where I wove that character insecurity into the story.

Another aspect of factual experience I used in that story pertains to the plastic bassinets they keep newborns in at a hospital nursery. During maternity rotation as a nursing student, one of the assignments was to hold and rock the babies. (Oh boy.) I remember sitting in a rocking chair and waiting for one of the nurses to bring me a newborn. And I don't know if it's because they keep the nursery excessively warm, or because I was so nervous, or because the baskets were old, or maybe the stainless steel trollies were bent, but the basket sides were slightly warped, so as I sat waiting and looked out across the rows of babies, their little cocooned bodies and faces also appeared warped through the plastic.

Every writer knows they should do some research when writing a story if they don't already know their subject matter or supporting details, but there's a limit on how much of that knowledge to use. This "right" amount will come with time and writing, beta reader feedback, rejections and acceptances, editor's comments, and so on. Plenty of writers go down the "rabbit hole" of research for hours, days, even months, or years. Some will work every bit of research into their story; more experienced writers will use what they'd learned in brief. It's this subtlety in a power-packed sentence or few that separates the masters of the genre, in my opinion.

Another fantastic way to get facts for your fiction is to reach out to other writers. From ice road truckers, military soldiers, to rheumatologists, I've found a plethora of knowledge within the horror community. I'm also a member of the Public Safety Writers Association as well as take part in several other online writing communities, including one on trauma.

When I first started working on this piece, I had an altogether different idea about what I planned to write, but as I kept thinking on it, I realized my original intention went a lot deeper, and I knew I had to dig down and relay what was at the base of what I thought might be more helpful to a newer writer. As writers, we all want readers, and the best way to connect with readers is give them something early on they can relate to, and one of the better ways to accomplish that is with a bit of factual information in one form or another.

Because it can't be better said—or sung—that your fiction will resonate more with readers if you've got some truth behind it.

Rena Mason is the Bram Stoker Award® winning author of *The Evolutionist* and *East End Girls*, as well as a 2014 Stage 32 /The Blood List Search for New Blood Screenwriting Contest Quarter-Finalist. She is currently co-editing an anthology for the HWA Presents series. She is a member of the Horror Writers Association, Mystery Writers of America, International Thriller Writers, The International Screenwriters' Association, and the Public Safety Writers Association. An avid scuba diver, she enjoys traveling the world and incorporating the experiences into her stories. She resides in Olympia, Washington. For more information visit her website: www. RenaMason.Ink.

So You Want to Be in a Horror Anthology?

James Aquilone

You poor, poor thing. Why do you want to torture yourself? Is it because of all the Eli Roth movies you've been watching? Don't you know you'll (most likely) be *rejected*? Better to lock your short story in a heavy oak trunk and drop it into the dark sea, where, hopefully, the kraken devours it. Save yourself the trauma and misery of having your literary dreams crushed by a heartless editor.

Did I scare you away? No? Great. Horror writers shouldn't scare easily. If you want to be a professional writer, you'll need to get published (and paid)—and you'll need to endure the pain. (Bonus Tip: Channel the suffering and torment of submitting to anthologies into your horror fiction.)

On the bright side, you wrote, rewrote, got feedback, rewrote again, and have a complete horror story. Congratulations! Now it's time to send your baby into the cold, cold world where it will be scrutinized by strangers! But don't worry. Follow these tips and you'll start seeing the acceptances pile up, and maybe—just maybe—the pain lessening.

Get Over Your Fear of Rejection

Rejection never feels good, especially when you're starting out. How do you get over it? Submit, submit, and submit. It gets easier, and it's a numbers game. The more stories you have out on submission the better your chances of getting an acceptance. Trust me, if you keep writing and sending out stories, you *will* get acceptances. You'll also get *more* rejections, but that comes with the territory. If you have a ten percent acceptance rate, you're doing well. And it's not unheard of for a story to get more than a dozen rejections before finding a home. Persistence is your friend.

Don't Take Rejections Personally

There's only one reason why a story is accepted: It's good. But there are many reasons why your story can be rejected—many of which have nothing to do with its quality. Many anthologies, or any fiction market, for that matter, accept between only one and five percent of submissions. And many of these anthologies get several hundred to several thousand submissions.

A lot of things need to align—some may say the stars need to be right—for your story to get an acceptance. Your tale can be passed up because it was too long . . . It didn't fit the theme . . . It was too similar to another story in the anthology. You can be rejected before the editor reads the first sentence because you botched the cover letter or formatting.

Go Short

When you're trying to land your first sales, the shorter the story the better. Longer stories are much more difficult for newcomers to sell. Anthologies have word-count limits. They can be anywhere from 75,000 to more than 100,000 words. If, say, you write a 10,000-word story, you'd be taking up ten percent or more of the book. Most editors are reluctant to give that much space to a beginner. That's not to say you shouldn't write that long story, but be aware that it will be harder to get an acceptance. Plus, the longer the story the better it needs to be. No one wants to read a so-so 10,000-word story.

Don't Settle for Any Anthology

When choosing where to send your story, always start at the top. That means send your masterpiece to the top market first (highest paying, most prestigious; however you measure it) and work your way down. This could be more time consuming, but it will pay off in the end, as you'll have a better chance at landing a big market. Many beginning writers take the easy sale and go straight to the $5-flat-fee or even the non-paying anthologies. (Bonus Tip: Never submit to non-paying markets.)

Follow the Guidelines

Read the guidelines. *All* the guidelines. If the editor wants werewolf stories, don't send a zombie story. If they don't accept simultaneous submissions, don't submit your story anywhere else until you get a response. Ignoring this rule can be disastrous. I had someone commit this sin during the open submissions period for an anthology I was editing.

The writer withdrew their submission after getting an acceptance from another anthology. We had stated in our guidelines that we didn't allow simultaneous submissions. Not only did this person waste our time, but the other anthology was paying only 1 cent a word, while mine paid 8 cents. The kicker: the writer's story was one of our highest rated and most likely would have been accepted. Follow the guidelines. Start at the top.

Stand Out

Anthologies have a theme (usually) and a limited amount of space, while still needing variety. As a consequence, editors often have to pass on great stories because they're too similar to another one they already accepted. To avoid this, write a unique story, stand out in some way, do something different. Write a tale only you can write.

Format Your Story Properly

Many a story has been eighty-sixed because of bad formatting. Some editors won't even read your submission if you don't follow basic formatting guidelines. Sending your story in triple-spaced Comic Sans is a clear sign you're not a professional. Overworked, bleary-eyed editors will use bad formatting as an excuse for a quick rejection. (Bonus Tip: Don't insert a copyright notice in your story.)

Keep Your Cover Letter Simple

Yes, you could be rejected for a terrible cover letter. Having no letter is better than a bad one. Here are some things you shouldn't do.

- Do not misspell the editor's name or the title of the anthology.

- Do not ask how you're getting paid. (Yes, people ask that.)

- Do not suck up to the editor. (Well, not too much.)

- Do not give a synopsis of your story, unless it's required.

- Do not say you had a great time writing the story or how hard you worked on it.

- Do not criticize your story.

- Do not insert images or graphics.

Do keep your cover letter short and sweet. Editors don't have the time to read a long letter. They may not even read your short letter.

Here's the form for a standard cover letter:

Dear [Editor's Name],

Attached is my story, "[Title of Story]," for consideration in [Name of Anthology]. I've been published in [Name of Market], [Name of Market], and [Name of Market]. I'm a member of [Name of Pertinent Organization].

Sincerely,
[Your Name]

That's it. Simple. The cover letter is not your place to pitch the editor or sway them. The story is the place to shine. If you haven't been published before or you're not a member of any groups, leave those parts out. (Bonus Tip: Don't forget to attach the story before hitting "Send.")

Final Word About Rejections

If you're doing this right, you will collect dozens and perhaps hundreds of rejections. When you get rejected, move on, send the story to the next market on your list, and write your next piece of fiction. And never argue with an editor about a rejection or respond to it, unless you get a personal note.

The odds may seem against you, but remember, many of the stories that editors receive are, to put it kindly, not so great, and many of the writers will commit the faux paus listed in this essay. If you write a strong story and send it out in a professional manner, your odds will go up. If you don't let rejections stop you and you keep polishing your story and sending it out, you'll get an acceptance. I promise. You're just going to suffer a while until the literary stars are right. Remember: Life is suffering. Writing, more so.

James Aquilone is a writer and editor from Staten Island, New York. His Dead Jack novels have been optioned for TV and film. He›s also the managing editor of *Weird Tales* magazine. For more info, go to JamesAquilone.com.

Horror's Dark Legacy

Tim Waggoner

Our society has long recognized that while all people may be created equal, they haven't always been *treated* as such. Recognizing a problem, however, isn't the same as actually addressing it, and we still have a long way to go before everyone is valued and respected equally. Thanks to Black Lives Matter, the #metoo movement, and the growing awareness of issues affecting the LQBTQ+ community, America is currently undergoing a reassessment about how *all* its citizens are treated, not only in day-to-day life, but also in our entertainment—including horror fiction and film.

Horror relies on fear of the Unknown. If something is known, even if it's a threat, it can be understood, dealt with, and conquered. But if something is *unknown*, it can't be understood, at least not easily. We don't know what it is, what it can do, what it wants, or how to stop it. The Unknown equals uncontrollable, and loss of control is at the heart of horror. Horror also relies on fear of the Other. The Other is anyone or anything different than you are. Technically, anything living that's NOT you can be classified as Other. The Other's background, beliefs, motivations, moral code, and abilities are all unknown, and because of this, we don't know how to regard or deal with the Other. The Other may see you as a threat, may want what you have, want to dominate you, may want to BE you. Difference, when viewed through a lens of fear, can equal distortion, and a distortion of the natural is one way we define that which is monstrous.

I think you can see where I'm going here. Horror fiction draws on the darker aspects of the human imagination for story material and themes, but fear of the Other all too often means fear of our fellow human beings who we perceive as being different than we are. As horror writers in the past plumbed the depths of their psyches in pursuit of story material, it was only natural that they drew upon their own prejudices for their stories, without being aware that their fears of the Other even *were* prejudices.

This resulted in racist and sexist tropes that became part of horror's tradition—the savage natives who practice forbidden dark rites, the woman who uses her unnaturally powerful sexuality to lure unsuspecting men to their demise, the aged crone or wizened old man who is a symbol of death and madness . . . These tropes entered horror's language and its shared culture, and writers adopted them without ever being aware of where they originated—or they adopted them because these tropes spoke to their own unexamined prejudices and feelings of distrust toward the Others in society. But if we wish to avoid harmful stereotypes in our fiction—and we should—we need to be aware of how they've been used in horror fiction in the past, how to identify and avoid them in our own work, and how we can use them in positive ways to comment on social issues without hurting others.

Sexism in horror

In horror fiction, women have long been portrayed in one of two ways: as prey or as predator. Women are victims of a story's Big Bad, and they're often dispatched in cruel, sadistic ways—especially in film—giving rise to the phrase *torture porn*. Strong women comfortable with and in control of their sexuality are often portrayed as symbolic or literal predators, using their bodies to lure men into a false sense of security before they strike. These portrayals of women reflect a stereotypical male fear of being controlled by women and the need to establish dominance over them. Think of the images on horror movie posters of the 1950s and 60s: a woman screaming as she cowers in front of a hideous monster. In other versions, she's held by the monster, who—the image implies—is going to carry her off and do whatever it wants to her. All too often, women are used as vehicles to generate horror in stories as opposed to being fully realized characters. They're reduced to blood-curdling screams and terrified expressions as they are violated physically, mentally, emotionally, and spiritually.

Racism in horror

Anyone from a background different than a reader/viewer in terms of race, religion, culture, region, language, codes of behavior, etc. can be perceived as Other. This Othering demonizes a group of people as not quite human at best and inhuman at worst. The cultists in Lovecraft's fiction were often depicted as non-whites, reflecting the author's own fears and prejudices of those he perceived as Other. Voodoo priests and priestesses, always black, are either threats to the white heroes or—more rarely—assist them in their struggle against evil forces (aligning them with the magical negro trope, the black person with mystical knowledge or abilities who exists only to help and guide a white protagonist).

Asian and Native American characters are also portrayed as possessing ancient knowledge that can be employed to benefit white heroes. In horror movies, black people are often the first to die, their characters existing solely to add to the overall body count, a situation so common that it's become parodied in metafictional commentary, such as in the film *Deep Blue Sea*. Whatever form Othering takes—whether portraying people of color as threats, victims, or magical advisors—it's dehumanizing.

Homophobia in horror

Sexuality is powerful, private, and intimate. It's a core aspect of what it means to be human, and people often have mixed emotions about their own sexuality—fear, joy, worry, desire, guilt. Sex can be a bonding experience, but also an alienating one, involving power, dominance, and submission. With sexuality comes high degrees of vulnerability and insecurity, which of course leads to worry and fear. For a long time, homosexuality was viewed as a great Unknown and a threat to cis society, and cis sexuality still viewed by many as the default—as "normal."

Gay characters in horror literature and film—especially effeminate men—were often depicted as sinister deviants, if not as outright monsters. The vampire Carmilla is one of the most well-known examples of a lesbian monster in literature, but there are also the gay hitmen Mr. Wint and Mr. Kidd from James Bond lore, and the gay twin brother killers from Dean Koontz's *Whispers* (which throws incest into the mix for good measure). And many Disney villains, such as Captain Hook and Scar, are depicted in ways that hint—and sometimes *more* than hint—that they're gay, as if their sexuality is another indicator of their evil natures.

Transphobia in horror

Many of the same attitudes toward gay people—their very identity being an indication of evil, for example—apply to trans folk in horror fiction, but trans folk are threatening to cis people for an arguably deeper reason. They threaten stereotypical ideas of gender identity, and gender identity is one of the foundational aspects of how children are taught to view themselves and the world. Trans folk also raise the specter of profound psychological and physical transformation for a cis audience, not just in others but, potentially, in themselves as well. Classic transphobic horror depictions include Norman Bates in *Psycho*, Buffalo Bill in *The Silence of the Lambs*, the title characters in *Dr. Jekyll and Sister Hyde,* and the killer in *Sleepaway Camp.*

Ableism in horror

In horror fiction, physical and mental distortion are regularly viewed as monstrous in and of themselves. This attitude goes back to some of the most ancient beliefs of our species, when disabilities, injuries, and illnesses were thought to be punishments inflicted by the gods, and people with mental illness were viewed as possessed by demons. In children's fairy tales, heroes are beautiful, villains and monsters ugly. One's outer form mirrors their inner nature. Examples of ableism in horror abound: Frankenstein's Monster, the Phantom of the Opera, Quasimodo, the urban legend of the maniac with the hook hand, and the thousands of violent, depraved mentally ill killers slashing their way through fiction and film.

Other -isms in horror

Many additional types of Othering find expression through our horror. Classism: murderous villagers or country folk who worship ancient gods and/or practice cannibalism (feeding on civilized people, of course). Ageism: sinister old people with dangerous knowledge and abilities, such as witches, wizards, and seers. Anti-intellectualism: smart people with education that are mad scientists, diabolical scholars, evil schemers or misguided fools that endanger the heroes . . . I could go on, but basically anything about humans that could be perceived as being Other could go in this section.

Does horror need -Isms to be horror?

In a word, no. While fear of the Unknown and the Other might rise from our own prejudices and discomfort (or through observing those of others), how we present these elements in our fiction to readers and viewers doesn't have to perpetuate harmful stereotypes.

How to avoid -Isms in your horror

First, become aware of any prejudices or stereotypical views of people you might harbor, whether consciously or subconsciously. This might require some uncomfortable self-examination on your part, as well as some difficult conversations with friends, relatives, and significant others. Make a list of these areas and do some research on stereotypes to learn what depictions and attitudes people in marginalized groups find ignorant, insulting, and harmful. When you write, make sure your characters are well-developed individuals, not just types. Try to avoid horror stereotypes and clichés, such as the mad scientist, the "savage" cultist, the homicidal lunatic, etc. Use sensitivity readers who are members of groups your characters belong to.

How to use -Isms in your horror

Movies and TV series like *Get Out, Lovecraft Country, You're Next, The Stepford Wives, Dale and Tucker vs Evil* comment on and critique various societal attitudes and stereotypes, and you can too. Give —isms of varying degrees to your characters—both heroes and villains—to make them more human and to propel the plot.

Maybe one of your good guys is uneasy around trans folk. Maybe one of your bad guys is creeped out by extremely old people. You can use both of these qualities to strengthen your story and challenge your characters by putting them into situations where they have to confront their prejudices and see whether or not they overcome them. You can put a spin on —isms and turn them on their heads. If one of your characters believes people from a certain background are all the same—for example, that all white country folk are uneducated, gun-loving, violent, intolerant religious nuts—have them encounter a character who explodes that myth such as a pacifist, atheist organic farmer who's as liberal as they come. Having your characters' viewpoints challenged and expanded can do the same for your audience, making your fiction richer and more impactful in positive ways.

Horror might have a dark legacy when it comes to its depiction of marginalized people, but by being aware of past portrayals and working to counter them in your own fiction, you can help create horror's future.

Resources for further reading

- ☠ "Gender in Horror Films." https://en.wikipedia.org/wiki/Gender_in_horror_films

- ☠ "The Misogynistic Portrayal of Women in Horror Films." https://dailytitan.com/opinion/the-misogynistic-portrayal-of-women-in-horror-films/article_24b47414-d0c9-53d0-9a9a-ea8885a67c71.html

- "Racism in Horror Films." https://en.wikipedia.org/wiki/Racism_in_horror_films

- "American Nightmare: Racism and Horror Cinema." https://www.motelx.org/en/sections/american-nightmare-racism-and-horror-cinema

- "LGBTQ+ Representation in Horror." https://thecurrentmsu.com/2020/02/12/lgbtq-representation-in-horror/

- "Queer Coding in Horror Films." https://controlforever.com/read/queercoding-and-horror-films/

- "Villainizing Bodies and Minds: Ableism in Horror Movies." https://femmagazine.com/villainizing-bodies-and-minds-ableism-in-horror-movies/#:~:text=The%20horror%20genre%20in%20particular,and%20mentally%20similar%20to%20them

Tim Waggoner has published over fifty novels and seven collections of short stories. He's a three-time winner of the Bram Stoker Award and has been a finalist for the Shirley Jackson Award, the Scribe Award, and the Splatterpunk Award. He's the author of the acclaimed horror-writing guide *Writing in the Dark,* and he's a full-time tenured professor who teaches creative writing and composition at Sinclair College in Dayton, Ohio.

Thank you to Tony Acree and the whole team at Hydra Publications, Greg Chapman for the artwork and cover design, as well as the writers and editors who put flesh on the ideas.

Michael Knost is a Bram Stoker Award®-winning editor and author of science fiction, fantasy, horror, and supernatural thrillers. He has written in various genres and helmed multiple anthologies. His *Writers Workshop of Horror* won the 2009 Bram Stoker Award® in England for superior achievement in non-fiction. His critically acclaimed *Writers Workshop of Science Fiction & Fantasy* is an Amazon #1 bestseller. *Return of the Mothman, Barbers and Beauties,* and *Author's Guide to Marketing with Teeth* were all finalists for the Bram Stoker Award®. Michael received the Horror Writers Association's Silver Hammer Award in 2015 for his work as the organization's mentorship chair. He also received the prestigious J.U.G. (Just Uncommonly Good) Award from West Virginia Writer's Inc. His *Return of the Mothman* is currently being filmed as a movie adaption. He has taught writing classes and workshops at several colleges, conventions, online, and currently resides in Chapmanville, West Virginia with his wife, daughter, and a zombie goldfish.